Praise for *Branding Between the Ears*

Branding Between the Ears offers a fascinating insight to the world of branding. After reading this book your brain will never look at brands the same way again.

> —**Martin Lindstrom**, *New York Times* bestselling author of *Buyology*, *Small Data*, and *The Ministry of Common Sense*

Branding is much more than a slick logo and sexy television commercials. *Branding Between the Ears* delves deeper into the reasons why some brands become cultural icons while others flop.

> —**Nir Eyal**, bestselling author of *Hooked* and *Indistractable*

Branding Between the Ears should be mandatory reading for brand managers, product managers, CMOs, and consumer business leaders. Easy-to-follow case examples illustrate the importance of understanding human psychology and why people behave the way they do. In a world where brands and corporations need to have a sense of purpose to build lasting businesses and motivate their employees, the ethical considerations framework (canonical, categorical, sunshine) should be on every marketer's desktop.

> —**Titi Cole**, Chief Client Officer, Head of Global Consumer Banking Operations, Citigroup

In this digital age where consumers are overwhelmed with information and options, it's more important than ever for brands to connect at a deeper level in order to break through. *Branding Between the Ears* lays out a compelling science-based path to what creates a truly iconic brand—unearthing how market shapers from Google to Guinness to Allbirds have systematically unlocked powerful psychological triggers that embed them into consumer's lives. And the book gives every business and brand leader a clear and pragmatic path to getting to greatness if they are open to thinking differently about creating the consumer connections that build cognitive brands.

—**Margo Georgiadis**, Partner at General Catalyst, former CEO of Ancestry and Mattel and one-time President of Google Americas

A terrific playbook for reimagining brand building and architecture that is science based and illustrated with powerful real-world examples. A must-read for every marketer.

—**Ravi Dhar,** Director, Yale Center for Customer Insights and Professor of Marketing, Yale School of Management

This book shook the very foundations of my decades in brand management; and meanwhile the answers were always there—*Branding Between the Ears*. Through a combination of fascinating brain science and rich real-world examples, Dayal reinvents the art and science of brand building.

—**Gina Boswell**, former President, Unilever US Customer Development, and EVP Chairman, Unilever UK & Ireland

Impressive depth and rigor, with excellent insights and practical lessons!

—**Sanjay Khosla,** Senior Fellow, Kellogg School of Management, Northwestern University, former President, Mondelez International

A treasure trove of new insights into how to build a brand. Wish I had this knowledge early in my career.

—**Micky Pant**, former CEO, Yum Restaurants International

Brand is and will always be powerful. The issue is how to create it. In this book, Dayal does a superb job at showcasing why old methods of branding are failing, and why Cognitive Branding is the new pathway forward.

—**Mathew Sweezey**, Director of Market Strategy Salesforce and author of *The Context Marketing Revolution*

Branding Between the Ears makes you think, feel, and see differently and provides actionable ways on how to truly unleash the power of Brands in ways that marry art and science to gain a sustainable edge. This is a must-read for every marketer in the world.

> —**Rishad Tobaccowala**, author of *Restoring the Soul of Business* and former Chief Growth Officer, Publicis Groupe

Occasionally a book transforms an industry. When it comes to attracting customers, *Branding Between the Ears* is that kind of a book. If you want to understand and empathize with prospects to ensure they choose your goods and services, *Branding Between the Ears* is a must-read. Sandeep Dayal weaves behavioral research, neuroscience, and vast marketing experience into a resource that will transform the way you connect with and deeply engage your target audience. Be ready to not only become top of mind with your customers but top of heart as well. Thank you Dayal for this masterpiece in marketing thought leadership.

> —**Joseph Michelli, PhD**, *New York Times* #1 bestselling author of *Stronger Through Adversity*, *The Airbnb Way*, *The New Gold Standard*, and *The Starbucks Experience*

For decades, marketing professionals have been like Formula One drivers racing around the course with blindfolds on. We've tried to change the way consumers think without knowing how they really think. By taking us deep into brain science, Sandeep Dayal's new book lets us drive with our eyes open. *Branding Between the Ears* contains the most important advice given to marketing professionals in decades.

> —**Rajan Anadan**, Managing Director, Sequoia Capital India, former Vice President, Google India & SEA

This brand marketer's guide to the consumers' mind is chock-full of vivid anecdotes that will help you build brands that glide into consumers' minds, that stick, and that generate enduring dividends. Read it fast, then again, slowly.

> —**Niraj Dawar**, Professor Emeritus Marketing, Ivey Business School, Western University, Canada, author of *Tilt*

Sandeep has put together an amazing wealth of knowledge here—brand leaders better read this because the rest of the market is going to exactly that and act on it to challenge them! Wish I had had this book to guide me 20 years ago.

> —**Raghav Prasad**, Division President, Sub-Saharan
> Africa, Mastercard

Brand building is the X factor that will distinguish tomorrow's unicorns and superstars from the rest. However, the knowledge and skills underlying the development of iconic brands remains something of a mystery. Sandeep Dayal's new book, *Branding Between the Ears*, is a tour de force for it deftly describes how brain science—psychology, neuroscience, and behavioral economics—is revolutionizing the art and science of branding and brand building. Entrepreneurs and corporate managers will start with a distinct advantage if the ideas espoused here are reflected in their playbooks.

> —**Ram Shivakumar,** Adjunct Professor of Economics
> and Strategy, Booth School of Business,
> University of Chicago

Undoubtedly, a down-to-earth eye-opener! Highly recommended for business executives who want to compete more effectively for the demanding consumer of today. Dayal's insights, when applied across-the-board, well beyond the marketing enclave, can have a clear impact on not only the brand, but also the customer's experience of the company and its products.

> —**Jorge Alfaro Lara**, former Head of Consumer Bank,
> Banco Santander Mexico

The marketing landscape is constantly shifting and evolving, with consumer expectations becoming increasingly higher. Successful marketing isn't just about creating brand impressions with tons of ads; it must reach consumers in a persuasive and compelling way to get them to buy products as well. This is why, by decloaking the workings of the brain, showing how it reacts to brands and prompts purchasing decisions, *Branding Between the Ears* becomes a must-read for all marketers.

> —**Sherina Smith,** Vice President of Marketing,
> American Family Insurance

It's a rare business book that combines breakthrough thinking with actionable insights, but *Branding Between the Ears* does both. Marketers and brand builders who are looking for a forward-looking framework to guide their efforts will find it here. This blend of consumer psychology and analytic insights, which the book introduces as "cognitive branding," is the future.

—**Christiana Smith Shi,** Founder and Principal at
Lovejoy Advisors, LLC, former President,
Direct-to-Consumer, Nike Inc.

Branding Between the Ears is a timely road map for helping successful marketers take their work to the next level. We have always known that all brand purchases happen in the brain, sometimes in an instant and sometimes over years. Sandeep's book is a great guide to how marketers today can simplify the complex working of the brain into actionable insights and executable strategies. I would recommend the book to every marketer and consumer specialist. It will make them better.

—**Vipul Prakash,** Chief Operating Officer, MakeMyTrip,
former Chief Marketing Officer, PepsiCo India

Insights from the brain sciences are starting to pop up with increasing frequency among marketing practitioners and consultants, but for the most part they are still deployed tactically and superficially—providing a minor tweak here or there to grab more attention or turn a website visitor into a website shopper. Sandeep Dayal's *Branding Between the Ears* offers something radically different: a blueprint for integrating brain science insights into the very fabric of brand strategy. With fascinating case studies covering a wide range of industries, Dayal shows how "cognitive brands" can leverage brain science to create meaningful and long-lasting customer relationships, based not on clever marketing hacks but on a deep understanding of consumers' wants, needs, and goals. Be forewarned: reading this book will forever change how you think about brands, marketing, and your customers' brains.

—**Steve Genco,** author of *Intuitive Marketing* and
Neuromarketing for Dummies

In times when the marketing practice has grown increasingly tactical, it's heartening to read a marketing book that addresses the core issue of understanding the mind and shaping the behavior of a consumer. As online marketers chase digital likes, shares, and follows and offline marketers optimize media and shelf space, this book offers practical advice on maximizing space where it matters most: Right Between the Ears! Sandeep's book harvests the latest in brain sciences to help real-world practitioners unlock the conscious and subconscious keys to lure consumers to their brands. Easily, the most powerful marketing book to come out in decades!

—**Lloyd Mathias**, former APAC Marketing head of HP, CMO of Motorola South Asia

BRANDING

BETWEEN

THE EARS

BRANDING

USING COGNITIVE SCIENCE TO BUILD LASTING CUSTOMER CONNECTIONS

BETWEEN

SANDEEP DAYAL

THE EARS

NEW YORK CHICAGO SAN FRANCISCO ATHENS LONDON
MADRID MEXICO CITY MILAN NEW DELHI
SINGAPORE SYDNEY TORONTO

1 2 3 4 5 6 7 8 9   LCR   26 25 24 23 22 21

ISBN   978-1-264-26984-6
MHID   1-264-26984-6

e-ISBN   978-1-264-26985-3
e-MHID   1-264-26985-4

Library of Congress Cataloging-in-Publication Data

Names: Dayal, Sandeep, author.
Title: Branding between the ears : using cognitive science to build lasting customer
  connections / Sandeep Dayal.
Description: 1 Edition. | New York : McGraw Hill, [2022] | Includes bibliographical
  references and index.
Identifiers: LCCN 2021029465 (print) | LCCN 2021029466 (ebook) | ISBN
  9781264269846 (hardback) | ISBN 9781264269853 (ebook)
Subjects: LCSH: Branding (Marketing) | Marketing—Psychological aspects. |
  Cognitive neuroscience.
Classification: LCC HF5415.1255 D39 2022 (print) | LCC HF5415.1255 (ebook) |
  DDC 658.8/27—dc23
LC record available at https://lccn.loc.gov/2021029465
LC ebook record available at https://lccn.loc.gov/2021029466

McGraw Hill books are available at special quantity discounts to use as premiums and sales promotions or for use in corporate training programs. To contact a representative, please visit the Contact Us pages at www.mhprofessional.com.

To all of my teachers,
For what I have become

CONTENTS

PART THREE
COGNITIVE BRANDS: EXECUTION

PART

HOW BRAIN
SCIENCE IS
REVOLUTIONIZING
BRANDING

ONE

BRANDS THAT ROCK

E pic brands in the marketing sphere and chartbusters in the music world have one thing in common. No one seems to know how to make one. They come out of nowhere, like sweet accidents that rock our worlds.

Take the recent hit, "Dance Monkey," from Toni Watson, known professionally as the artist Tones and I.[1] I like the song because it has exactly the kind of effect I want my brands to have on consumers. The words of the song speak to the trance-like hold that some street dancers can have on bystanders, when neither they nor the performer can let go of the moment. Who knows what they see, hear, and feel, we just know that no one wants the music to stop.

Yet even Watson's managers warned her not to expect too much from the song. After all, she had spent a mere 30 minutes creating the number. Maybe it could do well with live audiences, but it would never be a big radio song, they thought. Well, that was before it went to number one on the charts in 20 countries, was streamed 1.1 billion times on Spotify, and was viewed on YouTube 700 million times.

As a busker living out of her van in Byron Bay, near Brisbane, Toni had struggled for recognition of her music beyond the streets of the small coastal town. The song itself is a bit like nothing else actually, sung in a sort-of syncopated, helium-tinged voice with a seventies synth and thumping bass. Yet every time she sang it in the streets, no one would just walk by. They would stop, listen, tap their feet, and some danced. Locals and tourists, young and old.

It is hard to tell when a song comes together like that. But when it does, everything about it is just right—the voice, the lyrics, the beat, and the notes and tones. No one knows what that secret sauce behind a number one hit is. But we know something about it makes our brains rock.

And that is what *cognitive brands* do. Like "Dance Monkey," they stop us dead in our tracks, and we can't walk away from them. Until now, designing iconic brands was just as much of a mystery as composing a chartbusting rock anthem. Advances in brain sciences have changed all of that. We now know a lot about shaping consumer choice and behavior.

Brands that rock our worlds are those that work the way our brain does. They hold the conscious and subconscious keys that unlock sensations of the experiences and fantasies stored in our minds, to make us happier and lure us to the brand. So while we still don't know much about creating head-bashing rock anthems, thanks to recent advances in brain sciences, we are a lot smarter when it comes to making hit brands.

In this book, I will show you what cognitive brands are, what's in them, and how you, as a practicing marketer, can build them. But before I do that, let me press the rewind key and take you back to where I began my journey into the brain science behind these brands.

FROM THE ASHES OF A BOOM AND BUST

In January 2000, I worked at McKinsey's Chicago office in the digital marketing practice as an associate principal, a respectable senior grunt. One particularly unrepentant Friday evening, with skies of molten gray, most people had left the office for the day. And yet, I sat glued to my desk. Something was very wrong.

Those were heady times, and the first dot-com wave was in a drunken swell. The NASDAQ had doubled in value just in the prior year. Traditional offline businesses felt like they were on the sinking end of an existential crisis and were clamoring to be on the web. Even at McKinsey, many of the brightest minds jumped ship to launch their own startups in their parents' grungy basements. Venture capital funding was available on demand to anyone with the artistry to sketch out an idea on the requisite coffee-stained napkin.

Amid this feeding frenzy, I was sweating nervously over the reports trickling in from the field. My clients, who had invested heavily into building slick websites, griped that consumers were not buying their brands as quickly as they had thought and that their sales were nowhere near the exponential growth rates needed to justify the sky-high stock market valuations for such companies.

As the anointed tech marketer at McKinsey, it fell upon me to sniff out the answer. But it was too late already. Businesses began to fall to the earth from their skyward perches like swatted flies; among them, storied brands like AOL, Webvan (online only groceries), Pets.com, Wingspan (online only bank), eToys, Flooz.com (Internet currency), and Esurance.com to name just a few. In the ensuing 18-month bloodbath, the NASDAQ would fall by more than 50 percent, erasing any monetary trace of the first internet bubble.

In the following months, I travelled the country speaking to many different Joe-and-Jane consumers. Some were buying a lot online and others not very much. Some used to buy a lot and then just stopped and vice versa. "Tell me why? What happened? Tell me how?" I asked them. In 2002, I cowrote an article with David Court that presented what we believed was the answer from our autopsy of the fallen kings: *Consumers were simply not ready to go online!*

What we found was that it wasn't enough for brands to have a value proposition—to say that they were better, cheaper, or more convenient. Brands needed a serious strategy for changing people's minds and attitudes about shopping online. The article "Beyond Behavioral Bounds," which was published in *Marketing Management*, a publication of the American Marketing Association,[2] expressed the dilemma as follows:

A new riddle confronts multichannel marketers: Why is it that even consumers who are fully aware of the benefits of shopping online still fail to do so? Why does a person wait patiently in line while his grocery store clerk completes a price check on the mystery vegetable being bought by the person ahead in line—when he could have his groceries delivered to his home? Why does he continue to buy and write checks and buy and lick stamps to mail bills—when he could use free bill paying services from an online bank? The answer to unlocking this second wave of consumers lies not in redesigning the online value proposition or advertising more, but in resolving the mysteries that percolate at the intersection of good marketing and consumer behavioral psychology.

In the article, we outlined ways to unshackle consumers from their behavioral chains through what we dubbed as "tactical accelerators." One such tactic, christened *Invisible Decisioners*, was described as follows: "In a world of proliferating products and features, many consumers simply feel ill-equipped to make decisions. Rather than scare them off with a lot of options, marketers should instead reduce stress by choosing invisibly for them. The real trick is knowing when to give consumers choice and control and when to take it away."

As an example, we pushed banks to automatically sign up customers for online payments to their utility companies, the identities of which could be ascertained by their address. Even then, almost 20 years back, this really wasn't a stretch. After all, the banks already did enroll customers for debit/ATM cards automatically.

Unknown to us at the time, a University of Chicago economist, Richard Thaler, was working on a very similar idea in the arena of public policy, which he ultimately described as *libertarian paternalism*—not limiting choices available to people (preserving liberty) while invisibly engineering their environment to help them make better choices for themselves (acting a bit like big brother). Thaler's behavioral theories, published in his widely acclaimed book *Nudge*, are familiar to many managers today.

Another tactical accelerator that we uncovered in our research was called *viral advocacy*. Today, peer reviews are among the biggest drivers of online sales, and viral advocacy has led to the rise of an industry of influencers, who on Instagram and YouTube determine the fate of many online and offline brands. As a marketer, I was hooked; it was the start of my obsession with solving the mysteries of the consumer mind through behavioral sciences.

FROZEN CONNECTIONS

Fast-forward 10 years. In 2010, my company, Cerenti, was working in Mexico with Scotiabank on their credit card portfolio. Consumers held credit cards from many different banks. Our task was to understand which ones would wind up in a person's wallet and be used most.

In one of our focus groups, we bumped into José Moreno, a used-car salesman, who confided that his favorite card, the one with the fattest loan balances, was not in his wallet at all. In fact, it was frozen into an ice cube and buried deep inside a freezer tray at his home. This way, he explained, whenever his wife and he were tempted to buy something impulsively, they would need to trudge back home and thaw out the card. In those intervening few hours, the urge to splurge would hopefully pass.

"*En serio* [Really]?" I asked, as scribes on my team struggled to take appropriate notes. "Dead serious, amigo!" was the response. "Wouldn't it be better to just leave the card in the wallet and count 100 sheep or something?" I countered. "Nope," José assured me, "I have tried that. Only the ice cube works."

Gradually, we understood that several customers viewed their credit card as a kind of person, a "best friend" that could become "the fiend from hell" at the drop of a dime. They wanted to be responsible but often could not help being tempted by the monster OLED TV or electric cascading chocolate fountain on sale. The learning for us was that consumers had very different tendencies for action. Some in the exact same situation would do nothing, and others would go ahead and do something

entirely irresponsible. I discuss this later in the book as the personal conative energy in each one of us.

Conation is a fascinating aspect of cognitive brands and leads consumers from indecision to purchase. The answer for José-like customers was to offer a card product that allowed them to regulate their own
buying behavior. Large purchases could trigger a hold, requiring the customer to call a toll-free number and speak to a service representative for
its release. The process delay was as good as an ice cube melting or better.
During the call, they could also be informed about the impact on their
minimum monthly payment should they proceed with the purchase.
Nowadays, all that can be done automatically with a text message, but few
card companies provide such a service.

If marketers have been slow to understand that these are not behavioral quirks but predictable human tendencies and reflections of how the
human brain works, confidence tricksters are fully up to speed. In one
common case, the play action runs as follows. Jack "Works-All-Day-at-
Starbucks-Instead-of-Office" is happily sipping his coffee and plugging
away on his laptop. Peggy Steel plops herself in the adjacent couch with
her best "I'm-so-harmless" smile. After half an hour or so, she asks him
for a teeny favor, "Could you watch my laptop while I go use the little girl's
room?" He obliges. Another grande mocha latte later, Jack needs to run to
the little boy's room for his turn at biologic relief. Of the 20-odd customers in the house, you guessed it, he asks Peggy to keep watch on his stuff.
After all, she owes him, right? Jack returns 10 minutes later to find nary a
whiff of Peggy or his laptop anywhere.

This tactic relies on a behavioral factor called the reciprocity bias to
work. People buy the brands they trust, but trust is a funny thing. Think
for a moment. Would you leave your computer with a random stranger at
Starbucks? Would you leave it if they had asked you to watch theirs? If the
laptop costs $1,000 to replace, would you leave 10 crisp $100 dollar bills
with a stranger at Starbucks to watch for you? Yet, these are all the same
scenarios. If you set your mind to studying common crooks, you would
learn a lot about the little-known cracks in human behavior and how to
work them to your advantage. We will learn later how cognitive brands

can use vibes to forge deep bonds with consumers so they embrace their brand propositions more dearly.

THE MARCH OF COGNITIVE SCIENCES

Even as I was searching for ways to disentangle the mysteries of consumer behavior in my work with clients, elsewhere, the news was really good. Brain scientists around the world were busy. Lots of work was going on in figuring out why people do the things they do. The research into the workings of the human brain has been accelerating at a breathtaking pace. Let's take a snapshot of the many different fields where this is happening.

In 2002, a Princeton psychologist, Daniel Kahneman, won the Nobel Prize for his research on behavioral sciences. This was shocking for two reasons. To start with, there is no Nobel Prize for psychology. It does not exist! So instead, he had to win it in economics for his work on *prospect theory*—which we will apply in a later chapter—without ever having completed a single course in economics. Couple that with the fact that classical economists at the time did not consider the field of behavioral economics to be a thing, let alone be awards worthy.

Kahneman was followed by Yale's Robert Shiller, who won a Nobel Prize for his work on behavioral economics in 2013, and by University of Chicago's Richard Thaler, who won in 2017. These intellectual titans and a cadre of other brilliant behavioral scientists who followed in their footsteps have transformed fields as diverse as economics, public policy, and investment finance. In the words of Richard Thaler himself:

> Behavioral science aims to understand why we make the choices we do. It offers a more robust view of human decision-making than economics or psychology alone, and can help explain consequential phenomena from the rise and fall of markets to how a person chooses an insurance plan. Society's most pressing challenges are, at their core, behavioral.[3]

Likewise, two decades ago, there were very few psychologists studying human emotions as a discrete scientific field. Today, scores of specialists are devoted to researching every distinct human emotion, such as anger, humor, and sadness. Yale University even offers a fascinating, full-semester undergraduate elective, Human Emotions, taught by the highly accomplished Dr. June Gruber.[4]

Look deeper and you'll find that the science of psychotherapy has seen the birth and widespread adoption of cognitive behavioral therapy (CBT), which focuses on reshaping negative human behavior through a deeper understanding of the patient's thought patterns. If Dr. Aaron T. Beck pioneered CBT for psychologists, it was Dr. David D. Burns who brought it to the masses with useful tools and frameworks.

Across the board, researchers have brought a new level of scientific rigor to the methods for understanding human behavior. For example, CBT has been found in controlled clinical trials to be superior to drugs like SSRIs (selective serotonin reuptake inhibitors) in successfully reshaping negative behavior to positive for a range of mental diseases. On a different path, researchers are using new imaging tools, like functional magnetic resonance imaging (fMRI) and positron emission tomography (PET), to map the synaptic taxonomy of different emotions and behaviors, which is allowing us to see the human brain and behavior in an entirely new light.

Interestingly, former US president Barack Obama foresaw a game-changing potential in the deeper understanding of the human brain. He seeded Project BRAIN (Brain Research through Advancing Innovative Neuro-technologies), with an investment of $100 million in 2013, billing it as the next "Space Race."[5] The stated goals of the project were to accelerate:

> the development and application of new technologies that will enable researchers to produce dynamic pictures of the brain that show how individual brain cells and complex neural circuits interact at the speed of thought. These technologies will open new doors to explore how the brain records, processes, uses, stores, and retrieves vast quantities of information, and shed light on the complex links between brain function and behavior.

You would think that studies aimed at understanding the links between brain function and human behavior emerging as a national priority would catch the wandering eye of marketers, right? Well, not exactly.

In this race to apply brain sciences to our very way of life, brand marketers are nowhere to be seen. The organization ideas42 specializes in applying behavioral sciences to social problems. It draws on and posts an online directory of experts from leading academic institutions in the world. The list boasts of over 100 gurus in 10 different domains, stretching from education and health to finance and international development. But marketers are MIA—missing in action. There are almost none on the list from marketing and branding, the two fields that live and breathe the art of shaping consumer behavior and choice.

Mind you, marketers have known for some time now that what people say they will do does not exactly match up with what they actually do, and a lot of time and resources have been devoted to analyzing the differences. Marketers in the consumer products world know that a "buy one and get one free" offer may work better than "buy two and get 50 percent off." Birth control pill marketers know that it is better for good adherence to let people take a pill every day versus for only the requisite 21 days.[6]

What is new is that now we understand a lot more about the mental machinery that makes us behave the way we do. We know why we do what we do. And that opens many doors to how we think about marketing and branding.

TAKE IT AND GO

As for me, after my moment of enlightenment at McKinsey post the dot-com crash, I knew that the path to great branding lay in embracing behavioral sciences and psychology. In 2003, I started my own consulting company, Cerenti, with a focus on helping brands grow. Given the freedom to mold my shop to my own fancy, I decided to double down on behavioral approaches. With a small band of young and irreverent marketing firebrands, we went where few others ventured, migrating from merely designing behavioral tactics to spur sales to rethinking brands. This was an important distinction.

Most marketers who turned to the new behavioral sciences devoted themselves to selling and retailing tactics, as had I in my days at McKinsey. They focused on finding clever tricks to optimize web pages and coax people into loading their virtual shopping carts. They helped retailers reorganize their shelves and re-channel traffic to increase the "shopping basket size."

Instead, we focused on using brain sciences to reinvent brands themselves, a much more ambitious endeavor. Our efforts, along with those of a visionary clique of clients, were instrumental in the creation of two of the world's hottest brands—PediaSure in the children's nutrition market and Humira in pharmaceuticals, both of which I discuss later.

The good news is that a lot of insightful work has already been completed by brain scientists and is ripe for the taking. At my company, Cerenti, we have been doing exactly that; not reinventing the wheel but devising new frameworks and adapting the extant body of research to real-world brands together with our clients. *Branding Between the Ears* is thus a blueprint for designing epic brands for marketers in industries as diverse as consumer products, pharma, credit cards, high-tech, and auto insurance.

The book lays out an entirely new approach, which I have dubbed cognitive branding, based on years of development and real-world testing, for designing and building epic brands. *To translate good theories to great business, you need three things: core principles, intuitive frameworks, and case studies. The principles give marketers the rules for playing the game. Frameworks allow them to apply the rules to their own brands. Case studies provide the conviction that all of it works. I provide all three in easy-to-understand terms.*

This book is written to guide and inspire you to use the work of the many brilliant, modern-day brain scientists with your own brands. It has a "let's get into it" mentality. Most of my clients are business managers who don't have the time to muck around through volumes of research on neuroscience and psychology. With this book, they can rest easy, confident in the knowledge that they don't have to. And yet for those who may feel the urge to delve into the science, it is cataloged in the footnotes.

Many books on marketing psychology make it a point to highlight the parts of the brain anatomy that relate to specific functions of the brain. While it is nice to know that there is such taxonomical research taking place in labs around the world, it is not particularly helpful to throw a bunch of challenging Latin terms at the practicing marketer. If you don't believe me, try this on for size:

> The [brain] circuit most associated with pleasure and reward is the mesolimbic pathway . . . located in the brainstem . . . Within [it] is an area called the ventral tegmental area (VTA) . . . [that] projects to the nucleus accumbens (thought to be the reward center). The neurotransmitter most commonly linked with the mesolimbic system is dopamine. Many people consider dopamine to be the driving force behind the human pursuit of pleasure.[7]

Ouch! Just reading that makes your head hurt! But all you really need to know is that systems in the brain create sensations of pleasure and happiness in response to a brand experience.

Slipping in science-laden language in your spiel can make you look creepily smart but serves no practical purpose other than intimidating your audience. For the most part, in this book, I have avoided it. I have left enough here and there so if indeed you were tempted to unnerve a disagreeable colleague, you could casually slip in a little, shall we say, Latin English into the conversation. This is a book for anyone with an interest in consumer psychology and branding by a lifelong marketer in the everyday language of nonmarketers. After all, aren't we all marketers at heart?

The stuff in this book is new and different. For that reason alone, it can feel a wee bit mind-bending at times. So having a map of where we are headed in the rest of the material can help.

In this chapter, we learned that cognitive brands are the hits they are because they work the way the brain does and are the key for unlocking the sensations of experiences and fantasies lodged in our minds. That was simply an introduction to the idea. We will explore more precisely how the brain works in the rest of Part One of the book. Then, in Part Two, we'll cover brand strategy, and in Part Three, brand execution.

Part One: How Brain Science Is Revolutionizing Branding

In Chapter 1, "Brands That Rock," I describe how advances in brain sciences are giving us a new and deeper level of understanding of how humans think and behave.

In Chapter 2, "Beyond the Illusions of the Past," I cover new findings from brain sciences that are shaking the foundations of branding as we know it today.

In Chapter 3, "Right Between Your Ears," I show a new model for how the brain works, so we can go on to design brands that work the way it does.

Part Two: Cognitive Brands: Design

In Chapter 4, "Brands That Work the Way the Brain Does," I show that cognitive brands are special and have three elements, namely, good vibes, sense, and resolve. This model replaces the soggy old brand constructs of the past that relied on mechanically laddering functional and emotional equities.

In Chapters 5 to 8, I explain in-depth what each of the three elements of the cognitive branding model is, with case studies from my client experiences and examples from my company's research.

In Chapter 9, "For the Love of Kids," I bring the cognitive branding model to life with a case study of PediaSure, a children's nutrition brand that my company helped to turn into a global blockbuster.

In Chapter 10, "Brands with Purpose," I discuss how cognitive brands can look to do good and pursue beneficial societal goals beyond just selling more.

Part Three: Cognitive Brands: Execution

In Chapter 11, "Tales from the Trenches—Brand Execution," I cover considerations in executing brand strategies in the real world, applying the latest relevant discoveries from brain sciences.

In Chapter 12, "Brand Sensations," I describe how our five senses can and must play a role in designing and executing brand experiences.

In Chapter 13, "Minding Your Manners," I cover ethical considerations in using brain sciences to manipulate consumers and provide a framework for making good moral brand design and execution choices.

In Chapter 14, "Where Do We Go from Here?" I talk a little about the future of cognitive branding and the required mindset for designing cognitive brands.

With that, we are ready to rock.

KEY TAKEAWAYS

The mystery of what makes some brands so iconic and others just also-rans is the stuff of urban legends in marketing. That coding and decoding, the mantra for how to make connections in the brain that drive consumers to buy the chosen brands, is the holy grail that marketers seek. Over the last several decades, countless scholars and practitioners have uncovered invaluable clues, but none present the whole story. Recent advances in brain sciences offer us a terrific look into our mental machinery, solving the mysteries of why consumers behave the way they do and how they choose the brands they buy.

As a result, there are three new truths in marketing:

1. Cognitive brands are the *keys to unlocking the sensations of experiences and fantasies in our minds.*

2. They do so because *they work the way our brain does.*

3. What's in them are three elements, namely, *good vibes, sense, and resolve.*

In the remainder of the book, we will dive deep into what exactly these new principles mean. In doing so, we will learn to master the art and science of cognitive branding. We start our journey in the next chapter by looking at some of the holy tenets of branding that today are under siege, and sort out what's not working and needs to change.

CHAPTER 2

BEYOND THE ILLUSIONS OF THE PAST

t is not the case that everything you knew about branding from the past is wrong, but maybe half of it is. And now we are learning a lot more about that half.

John Wanamaker, if he were alive today, would be a happier man. He is the guy who nearly a hundred years back memorably griped, "Half the money I spend on advertising is wasted; the trouble is I don't know which half." He is famous for saying that because, amazingly, until recently, he was mostly right. Not so much anymore. With the help of brain sciences, we are getting to be a lot smarter about what works and how. But marketers need to shed the illusions of the past and look at the new rules.

Let's start by taking a look at the widely acclaimed recent commercial for Enbrel, a drug by Amgen for patients with rheumatoid arthritis (RA), that has people reaching for their Kleenex boxes through misty eyes. RA is a degenerative disease and gets worse over time if left untreated. Thus it is natural for patients to worry about the possibility of losing their ability to walk and do things for themselves later in life.

As a marketer, you can't exactly say, "Take my drug or you will end up in a wheelchair." You might want to, but it's not nice. Enbrel cleverly threads this needle of propriety in its television commercials by using a child to voice his mother's fears. The spot opens by showing a mother in her thirties happily helping her young son with his drawing homework. The scene unfolds through his eyes as he intones his thoughts into words that go something like this:

> My mom's RA pain was intense. I wondered if she could keep doing what she does for us, which is kinda a lot . . . and if that pain can mean something worse?

The little boy is adorable, and just the idea of him "losing" his mom tugs at our heartstrings.[1] But there was a problem. In my in-depth interviews with tens of patients, many could recall the adorable little boy and his poignant story, but very few could remember that the ad was about a brand called Enbrel! With arms flailing in the air, they'd say something like, "What's that drug where the cute little boy talks about his mom? It's on the tip of my tongue, but now I can't remember."

Hmm. People remember your ad but not your brand? Not good! We will return to dissecting this ad a bit more in a later chapter, focusing on its good parts. For now, let's take a look at five tectonic shifts in how we have traditionally thought about brands.

EMOTIONAL BRANDING IS TRICKY AND MAY HURT YOUR BRAND

Marketers have long believed that emotionalizing brands is good. It strengthens a brand's connection with consumers who remember it better and are more loyal to it. The good news is that research shows that we indeed do remember emotional experiences better than nonemotional ones. However, when we witness emotionally charged events, we increase our focus on the central drama but decrease it on the peripheral details.[2]

In the Amgen ad, patients remember the boy because he was central to the emotional storyline, but not the brand, Enbrel, because it was a secondary, nonemotional detail. This kind of trade-off is particularly true when negative emotions are on display. Thus, over-the-top emotional branding can be effective and defective. The result? Ads that make us laugh and cry but do little for the brand.

No marketer understood this trade-off better than Steve Jobs. Between 2006 and 2009, Apple shot 300 commercials around their campaign "Get a Mac," but only 66 ever aired. In a number of amusing vignettes, the ads cast a cool and hip Apple Guy versus the uptight and techie PC Guy. So why did Jobs say no to some of the laugh-out-loud Apple versus Microsoft ads?

Justin Long, the actor who played the Apple Guy, inquired why one particularly hilarious ad, which featured Zach Galifianakis playing a drunken Santa Claus, had never aired. He was informed by Apple that "Steve Jobs preferred when (the ads) weren't super funny because he thought it would detract from the point of the commercial. He thought if people were too focused on the humor in it, they would lose sight of the product." Jobs was probably right about that, even though I note that the research shows that with positive emotions there is less of the focalizing that I described earlier. But hey, why risk it?

As a marketer, you have to be careful that the intensity of emotions around the storyline supports but does not overwhelm the main idea behind the brand itself.

In a similar vein, research by Ellie Parker and Adrian Furnham shows that sex doesn't necessarily sell either.[3] In their studies, people who watched sexually suggestive commercials on TV had no better recall of the brands than those who watched nonsexual ones. Further, people who watched advertisements between sexually laced shows may remember the shows better than the ads. The memory of the sexual episode itself may overshadow the recall of the brand.

Similarly, there has been a high concern among marketers that when super-hot models are placed in commercials, people may focus and remember the models but not the brands. I show later that to make emotional branding work, you have to embed the brand's own narrative into the overall storyline carefully.

YOU DON'T THINK, FEEL, AND ACT; YOU JUST DO IT!

To get inside the mind of a customer, brand marketers have always needed a theory of how the brain works. The traditional version of it goes as the Think, Feel, Act model or some other glorified version of it.[4] It says that given a brand stimulus, a customer thinks about what to make of it, considers how those thoughts make him feel, and finally, acts on the said feelings. The thinking piece is assumed to communicate the rational benefits of the brand to you, the feeling slice takes the emotional benefits to your gut, and the combination of the two is supposed to lead you to action or the buying-the-brand part.

As a theory, this model has been popular because it kind of makes sense. But here's the rub. Modern behavioral science shows that our brain works in this way only 5 percent of the time.[5, 6] That's pretty close to never!

Imagine this. You're cruising along on the I-20 freeway in Texas, and through the corner of your eye, you spot a billboard for the local smokehouse in Abilene, with the picture of a big, fat, and juicy brisket. You're hungry. You're tired. You're bored. The next thing you know, you hear a little rumble from your stomach, you feel your mouth water, and you can almost smell the charred end tips on the meat. Hmm. But wait, if the Think, Feel, Act model is true, then you would have thought about the proposition first, and only then felt aroused, and allowed your mouth to salivate. And wouldn't you have realized it was a bit pointless to slobber over an interstate billboard and dispensed with that and the stomach rumbling part? Think, feel, and act can be sequential, but don't have to be so in brand experiences, and usually aren't.[7]

Brand experiences are stored in our memories as cognitive bundles. Each bundle contains smart information on a curated set of your interactions with the brand—what the stimulus and context were, what you thought and felt about it, how each one of your five senses reacted, what choices you made, and the actions you took at the time.

The next time you feel the same stimulus in the appropriate context, the entire cognitive bundle is released in a flush. You choose and act even as you think and feel. These bundles of experiences are unleashed only when properly triggered. In other words, the brand message has to be just so for the cognitive bundle to unleash the full glory of the stored experience.

Thus cognitive brands are the keys to unlocking the sensations of past experiences or, as we shall see, even harbored fantasies. When properly keyed, the essence of the prior experiences is relived, detonating like a liquor-filled chocolate in the mouth, releasing magnificently the captive flavors and aromas as a single explosion.

The cognitive bundles in our brain evolve constantly. As new encounters take place with the brand, more information may be appended to previously rendered cognitive bundles. This reduces the future effort necessary to decipher sensory inputs.

If you happen to smell chocolate chip cookies while walking through a shopping mall, and they smell just the way they used to when your mother made them when you were a kid, all of that will immediately come back to you in a flash even though the food court in the mall is not your house and that certainly is not your mother behind the counter. You may not actually remember your mom's cookies vividly, but you experience what is called the *affective residue*[8] or sensations of those past experiences.

In a twist, the mall lady may serve her cookies with a homemade mint sweet cream sauce, and now you have another memory of an elevated experience added to the "chocolate chip cookies" cognitive bundle. This continuous enrichment of the stored experiences makes you more discerning about your future brand choices and keeps raising the bar for marketers.

CHOICE IS MOSTLY SUBCONSCIOUS OR LOWLY VIGILANT

Brand marketers so far have worked under the thesis that people make choices rationally or emotionally. Instead, Daniel Kahneman points out that there are two processes, which he dubbed System 1 and System 2, by which the brain works, either of which can be rational or emotional.[9] This new model creates unique opportunities for marketers to influence behavior subconsciously and consciously. Mastering these two systems and how they work with each other is the path to engineering consumer choice in the future.

System 1 is a collection of processing capabilities that the brain uses to make decisions by relating things to its past learnings and experiences. For that reason, it is referred to as the associative component of the brain, and because it draws on what it already knows, it is fast and instinctive. In some cases, it taps literal memories like, "What did I do the last time someone threw a rotten tomato at me?" In other cases, it connects the dots with similar experiences, as in, "What do I do now, when someone is throwing a different vegetable at my face?"

System 1 is adept at responding to situations by applying beliefs and cognitive biases we have developed over the years. When brands align their message to such preexisting wisdom, they are adopted by consumers with minimal introspection. In other words, the brand choice is made with low vigilance and in some cases subconsciously, without any vigilance at all.

If you are a brand marketer, you can see how this could be exciting— and especially so when you consider the fact that humans use System 1 to make choices 95 percent[10] of the time. This is why, often when you come back from a trip to the grocery store, you may find things that you hadn't noticed you were buying ("Did I really bring back another tub of the Chunky Monkey ice cream?"). And this is why you may have more ugly Christmas sweaters in your closet than you really need.

System 2 is the vigilant and deliberative part of the brain. Unlike System 1, which is always on, System 2 kicks in only when a more complete analysis of the situation is warranted. These are the faculties of the brain that we use when faced with complex or higher-risk brand choices. In a later chapter, I discuss how marketers must awaken System 2 in their consumers when their products and services are so different from convention that people have to change their mindsets to accept them.

System 2 methods for driving choice present a steeper hill to climb and take more time than System 1 processes but are unavoidable for some brands. This is why people did not start buying groceries online immediately during the first dot-com boom of the early 2000s, but now they do. This is why people did not cut the cord on their landlines with the advent of the cell phones, but now most have.

In today's world, marketers must be smart about how they use System 1 and System 2 drivers to design their brands. The two systems work seamlessly inside a person's brain. So while marketers can appeal to a consumer's System 1 for an instinctive choice in many cases, the more conscious and deliberate System 2 will override System 1 when it really counts. So yes, I will not come back with that tub of Chunky Monkey every time from the grocery store. Maybe only the first five times.

Conversely, when System 2 has done all the evaluation it wanted to, it is not going to waste time and energy on it in a future similar situation. It will encode the experience into System 1. This is how System 2 encodes brand loyalty.

The first time you used Uber, you probably had to think a lot about it. You had to download the app and decide to entrust your credit card to it. But now, anytime you need a ride, you just Uber it. As a matter of fact, I see people call an Uber and wait 10 minutes for it, even when there are taxis parked right across the road. Although, arguably, sometimes that may be due to other advantages that Uber offers—like the convenience of noncash payments—mostly it's just the mental momentum of repeating a choice that had been investigated and made earlier, a Pavlovian reflex.

THE WHAT AND HOW
OF BRANDING LIVE AS ONE

Traditionally, marketers work on their brand execution strategies only after they have finished developing their brand positioning. Yet behavioral science tells us that it matters not just what you say but also how you say it.

Let's go back and take a look at what happened in the highly charged US presidential election of 2016. Border control, gun violence, and access to healthcare were three important issues for swing voters. In the traditional branding lingo, you would call these *preference driving equities*. While both Donald Trump and Hillary Clinton were addressing these issues, they were doing so very differently. Trump warned Americans about everything they stood to lose: You'll lose your jobs to a flood of immigrants. You'll lose your guns to the government. And you'll lose your doctor to Obamacare. In contrast, Hillary Clinton was trying to build a vision of the great shining city on the hill. She talked about how open immigration would attract the best talent from across the world, how gun control would make the streets safer for children, and how an expanded Obamacare would mean better health for all. So why did so many swing voters respond favorably to Trump?

Well, because of how he said it! There is a cognitive bias known as "loss aversion" that says that all else being equal, people are more sensitive to what they stand to lose versus what they could gain, even when the amount of loss or gain is the same. Trump, in massive rallies across the country, honed his message of losses to perfection as made evident in the "Make America Great Again" chant of his followers.

In psychology, there is also something called the *framing effect*.[11] It says that our choices are influenced by the way they are framed through different wordings, settings, and situations. Given two equally attractive choices, you will have a preference (and pay more) for the one that is framed better. *For brand marketers, the lesson is that the* what *of branding cannot be separated from the* how *of branding. Brand positioning and activation live and breathe as one.*

In 2005, I was working with Keli Bennett, who was then already a hotshot consumer marketer working on Humira,* Abbott's wonder drug for treating rheumatoid arthritis. Keli was among the few marketers to

---

* The events described in the following passages about Humira have been fictionalized to hide any nonpublic information and preserve the privacy of the individuals mentioned. The narrative is thus designed to be instructive rather than accurately biographical or historical.

have seen the potential for cognitive branding far ahead of her industry peers in the pharma world. Her pioneering efforts may have done more for shaping what consumer marketing for biologic drugs is today, than any other single person.

Research from the market showed that patients felt like they needed a weapon against their disease, a smart bomb that could go kill the disease. Yet as we debated the topic further, it also became evident that the perfect weapon positioning that tested well in surveys and focus groups was actually hard to activate. How do you turn a patient's body into a battleground? After all, in which war does the battleground win anything? Would you do commercials with bombs exploding inside the patient's body? A deadly warrior hacking at the innards? In-depth discussions with patients slowly uncovered concerns that led Keli to pursue other more feasible avenues that contributed to making Humira what it is today. In this case, the *what* of the branding was pretty solid, but the *how* was inexecutable.

THERE'S SOMETHING TO THE BRANDS OF OUR DREAMS

In conventional branding, there is a fear that consumer attention spans are short. Thus marketers dumb down the brand message in hopes of getting it across within that fleeting moment of attention. They look for magic phrases like Ali Baba's "open sesame" that could help them wondrously open the mouth of the treasure caves inside consumers' minds. Research shows that this happens only when the customer is already inclined to buy your product. But then what do you need marketing for? In real life, we make choices quite differently. What we learn about a brand lingers in our minds, at some point begins to make sense and leads us to go buy it. It may be fast or slow. Think about those delayed aha moments that we all experience from time to time.

In 2004, I had a team working on Humira, a year or so after its launch. At the time it was struggling to gain traction in the market. Its nemesis was Enbrel, a drug from Amgen, that worked equally well and in pretty much the same way. There were two differences between the drugs, and neither seemed to matter much to physicians prescribing the products. The first difference was that Humira would have to be self-injected by patients once every two weeks and Enbrel twice a week.

However, biologics were relatively new to the market and doctors were very worried about their long-term effects. Since Enbrel had entered the market three years earlier, there were thousands of patients already on it and it was a known quantity. As a result, while Humira was obviously a more convenient drug for the patient, the doctors didn't care a whit about that. The second difference was that Humira was manufactured from "fully human" cells, as opposed to Enbrel, which was made using part-animal cells. Again, there was no clinical data to suggest one was better or worse than the other. Thus, Humira was struggling to break through the status quo bias for the tried-and-true favoring Enbrel.

To figure out how to put some wind in the sails of Humira, we crunched our databases to look for physicians who had changed their behavior, from prescribing very little of Humira to prescribing a lot. There were only a handful across the country and one of them was a Dr. Katz. I decided to jump on a plane and go meet him.

There I was sitting with Dr. Katz in his busy practice outside a retiree town in sunny Florida. I didn't wait long to pop the question, "So what gives, doc? How come you went from prescribing Humira to only 6 percent of your new patients to 83 percent?"

"So, you understand that I don't like switching patients willy-nilly from one drug to another once I start them, right?" he asked. I nodded. It was common knowledge that switching patients was inadvisable. Any biologic drug we take triggers in our system the production of antibodies that resist the drug. Hence, once a drug settles in and is working, you don't want to muck around with it. If you try a new drug, these antibodies may block it from working, and the new antibodies that the new drug gives rise to may stop the old drug from working, leaving you flat out of options. You get the idea; switching is bad.

"You know, for the first year that your drug was in the market, I really saw no upside to trying your drug for my new patients. Humira was the last resort for patients for whom Enbrel failed to work," he said. I nodded again. That is exactly what most other rheumatologists were doing.

"And then one day it hit me," he continued, suddenly energized. "If I used Humira first on new patients, I would have to risk fewer switch-overs!" Confused, I responded, "But you said earlier both drugs work equally well." "Well, what happens is that some 10 to 15 percent of the patients have a form of the disease that for unknown reasons requires a higher dose." Dr. Katz said. "With Enbrel, since it is already twice a week, I can't double it. With Humira I can always go to once a week versus every other week and not have to switch."

"But then you would only be writing prescriptions for those few patients that needed the higher dose? Why the 80 percent of all new patients," I persisted. "Simple. I don't know which patients will require a double dose until I actually start them on the drug. So if I always start them on Humira, I know I won't have to switch them as often because I can always step up the dose as a fallback! That was a big aha moment for me. I can't believe it took me a whole year to figure it out," Dr. Katz said, beaming proudly at his own discovery.

As marketers, it was an epiphany for us too. We had always thought that Humira's main advantage was its less frequent, more convenient dosing for the patient. Instead, it was the flexibility to increase the dose if needed. When we tried the latter argument with other rheumatologists, we got the same reaction: "I hadn't quite thought of it that way, but now that you mention it, it makes a whole lot of sense."

With the help of a new brand message and a host of other innovative marketing programs, Humira would go on to become one of the world's largest global brands, with over $20 billion in annual sales today.

Unlike System 2, System 1 processes in our brain are always on, scouring past experiences and making finer and finer connections. And then one day, the light bulb goes on; a flash of lightning, out of the blue. If you have emerged from your morning shower with a sudden epiphany, you know now what I'm talking about.

When the brain encounters stimuli that are too overwhelming to fully resolve, it records the information and tags it for subsequent processing. It took our Dr. Katz a whole year and us longer. *In other words, marketers need not be afraid to overload the consumer with useful brand information. Don't dumb it down.*

Marketers can make aha moments easier for customers by leaving a trail of breadcrumbs for them to follow to the ultimate answer. Brand promises that connect with a customer's prior beliefs, experiences, or learning can help do exactly that. This is in part due to a process that psychologists call *processing fluency*. When we explained to physicians how Humira could give them greater treatment flexibility, they could get to their own aha moments faster, because they already believed switching patients was a bad idea. Baby steps and breadcrumbs work far better in branding than tall tales and grandiose visions of nirvana with your brand.

For the sake of completion, I should mention that there is even a question around whether some epiphanies occur while we dream. A recent article in the *Wall Street Journal* posed the question, "Can a person learn while sleeping?"[12] It cites research by Sanam Hafeez, a neuropsychologist at Columbia University, who explains that while the brain is bombarded by various stimuli all day, sleep is the time when the brain can filter, categorize, and consolidate that information. "As it tunes out all distractions, the brain encodes information and decides how important a memory or piece of information is," Dr. Hafeez said.

There is actually a word for this, namely *hypnopedia*, or sleep-learning, whereby researchers have shown that during some nondreaming cycles of sleep, the hippocampus, the area of the brain related to memory and learning, is activated.[13]

Who knew! Maybe there is something to the idea of the brands of our dreams? No? Well, sleep on it, will ya?

KEY TAKEAWAYS

Traditional branding approaches are built on a foundation of many half-truths. That has been the case because until now, we knew no better. Today, brain science is shedding light on what's right and wrong with our brand premises. Here's what we are learning:

- Emotionalizing brands does work because consumers remember such narratives more easily and for longer. However, if you are not careful, they will remember the emotional elements of the story but not your brand.

- It seems logical to believe that when presented a brand choice, the brain would first think about it, then check to see if it feels good, and finally prompt the consumer to buy it. In fact, whenever possible, the brain works mostly by comparing current brand experiences with related ones from the past, and thinking, feeling, and acting similarly, not necessarily in any order.

- Marketers like to highlight the rational and emotional benefits of their brands. The brain works differently. It uses two processes, System 1 and System 2, which use association and deliberation to make choices.

- While the brain is perfectly capable of conscious and subconscious choice, most of the time it works with the latter, skipping a detailed evaluation of the brand benefits.

- Brand strategy and execution must be considered as one and the same and planned together rather than sequentially, as it normally is. The *what* and *how* of a brand have to be designed as one or its message may be lost.

- Marketers assume that consumer attention spans are short and try to deliver their messages in small bites. In fact, brands can present longer and more complicated messages because the brain has the machinery to listen now and figure it out later.

This chapter was a sneak peek into how the foundations of branding are shifting. In the remainder of the book, we will learn exactly how to use this knowledge to design epic brands that work the way our brain does. In the next chapter, I present a new model of how the brain works when choosing among brands.

CHAPTER 3

RIGHT BETWEEN
YOUR EARS

Psychologists sometimes like to point out that everything about sex happens not where you might think, but between your ears. Everything about branding, too, happens not on perky store shelves, or dazzling billboards, or streamed OLVs (online videos), . . . but in your brain. That's right, *everything about branding happens right between your ears*!

If you pause for a minute, both premises should be obvious. All that we see, touch, hear, smell, and taste is a sensory stimulus to the brain that triggers a conscious or subconscious response. But all of it is simply what the brain makes of it. Even when it isn't. That is why amputees, nearly all of them, feel the presence of a phantom limb: because their brain believes it's there.[1]

It's not just limbs; it's everything. The notion that all reality is contrived in the mind has been around for a while, starting with Indian Vedic philosophers who lived in 1500 BCE to more recently, the Keanu Reeves character, Neo, in the movie *The Matrix*. In the latter, the wise old

Morpheus gives Neo the choice of taking the red pill and facing the bitter reality, or taking the blue pill and living in a dream.

Morpheus says, "This is your last chance. After this, there is no turning back. You take the blue pill—the story ends, you wake up in your bed and believe whatever you want to believe. You take the red pill—you stay in wonderland and I show you how deep the rabbit hole goes." Ironically, in the real world, the only choice of reality is that of the blue pill, the one that our senses can perceive, and then what our brain makes of those perceptions. It is all right between our ears.

Even though we cannot have true reality, we do have volition. Volition is considered by philosophers to be the tiebreaker that distinguishes humans from animals.[2] And the fondness for shaping volition is what separates brand marketers from normal people. To understand how volition, or brand choice, comes about, we need to take a peek at how the brain works.

There are many mysteries and myths surrounding the human brain. Today, with what we know, hopefully there are fewer of both. So, no, humans don't just use 10 percent of their brain capacity, leaving the remaining 90 percent for telekinesis and other untapped feats.[3] We use all of our brain, most of the time. And no, there aren't people who are left-brained and artsy or others who are right-brained and logical.

Rather, brain scans show that humans don't favor one brain hemisphere over the other, nor is one hemisphere dominant for some.[4] So sorry, you cannot segment your customers as left- and right-brained, but you could use a mix of brand strategies to appeal to their creative or logical sides. And finally, AI-based computers won't displace humans anytime soon. The brain does innumerable things better than the best supercomputers, despite being slower and having less memory. Less is more! Why? Because our brain does not work the same way as computers.

The human brain consists of over 80 billion neurons, each of which, on an average, connects to 10,000 others, forming a network with a hundred trillion connections.[5] While supercomputers can now beat the best human minds in games like chess and Jeopardy, even the garden-variety brain can beat a supercomputer in a multitude of everyday tasks.

For example, it is difficult for computers to understand a sentence like, "Some people think that sleeping at the wheel in their self-driving Teslas is hip, but it's just pulp-brained!" Computers would also have a hard time figuring why a movie like *Aliens* is scary given that the extraterrestrial in question is nonexistent and known to you to be fictional. So how *does* the human brain work?

A WORKING MODEL OF THE BRAIN

Marketers have always felt a need to have a model for how the brain works. It gives them more confidence in their assertions. Remember, we talked about the rational plus emotional model of the brain and the Think, Feel, Act model. Since I trashed both of those, I feel I owe you a replacement.

I am not going to discuss what part of the brain does what. If you have a thing for anatomy, you can get the basics from lessons taught to elementary-middle school kids (yes, they make them super smart these days).[6] My goal is to give you a brand marketer's stylized version of the functions of the brain, as shown in Figure 3.1. For where we are going, that is more useful. I divide the brain into four main functional subunits:

1. Associator

2. Deliberator

3. Learner

4. Conator

It is a bit dicey to have to explain four things. So I'm going to do it fast first, and then slow with an example.

Every brand stimulus or experience is evaluated either by the *Associator* using System 1 or the *Deliberator* using System 2 processes for whether or not they make any *sense*. In other words, the brain looks at

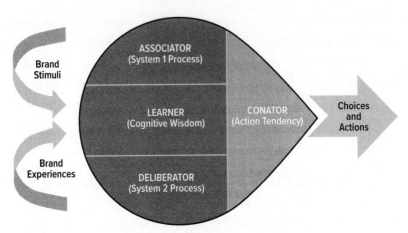

Figure 3.1 Functional model of the brain.
(*Courtesy:* Cerenti Marketing Group, LLC)

whether what the brand says makes sense instinctively or critically. If it does, then that constitutes a recommendation for the brand. It is a good choice.

But a recommendation is not the same thing as a purchase. The *Conator* scores how happy you would be with the proposed choice and how well it fits with your goals and then *resolves* to act or not act. The *Learner* subunit stores all of the information surrounding the event, including the recommendations and actions, as accepted wisdom for future reference. In this way, things that turn out well may give good *vibes* automatically in the future.

Now, let's take a deep breath and work through an example to understand each part of the brain in more detail.

> Oh, Look! We have some help! There's Jane at the Saks Fifth Avenue store on Michigan Avenue, eyeing a sultry mannequin swathed in an Eileen Fisher funnel neck sweater. Oh, yeah! She can totally see herself in it. She remembers how gorgeous she looks in pullovers like that and can perfectly imagine how her friends will drool over it. A smile breaks upon her lips, she feels a little warm and fuzzy, and her hand reaches out to caress the Italian cashmere.

Ok, stop action! We are witnessing Jane's *Associator* recall past brand experiences from the *Learner* subunit. Everything she felt in that moment, from the feel of the wool on her skin to the projected gratification from envious looks of her women friends, wafts out from cognitive bundles stored in her brain from previous encounters. Because she buys from Saks often, she also feels good vibes from the *Learner* about buying anything from there. After all, when has that ever gone wrong? Instinctively, the Eileen Fisher feels like a good idea.

The previous chapter showed that the *Associator* makes choices via System 1 by comparing present experiences to past ones. It could be an identical prior event or a similar situation. It works subconsciously or with low vigilance. Jane does not have to literally imagine herself in the sweater or the reactions of her girlfriends. Those sensations happen in the blink of an eye all by themselves.

In one sense, the *Learner* is a memorizer. It records the entire experience—what the situation was (context), what choice was recommended by the *Associator* or *Deliberator*, what action was taken, how good it felt, and how well it turned out—all as a single cognitive bundle. The *Learner*, of course, catalogs its own experiences in this way but is also capable of filing away brand choices of experts or endorsers it trusts.

But notice that I did not call the *Learner* subunit the "Memorizer." That is because while it does record experiences, it also learns from them continuously. Like the *Associator*, it is always on in the background, becoming a little smarter with each passing day. If Jane buys the sweater and is thrilled with it, until a month later when it starts pilling excessively, the *Learner* unit is going to take note and edit its memory so that she does not make the same costly mistake again.

The *Learner* also looks for relationships across experiences and will enhance the recorded information with hashtags like #Cashmere, #Sweaters, #LookAwesome, #LoveYouEileenFisher, and #SaksForever. It makes these connections whenever it has time to spare, possibly even while we sleep. The *Learner* is spectacular as a neural net that crunches data over time and makes us savvier shoppers. It is an evolving repository of what I call our individual "cognitive wisdom." It may not always be right, by the way, but it is our personal cache of knowledge, our conscious and subconscious guiding light.

OK. Let's get back to Jane. Lights! Camera! Action!

Jane picks up the sweater and stares at it. It's her favorite color, a lemon-zest yellow. As she drapes it over her arms, the price tag hidden deep in its folds slips open: $358. Ouch! She remembers that there are exactly zero dollars left in her monthly splurge-on-Jane budget. The unhappy face of her husband glowering at last month's Visa bill flits momentarily by an open window in her mind. Undeterred, she flips out her iPhone and googles for a better price.

Wait! The Eileen Fisher is not available anywhere, but she can get a cashmere mock neck in heathered chai, a color that is "in," from Everlane, for a paltry $228. Not exactly an Eileen Fisher, but good, very good.

All right. Stop action!

Even as the *Associator* in her brain reveled in the idea of donning the cashmere Eileen Fisher, there was a part of it that said, "Hmm. Sounds good, but I am not 100 percent sure," and it referred the matter over to the *Deliberator*.

The *Deliberator* is the System 2 subunit of the brain, adept at resolving situations that pose risks and complications. It can frame issues, weigh the pros and cons, apply theorems, follow algorithms, and perform computations in all kinds of neat ways. It takes effort to put on this kind of a show, so System 2 would rather avoid it if it can. In this case, the *Deliberator* helps Jane solve her three-dimensional shopping dilemma of $358 of awesomeness versus a likely derailed husband versus a $228 consolation prize. It tells her that going for the latter would be wise.

The *Learner* unit, by the way, also appends a confidence score to any recommendation to account for the "I'm not 100 percent" factor when it encodes the experience into the memory. That matters because answers with high confidence will not be questioned in the future and will pass through with low vigilance. For marketers, that means that their brand will be repurchased reflexively without further thought.

Now, everything I have said so far could happen, and yet nothing happens. The *Associator* likes the idea of the Eileen Fisher. The *Deliberator* cautions that the cheaper Everlane is the sensible choice. Jane may buy the Eileen Fisher or the Everlane, or simply walk away.

Brain sciences tell us that as humans we are programed to pursue happiness. Happiness is serious business, not in a manner of speaking, but literally, and involves neurochemical reactions of hormones like dopamine, norepinephrine, and oxytocin in our brain that give us actual warm fuzzies.[7] That dopamine rush is what makes her want the sweater in the first place and then want another one to keep the feeling going. The *Conator* subunit of the brain can forecast happiness; that is, it makes a guess as to how happy Jane will feel with each decision and calibrate it against her goals.

So what happens next?

Jane grabs the Eileen Fisher, marches off to the nearest sales counter, and is soon thereafter seen leaving the store with a glossy, black-ribbon Saks shopping bag and the biggest recorded smile in the history of the planet.

In this case, the happiness that Jane feels from the idea of looking stupendous in front of her friends proves too hard to resist. She goes for it.

Conation is one of the thousand most obscure words in the English language.[8] For brand marketers, it shouldn't be, because *conation* is defined as a person's innate tendency for action or resolve. Without it, you would create brand preferences but not brand buys. The *Conator* subunit is different in each of us and drives us to pursue different goals. Kathy Kolbe, a specialist in this field, attributes this to each individual's MO, or method by which their system operates.[9] So the same brand stimulus can have a distinct effect on different people.

Hold on! Did I mention that Jane was shopping at Saks with her identical twin, Joyce? Most people can't tell them apart, you know. Joyce, too, looked at the Eileen Fisher pullover. It left her unmoved. She passed quickly on it, picking up a $79 "Save the African Rhino" camouflage-green sweatshirt instead.

Even though the identically bodied Joyce would look just as gorgeous as Jane in the sweater, going around dressing to impress friends is not her thing. She would be happier doing something for the good of the world with her money. That is her *conative MO*. It is that kind of happiness that matters to her goals.

The *Conator* captures what cognitive marketer Steve Genco describes as the two *universal* motivations that drive consumer behavior.[10] The first is *aspirational,* a desire to be happier and better off tomorrow than today. And the second, related to having an *identity*, is a need to feel good about who we are and how we are perceived by others.

If all of this feels a little confusing, it really isn't. But it is different from how we have been used to thinking about consumer choice. Jane chooses to indulge her fantasies despite her own better judgment. Joyce saves a mammal on the other side of the planet. It's what our brain does; it connects our choice with our happiness. This understanding of how the brain functions leads us to a different framework for designing brands that work the way the brain does. In the following chapter I do exactly that and present a new model for architecting what I call cognitive brands.

KEY TAKEAWAYS

Cognitive brands work the way the brain does. So if we are to be successful in designing great brands, we need a solid understanding of how the brain works. This chapter provides a functional view of the marketing brain, which we see has four modules that work seamlessly together:

- The *Learner* subunit is where the brain stores its wisdom of the ages. All past brand experiences lie here, along with annotations on what the associated thoughts and feelings were at the time and what actions were taken.

- The *Associator* is one of the two choice modules in the brain. When presented a brand proposition, it subconsciously draws on its learnings from similar experiences in the past and tends to make similar choices for or against the brand.

- The *Deliberator* is the other choice module in the brain. It works by analyzing a brand experience in detail with sophisticated tools and methods. It is mentally taxing and thus sparingly used.

- The *Conator* is a module in the brain that resolves whether or not to act on the choices proposed by the *Associator* or *Deliberator*. It is different from person to person and defines their MO for taking action. If a choice seems iffy to a particular consumer given their own MO, the *Conator* may decide to park it and not have the consumer buy the brand. The consumer may like your brand but not want it.

Now that we know how the brain is organized, we can design our brands to work the same way. That is exactly what we start doing in the next chapter.

PART
TWO

COGNITIVE
BRANDS:
DESIGN

CHAPTER **4**

BRANDS THAT WORK
THE WAY THE BRAIN DOES

G iven everything we have learned so far, you would think that the field of branding would be in the midst of a bloody revolution, with marketers tearing down the old walls, redrawing boundaries, and building new foundations and pillars. Let's review the facts.

Fact #1: Nobel Prize–winning pioneers like Kahneman, Schiller, Thaler, and a myriad others have turned the world upside down in fields as disparate as economics, social anthropology, linguistics, and neuropsychology, with a consilience of discoveries on how consumers behave and make choices.[1]

Fact #2: Branding is all about understanding consumer behavior and shaping customer choice to favor your brand. And yet, the art of branding is at a standstill. There is not a lot happening that hasn't already happened. And that is because marketers are either distracted or comfortable in their soggy old shoes.

Normally, the task of reinventing branding would fall upon the marketers at iconic consumer products companies like Kraft, Procter &

Gamble, and Campbell's, which have been the torchbearers of all that is new and good in the field. But over the last two decades, these companies have been looking nervously over their shoulders at a new kind of threat: private equity (PE) firms that were leading a charge that often entailed the acquisition and destruction of the great consumer brands.

3G Capital, a Brazilian investment house, bought companies with strong *momentum* brands, like the iconic Kraft Foods in 2015, and milked them dry. In what was proudly celebrated as a "margin expansion strategy," 3G would cut the power, stop investing in the brands, and look around for ways to prop the profits by remaking the products with cheaper stuff.

With more cash flowing in, a PE firm like 3G could add debt and reward itself with handsome dividends. For some years, the brands would continue to cruise along, and reporters would dutifully barrage the company for pearls of wisdom. Carlos Sicupira, a 3G founding partner, obliged, with one-line zingers like "Costs are like fingernails: they always have to be cut."[2]

By 2018, the wheels had come off the bus, the share price of Kraft, one of 3G's crown jewels, crashed, and the party ended. Yet, it takes time to get new religion. By then, the PE firms had cultivated a cadre of marketers who treated gilded brands like fingernails that always had to be cut. And worse, other consumer product companies committed their own hara-kiri proactively, starving brands and launching margin expansion strategies to preempt the possibility of a takeover by a 3G-like PE cousin.

If consumer marketers were distracted and impoverished, those in other industries, like pharmaceuticals, consumer finance, insurance, and automotive, suffer from an embarrassment of riches. Yet, in many cases, they are stuck in the ways of the past. For example, in the pharma world, where money flows like water on blockbuster drugs, the companies often are constitutionally married to old formulas borrowed from their consumer product company cousins. And those are not working. In one study after another, we found that pharma brands were lost in a "sea of sameness." Consumers often struggle to tell one brand apart from another. This is truly astonishing because I am talking about markets in which the companies as a group may spend $200 to $500 million per year on television and online advertising.

According to Nielsen, in 2018, pharma marketers smacked down $5 billion on television ads in the US market alone. Pfizer, all by itself, spent $1 billion, including about $200 million on Chantix, a smoking cessation drug, and $160 million on Xeljanz, a rheumatoid arthritis drug.

It is true that with that much exposure to advertising, consumers are generally more aware of their options and motivated to ask their doctors about new drugs. Yet, the differential benefit to individual brands is questionable. The sea of sameness problem is not limited to the pharma world; other industries, including automotive, insurance, and telecom, find themselves in a similar predicament, feeling the pressure to differentiate their brands.

The good news is that there is the proverbial light at the end of the tunnel. Consumer marketers have seen the folly of the "3G ways" and are slowly returning to a focus on brands. Forward-looking managers, from pharma to consumer insurance, are questioning the wisdom of their tired old approaches to branding and opening the doors to new ideas.

My company's work with clients across several industries demonstrates that the problem with branding lies not in the amount of money and time spent on commercials, the packaging, brand cues, or the creative strategy. Rather, it has to do with the way brands are being positioned. Their message fails to rise above the clutter, not because it is not being repeated enough but because it is not sinking in. *And it is not sinking in because it does not work the way the brain does.*

To understand why we are stuck, it helps to take a look at the branding approaches in use and what's wrong with them.

BRAND LADDERS DON'T QUITE WORK

One of the most common ways to design brands is to ladder rational and emotional equities into a point of difference. What does that mean? Well, you go ask people what is important to them in a product. Make a note of the top three benefits that consumers get from how the product works. These are called the "functional or rational brand equities."

Then you ask consumers how they *feel* about the benefits they receive from the product. Make a list of those, too, because they will come in handy as "emotional brand equities." Next, mix the two lists together and knit together a brand message. This is an exercise akin to the children's game of "I'll give you two words (or phrases) and you make a sentence with them." Once you have done that, and this is the most important part, say a little prayer! Figure 4.1 shows you a version of the brand ladder framework.

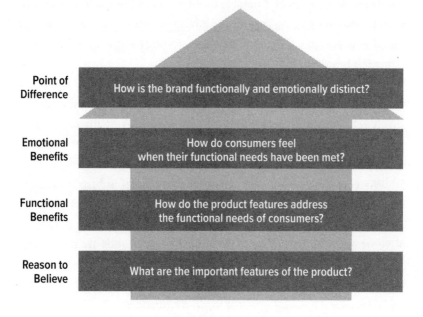

Figure 4.1   Traditional ladder-based branding approach.
(*Courtesy:* Cerenti Marketing Group, LLC)

Let's say that you sell ice cream. You may find that creaminess, a rational/functional benefit of ice cream, is important. You also observe that people eating ice cream seem happy, which is an emotional benefit. "Voilà!" You connect those two pieces of information into a tagline saying something like: "Sheer creaminess! Sheer happiness!" Sounds pretty cool, doesn't it? However, the whole idea that creaminess makes you happy is contrived. It may not stir a single neuron in your brain to make it care a whit. It is like a song with all the right elements, a great rhythm and outstanding vocals, and yet, it doesn't rock!

The idea of brands as a bundle of rational and emotional benefits has not changed much in the last 30 or so years. Yet, its seeds were sown centuries back. Rationalism grew out of the seventeenth century, as a reaction to the stifling faith-based dictates of the times, through the works of philosophers like René Descartes, Baruch Spinoza, and Gottfried Wilhelm Leibniz in the age of reason.

If people had stopped there, all we would have today is brands with functional benefits. But thanks to David Hume, and let's just give him the title of the father of emotional branding, we learned that humans also behave emotionally. Hume said, "Reason is, and ought only to be, the slave of the passions and can never pretend to any other office than to serve and obey them."[3] Pretty strong stuff!

In Book Two of *A Treatise of Human Nature,* Hume even published a taxonomy of human emotions. Imagine that! But wait, it's 2020 now. Hume did his thing over 200 years back. Now, we know a lot more about how the brain works. Isn't it time to put that knowledge into play?

This is not to say that brand ladders never work. Quite to the contrary, sometimes they work spectacularly well. Over the last century, marketers have built tons of iconic brands. But for every one of those, a thousand more are piled high on top of the soaring heap of brands you've never heard of. With that kind of a run rate, you have to wonder whether the brands that became hits were just lucky!

LIST BRANDING DOESN'T WORK EITHER

The other way that marketers run into trouble is when they try to brand their products as a list of benefits. It is tempting. After all, if the consumer has told you the three things that are most important to them in your product category, why not just say your brand is exactly those three things?

The trouble is humans are not particularly good at processing lists of disconnected benefits. I was recently chatting with the general manager of a pharma company who was in the midst of launching an exciting new drug for the treatment of atopic dermatitis. I asked him, "Hey, Don, so what are you saying about the brand?"

"Three things," he responded, without missing a beat. "First, it is a highly *effective* drug; second, it works *fast*; and third, it is, uh . . ." As he was talking, he was flipping open his fingers sequentially from a tightly wound fist in case the weight of the numeric count was lost on me, his solitary audience. And then, instead of the third finger snapping out, there was a seven-second silence as he struggled to recall the third benefit on his list. And then after several vigorous shakes of his hand to jog his memory, he cried, "And third, it is *convenient* for the dermatologist to use in his practice."

He turned to me, brandishing all three of the now unfurled fingers in my face for effect, "Well, what do you think?"

"It's brilliant," I responded. "If you can remember it. But if *you* are having trouble, how will *physicians* distracted by patients have any recall of it? Especially, when the brand message is being blurted out by a nervous young sales rep on a 30-second timer."

The challenge of list branding is that not all of its pieces connect into a real story. To understand why this does not work well, let us use a puzzle analogy. Think of your product as a 20-piece jigsaw puzzle, where each piece is a product feature or brand equity. Close your eyes and imagine that the puzzle depicts a Cézannesque painting of a happy-go-lucky peasant girl, riding atop a cart piled high with bales of hay and a donkey straining at its reins to pull it through a field brimming with daffodils swaying gently in the breeze.

Now we pull the puzzle apart and jumble up the pieces. Then I instruct you to rank each piece individually for attractiveness and pick the top three. You may pick one with the laughing face of the girl, one with the weary donkey, and a third with a flower. Well done! Now we say, knit these very cool pieces into a brand idea.

You go, "Hmm, donkey, plus flower, plus girl face." So in a moment of displaced brilliance, you say, "Use my brand and even a *donkey* can feel like a *happy girl* that will *flower* into her true potential."

Absurd, you say. Yet companies, all over, use this approach of knitting together unrelated attractive pieces to don their brand message all the time. This is wrong because our brain does not make sense of the world—in this case, the painting—in this manner. It does pick pieces, to be sure, as research has shown, but craftily only those that help it understand the picture.

Instead of following my instructions, you may have been better off picking three pieces around the donkey to show it carrying the burden of mankind, or three pieces around the peasant girl to show her ensconced in the happiness of youth, or three pieces around the swaying daffodils to show the indifference of mother nature to the travails of humanity. Even if some of those pieces were rather plain, you would have been more successful in telling a memorable story true to the essence of the painting. That is because those pieces connect together and say something. They work better because even though some important elements of the big picture are missing, the story told is true and sensible.

And so it is for cognitive branding. The idea is to take a few cognitive threads to knit together an engaging story that the audience can remember and find compelling. Not every brand equity that pops up as important in market research has to be a part of the story, but the equities that are in there must relate some compelling threads of the drama. In the process, you may, in fact, leave out some key equities. That's fine, don't sweat it. When customers are drawn to your brand, they will go on to discover the other parts of its story.

THE COGNITIVE BRANDING FRAMEWORK

In the following chapters, we will learn how to create the mental threads that weave together the fabric of iconic cognitive brands. Having invoked Cezanne in coloring our analogy, let's reflect on how the master thought about great art: "For an impressionist to paint from nature is not to paint the subject, but to realize sensations." *With cognitive brands, we look to find the keys that can unlock the sensations of past experiences or fantasies that live consciously or subconsciously in our minds and when thus keyed, make us feel happier.*

As we go through our lives, we experience sensations at every moment. If you thought that our brains recorded a snapshot from each of the five human senses, five times per second, for as long as we lived, a

75-year-old man would hold nearly 60 billion impressions. Good thing, then, that a person's brain has 80 billion neurons and one trillion interconnections amongst them in its neural net.[4]

All of this information is neurochemically burnt into our brain cells or sitting in little electrical charges in the synaptic net. That collection of chemicals, charges, and biologic materials represents who we are, what we know, what we hold as true, and how we think the world works. More to the point of this book, it governs how we, as consumers, make sense of the brands we buy. That knowledge is inscribed like biochemical tattoos in our brains. You can try to remove the tattoos and get new ones, but if you have ever tried that trick, you know how it goes. That is why what I call cognitive brands are designed to work the way the brain is programmed already over our lives. And that is why they work so well.

There are three possible elements in a cognitive brand: I call them *brand vibes*, *brand sense*, and *brand resolve* (see Figure 4.2). I say "elements" because they are a part of the brand that says something about its nature.

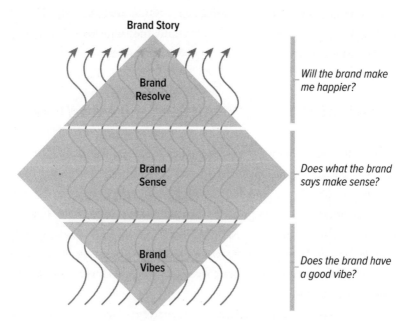

Figure 4.2   Cognitive branding framework.
(*Courtesy:* Cerenti Marketing Group, LLC)

It could do so in words, or with its logo and appearance, or with its smell and touch, or any other cue for that matter. And I say "possible" element, because not all need to be present formulaically in every cognitive brand.

The brain is very flexible in its working and can make sense of brands in a number of ways. We are going to be diving deep into the three elements of cognitive brands, their vibes, sense, and resolve, with a chapter or two devoted to each. But before we start on that journey, I want you to have a pocketbook summary of the concept.

I will say the following sentence over and over in this book. *Cognitive brands work the way the brain does.* Thus it is not surprising that the cognitive branding model closely mirrors the functional subunits of the marketing brain that I described in the previous chapters. The following is a summary explanation of brand vibes, brand sense, and brand resolve—and how these elements correspond to how the brain functions.

Brand Vibes

When consumers look at brands, a question they may ask is, "Does it give me good vibes? Can I trust it?" Brand vibes are a way for the brand to establish an empathetic bond or shared chemistry with the consumer. They allow the brand to say to the consumer, "I feel what you feel" or "I know what you are going through."

In other cases, they look to assure the consumer that the brand is in sync with their values. It sees the world the way they see it. Brand vibes are not the product's value proposition, but rather the amuse-bouche that preps the brain for the main course. When done in the right way, vibes make consumers more receptive to the core brand promise. Consumers feel like they are on the same wavelength as the brand—that they trust it and feel a bond with it.

Brand vibes connect with the prior positive experiences in the *Learner* subunit of the brain. They sort of put the brain in a good copacetic mood. Thus, when the main brand proposition follows, the *Associator* or *Deliberator* subunits in the brain are already predisposed to accepting it. In this way, vibes condition the brain to have a favorable disposition toward the brand. For brands that have a steep hill to climb because they are new and different or are starting with a trust deficit, good vibes can be an essential tool in the arsenal.

Brand Sense

The second question a consumer asks of any brand is, "Does what it says make sense to me?" From behavioral sciences we know that the brain works through the dual processes of System 1 and System 2 to make choices. Accordingly, cognitive brands can use what I term *System 1 Easers* or *System 2 Deliberators* to let the consumer assess whether or not the claims of a brand make good sense.

Easers use System 1 processes to make consumers believe that what the brand says makes good sense by working with the existing wiring in their brain. They target the *Associator* subunit of the brain and just go with the flow. Easers don't like to ruffle feathers; they look for ways to align with the consumer's own cognitive biases frictionlessly. You could say that Easers give the brand *instinctive* good sense.

Choosing is mentally taxing for the brain. If the brain can avoid that extra effort, it would much prefer to do so. Thus as the name implies, Easers look for ways to make brand choice sensible by making it feel easy. They can do so in a number of ways. For example, a brand Easer may make the choice feel *familiar* or similar to the good choices the consumer had made in the past. They can also make the brand choice easier by making it feel more *true* or authentic. They can make a choice simply *feel good*. And finally, Easers can make brand choice easy by finding a way to simplify it and making it *effortless* for the brain.

In contrast, Deliberators use System 2 processes to make consumers believe that what the brand says makes sense by egging on the brain to scrutinize the unfamiliar or dissect its existing biases and beliefs. They are harder to pull off because they involve laying new wiring or reinscribing tattoos in the brain. It is akin to converting someone to a new religion.

As the name implies, these processes draw on the Deliberator subunit of the brain, which as we know is loaded with an impressive toolkit of mental methods for comparing options and analyzing needs and wants in-depth. Thus you could say that Deliberators give the brand *reasoned* good sense. They do their thing to let the consumer know that everything about the brand checks out.

Deliberators try to influence brand choice by highlighting the value proposition of the product and, if need be, by *amping up its benefits* to make the choice feel like a no-brainer or *providing hard* evidence to make those benefits believable. In other cases, brand deliberators may look for ways to *mitigate the risk* of choice for the consumer. Finally, Deliberators can also *change the consumer's perspective*, or the lens by which they evaluate the brand, so as to shed better light on it.

Brand Resolve

The final question that a consumer may ask is, "Will I be happier if I buy this brand?" Brand resolve is responsible for pushing us off the fence of indecision and inaction. Without it, consumers would choose, but never buy. Resolve links brands with a consumer's goal of greater happiness and their conative drive to pursue it. In behavioral research, happiness is not an abstraction; it's a science. Brand resolve strategies aim to trigger the Conator, which is the action subunit of the brain.

Each person's resolve or tendency for action is different and has to do with their DNA. It relates to their inborn desire to be free and in control, feel good about themselves, and make the world a better place for themselves and others. That is ultimately what drives happiness. When brands enmesh themselves with this natural conative energy, they get the resolve and the brand buys they want.

I like to think that cognitive brands have great karma, what with all their good vibes, good sense (instinctive or reasoned), and good resolve. Together, I call them our *brand visers*. Got that? Vi-Se-R? It is a nice little acronym for remembering the three brand elements, *vi*bes, *se*nse, and *re*solve, and in old French, the word *viser* means "to aim."[5] With cognitive brands, that is what we are doing, isn't it? Aiming for the perfect sensations right between your ears.

It is time for marketers to move out of their comfort zones. Brand ladders and list branding have survived because marketers are fond of them, the same way that Grandma loves her old rocker. With the advance of brain sciences, we have something that is way better than that decrepit piece of furniture. We have cognitive brands.

Cognitive brands work the way the brain does, aiming for the vaunted sensations right between our ears. They connect with who we are and what we believe. They drive conscious and subconscious choices and make consumers happier.

Cognitive brands have three elements, namely, good vibes, sense, and resolve.

- Brand vibes build a unique bond or shared chemistry between the consumer and the brand, and pave the way for the main proposition.

- Brand sense helps consumers make instinctive or reasoned sense of their choices with System 1 Easers or System 2 Deliberators.

- Brand resolve helps consumers consider whether it is all worth the bother and prompts them to buy the brands that would make them happier.

In the next four chapters, we discuss how to design each of these three elements of a cognitive brand. We start in Chapter 5 with brand vibes.

CHAPTER 5

BRAND VIBES

Tugging at the Heartstrings

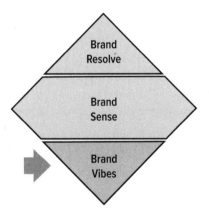

If you don't understand what I'm going through, how can you help me?

—LISA, PATIENT WITH RHEUMATOID ARTHRITIS

That simple question from Lisa, a patient in one of our focus groups many years ago, left me a little confused. As a brand marketer, I wondered:

"Why can't I just tell you what my drug will do for you? It is what it is. You make the call on whether you want it. Why do you need to know if I understand how you feel?" Nothing that I had learned in marketing by that time suggested that brands needed to have a special chemistry with their customers. Wasn't it supposed to be simply, "You've got a problem and I've got a solution?"

Rheumatoid arthritis (RA) is an invisible disease. Everything that goes wrong, does so inside the body, at least in the earlier stages. Outwardly, Lisa looks quite normal, even when she is far from it. Her joints hurt like hell and are so stiff in the mornings that she has trouble getting out of bed and being active. People who don't understand her condition can be quite mean to the poor soul.

At the parking lot in malls, shoppers glare at Lisa when she pulls up her car into a handicap spot. She looks fine to them. Her mother-in-law, who lives nearby and often has to drop by to help around the house, frequently loses patience and tells Lisa to drag her butt out of bed like everyone else and get the house cleaned. The emotional pain can hurt as much as the physical. As she told me that day, "You feel like you're wearing a mask for everyone else all of the time. Who wants to hear about your pain every morning? I just say I'm OK, but only *my* mom knows. She says, 'Lisa, you're not OK.'"

When my company did the branding for Humira, a drug for treating RA, soon after its launch, we worked hard with the AbbVie managers and their agency to create print ads that let the patients know that we understood what they were going through. In one version, they showed a mother tying her daughter's hair into a ponytail. In the picture, if you looked carefully, you could see that the mother's hands were very slightly deformed from the advance of the disease.

But that simple image had its own secret communication with the patients and their treaters; if you have severe RA, it would be difficult for you to have the dexterity in your hands to tie hair into a knot, unless the medication was working. The picture would mean nothing special to a normal person but would resonate deeply with a woman suffering from RA and her care provider. It showed that we knew that a mom with

RA could not get up in the morning and do what every other mother does routinely—help her little daughter get ready for school. Reaching into that hurt was the key to connecting with the patients like Lisa. They needed to know that we got it.

You don't require a textbook to tell you that people like to *connect* with people. Brand marketers don't necessarily know this, but it is true that when people think that you "get them," they are more likely to believe in whatever else you have to say. As a matter of fact, rheumatologists are known for spending a lot of time just listening to their patients. While general practitioners may see 40 to 60 patients per day, it is not unusual for a rheumatologist to examine just 12 to 15, or less than half of that.

By spending more time empathizing with what their patients are going through, rheumatologists earn their trust, and their patients are much more likely to follow their advice on eating right and exercising regularly. Despite the hundreds of millions of dollars spent on consumer advertising by drug companies, most patients still choose the drug that their rheumatologist recommends.

For marketers, brand vibes are elements that pave the road for the main brand value proposition and make it more likely to be embraced by the consumer. It is not a necessary step for every brand, but it can ease the pain, particularly when dealing with products that have a steeper hill to climb to adoption.

When brands establish a sense of kinship or empathy with consumers, they create positive feelings and trust. That positivity then rubs off on the brand as well in related processes that psychologists refer to as "misattribution" or "evaluative conditioning."[1] What happens is that when your brain processes two different signals, one of which you like a lot, together or in quick succession with one another, it can "mistakenly" halo the feeling of positivity around both. This is because the neural circuitry in the brain for processing both signals can overlap and things get mixed up.

Think of it like this. You are a woman and you pass by two attractive gents in a room. One of them is wearing a nice earthy cologne. You can't really tell which one and thus you may be primed[2] to have a generally good feeling about both. In the marketing world this happens often. When you see a brand, say, the latest perfume, J'Adore Absolu, by Dior, together with a celebrity endorser whom you like, in this case Charlize Theron, you tend to like it more.[3] That is, if you like Charlize Theron, which I do!

There are two ways for a brand to create good vibes and empathy with consumers—one is by understanding their angst or sharing their feelings, and second is by sharing their core values and getting on the same page with them. You should note that good brand vibes follow from this shared chemistry *without* necessarily a discussion about the product's attributes and benefits. If brands establish that personal connection with the consumer, all else follows more comfortably. It works for humans and it works with brands.

BRANDS WITH EMPATHY: I KNOW HOW YOU FEEL

A wonderful example of a company that understood the value of creating great brand vibes and connecting with its customers was Subaru. How Subaru came to be the "Lezbaru car," establishing a secret compact with lesbians, is truly one of the great brand stories of our lifetimes.[4] In the 1990s Subaru was an also-ran brand in the US car market, struggling to find a foothold against mega-competitors, Toyota and Honda. Its sole claim to fame, a car with all-wheel drive, was of appeal to rugged outdoorsy people and campers, but that market was not large.

In one focus group with such outdoors enthusiasts, a gay man made the offhand remark that five of his Subaru-owning friends were lesbians. The mid-nineties were a tumultuous period, rife with meaning-of-marriage debates in which businesses were not inclined to risk their brands by having any association with homosexuals. In 1996, in the era of "Don't Ask, Don't Tell," Bill Clinton had passed DOMA, the Defense of Marriage Act, which defined marriage for federal purposes as the union of one man and one woman, and allowed states to refuse recognition of same-sex marriages granted under the laws of other states. It was in that embattled environment that Subaru decided to make a remarkable gamble.

Under the leadership of marketer Tim Mahoney, Subaru, with more marketing grit than seen in ages, decided to plunge headlong into targeting lesbians as a core segment. The president of Subaru green-lighted the proposal, saying, "I don't need to invent a group to speak to. It looks like you've found a group of people we can talk to. So, this is a good thing."

And talk to their hearts is what they did. A stream of brilliant campaigns followed, wrapping messages about the all-wheel drive car in a variety of double entendres (see Figure 5.1) that connected a direct and secret hotline to lesbians everywhere in the United States with brilliant taglines like:

"It's not a choice. It's the way we're built.

Subaru All Wheel driving systems. In every car we make."

In other versions of the campaign, the first two sentences were replaced with other lines with hidden meanings:

"At least we've got our priorities straight."

"Get out. And stay out."

"Entirely comfortable with its orientation."

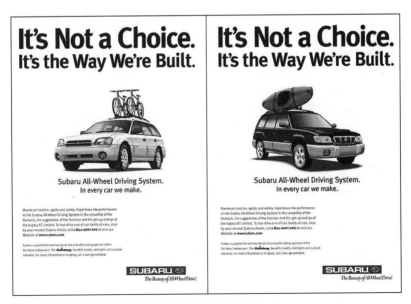

Figure 5.1   Subaru's double entendres.

The rest, as they say, is history. In 2000, Martina Navratilova, a lesbian tennis champion, shunned by other sponsors, became a spokesperson for Subaru as the campaign went mainstream. Sales took off, and during the recession years of the nineties, Subaru was the only car company in the United States to not lose market share.

Note that in the preceding taglines, the first statement (e.g., "At least we've got our priorities straight") is simply intended to establish the brand vibe. It creates an empathetic connection with the consumer. But without it, the brand message following it, "Subaru All-Wheel Driving System. In every car we make," is simply not the same. The vibes and special chemistry that Subaru forged with its lesbian customers were so strong that they trusted the company deeply and were inclined to buy their car.

It did not matter that there were other arguably better and more reputable cars to choose from. The lesbians had found their car. They knew that here was a company that stood with them, shoulder-to-shoulder in solidarity to face whatever it was that they had faced from an unsympathetic society. Even as Subaru took flak from right-wingers and conscientious objectors from different sides, for lesbians, there simply was no question of going anywhere else. It was Subaru all the way.

Subaru won the car wars by building a brand with empathy, that made the company a friend like no other to lesbian women at the time. The product itself, the all-wheel-drive car they sold, was not the real star in the print ads. Yet their customers had no doubt that the Subaru brand got them and could feel what they felt.

For those who think that opportunities for such deep brand vibes can only be seen in the odd market niche, the story of Dollar Shave Club, the unlikely David that took a punishing crack at Gillette, a sleeping Goliath, is instructive. The brainchild of Michael Dubin, a failed entrepreneur, the Dollar Shave Club disrupted a virtual market monopoly by tapping into the deeply felt angst among men—that the money they had to spend on buying shaving blades constituted highway robbery.

The business took off when one day a desperate Dubin decided to string together a video to put on the web. Filmed in a warehouse full of boxes of unsold blades, the 90-second film is pure angst, every drop of it.[5] Described by AdWeek as an act of "violent comedy," the ad starts with Mike introducing himself bluntly:

"Hi, I'm Mike, founder of Dollar Shave Club. What is the Dollar Shave Club? Well, for a dollar a month, we send high-quality razors right to your door."[6]

Then he gets up from his desk and starts pacing about,

"Yeah! A dollar!"

As the drama builds, you can see Mike getting all worked up.

"Are the blades any good? Nah! Our blades are f***ing great!"

By now, the words are flying fast and furious, as Mike smashes through a paper divider separating his office from the main warehouse.

"Do you like spending $20 on brand name razors?" he demands to know. "Nineteen go to Roger Federer. And do you think your razor needs a vibrating handle, a flashlight, a back scratcher, and 10 blades? Your handsome-ass grandfather had one blade . . . and polio."

And then finally:

"Stop paying for shave tech you don't need . . . and start deciding where you're going to stack all those dollar bills I'm saving you."

His message hit home, even though the Dollar Shave Club blades are not quite the same high quality as Gillette's and don't last as long. The clip was tagged by millions to their friends. And that's exactly what happens in the Twitter- and Facebook-fueled networked world of today. When people feel your brand vibes so deeply, they talk about you. By 2014, 50,000 people a month were being referred to the online store by fans. Mike's YouTube video has been seen by more than 26 million viewers.

While opportunities to find such gut-level connections with customers may be difficult to orchestrate, great vibes are a relevant consideration in every brand positioning. Showing the customer that you empathize with them works. As we saw in these examples, the interesting thing about brand vibes is that the angst felt by the consumer is not necessarily about the product specifically; rather it is about how people fail to understand what they are going through.

With Humira, patients felt the hurt that comes from people not understanding their physical limitations. In the Subaru's case, the angst flowed from people treating lesbians as illegitimate and unworthy of attention. With Dollar Shave Club, it comes from men feeling like they have been taken for a ride by blade manufacturers.

BRANDS WITH VALUES: YOUR VALUES ARE MY VALUES

If the first approach to good vibes is for the brand to say to consumers "I know how you feel," the second is to acknowledge that you share a common set of values with them or at least respect theirs. Values represent a consumer's idea of what is right or wrong. When brands adopt core values that consumers identify with, deeply and authentically, they build a fanatically loyal following of those who feel that by buying the brand they are doing what is right or stopping a wrong.

Research shows that people are more likely to pursue goals persistently when those are aligned with their values.[7] Yet, this is one of the most difficult paths a brand can take, and many that choose this path fail due to difficulty of staying true to a set of core values.

The first (and only) time I met Ben Cohen and Jerry Greenfield, the founders of the eponymous Ben & Jerry's company, was when they showed up one sultry afternoon with tubs of ice cream at the Yale School of Management where I was a student at the time. Lots of CEOs used to come to the campus to talk about their companies, but there was free ice cream involved here, so I made it a point to show up. The only thing was, they didn't sound like any of the other CEOs, and what they said didn't make a whole lot of sense.

Greenfield dwelled on how the company was dedicated to standing up for social justice and that ice cream, the only product they made, wasn't everything the business was about. Fresh from classes extolling the virtues of carefully architecting your brand around its product differentiation, to me then, Ben & Jerry's success appeared to be a fluke, a temporary aberration that too would pass. It didn't help that the duo also confessed that neither had been to b-school and that they had learned how to make ice cream from a $5 correspondence course from Penn State.

Yet, now 30 years later, Ben & Jerry's is still one of the grand American ice cream brands. How?

In a recent *New York Times* article, Greenfield explains "'Why has Ben & Jerry's been successful?' We usually say it's because of three things: really high-quality ice cream, great ingredients, very unusual flavors— and also *the activist social mission of the company*. Some other company could start making ice cream with big chunks the same way Ben & Jerry's does, but Ben & Jerry's having this activist, outspoken social mission— other companies can't copy that. It's not something you can just say. It has to be who the people are."[8]

That last sentence is important, because you can't change who you are like you can change ad campaigns. Once you wear your values on your sleeve, it is what your brand becomes and the box it lives in. No matter, though. That doesn't seem to worry the company at all.

Ben & Jerry's mission extends beyond simply writing a check for a charity, which most companies do. Instead, they are a loud and unrelenting voice in rallying for social justice issues spanning from voting rights to campaign finance reform. Witness their recent ice cream flavor, "Justice ReMix'd™," (Figure 5.2) dedicated to criminal justice system reform and Pecan Resist supporting "four organizations that are work-

Figure 5.2   Ben & Jerry's Justice ReMix'd™ Ice-Cream Flavor.

ing toward a more just and equitable future and peacefully resisting the Trump administration's regressive and discriminatory policies."[9] Ben & Jerry's brand values and vibes are impossible for the consumer to ignore.

As Rob Michalak, the Director of Social Mission Special Projects, in an interview with Forbes states, "We respect that some people will have a set of values that are meaningful and important to them, and we may lose some customers."[10] He continues to explain, "But . . . those who share those values are more deeply loyal. We did some internal research that suggested that those people are actually two and a half times more loyal than just regular customers—that's of great value. They understand that we stand for something and we're authentic about it."

Another quintessential example of a brand that wears its value on its sleeves (or maybe its shoes) is Nike, what with its decision to place the highly charged figure of Colin Kaepernick front and center on its billboard in New York's Times Square. In 2016, Colin, the star quarterback for the San Francisco 49ers, lit up a firestorm of controversy when he decided to kneel during the playing of the national anthem to protest racial injustice and police brutality against blacks in the United States.[11]

Donald Trump pounced on the opportunity to castigate Kaepernick as an unpatriotic liberal. In the furor that followed, Kaepernick failed to get a contract renewal with the National Football League and never played professional football again. Undaunted, Nike went ahead with making the young quarterback the star of their "Just do it" campaign.

The black-and-white poster (see Figure 5.3) was almost entirely covered by Kaepernick's face, with the words "Believe in something. Even if it means sacrificing everything" etched in stark relief across it. The idea of standing for one's rights was central to the values of many in the years of divisive politics that followed Trump's election. By buying Nike branded shoes, people were expressing their solidarity with the values that the brand and Kaepernick represented.

The strategy was a departure from the norm. Nike's brand is built around the idea of performance shoes. Most often, that strategy has been executed by securing endorsements from the world's top athletes, including Michael Jordan and LeBron James. In those instances, the

Figure 5.3   Nike ad featuring Colin Kaepernick.

brand was saying, "These shoes are so amazing that even Jordan plays his games in them."

The Kaepernick strategy was completely different. This was a brand forging a connection with its consumers through value based vibes, with a "what matters to you, really matters for us too" strategy that had little to do with the performance aspect of the shoes. In the aftermath of the campaign, while many Trump supporters rushed to rallies in which they dutifully burnt their old Nike pairs, quarterly sales and profits for the company grew rapidly.[12] Like I said, this path is not easy, but for brands with a clearly articulated set of values, it is also the only way.

HOW THE MASK BECAME A METAPHOR FOR A BRAND WITH VALUES

One of the enduring mysteries of the Covid-19 pandemic times is why wearing a face mask has become such a political flashpoint in the US. People have had fistfights, been unceremoniously tossed off of airplanes, pulled out their guns, and yeah, gone completely berserk over it.

In the middle of an interview, a fed-up Fox News anchor Chris Wallace turned to his stunned hosts and warned, "The president (Trump) . . . is in the most secure bubble in the world. . . . And he still got it (Covid). So, wear the damn mask!"

Wallace is a superb newsman, but he doesn't know brands. He is also an outlier among conservatives, for generally it is the case, that if you are for wearing masks, you are likely liberal, and if you are against it, you are likely conservative.

The mask has spawned a sharp divide because it has become a metaphor for political brands of values, for what the Democratic and Republican Parties stand for. Wearing or not wearing one is like asking Ben & Jerry's to give up their company's mission to fight social justice. Or like asking the Hobby Lobby store, owned by the Evangelical Christian Green family, to cover contraceptive use for their female employees as part of their medical insurance, despite their religious opposition to it. It is about the values those brands stand for.[13]

You say, "what?" But, stay with me for a second!

For Democrats, wearing a mask as advised by experts means believing in science and caring for others (it is more for protecting others from your infection than you from theirs). A belief in science is a belief in climate change, vaccinations, and evolution. A belief in social well-being, helping the needy, is about wanting healthcare, free education, and immigration opportunities for all.

For Republicans, not wearing a mask is about a belief in freedom and self-reliance. Freedom is about the right to bear arms, get education vouchers for sending children to religious schools, and not wear helmets while riding a motorcycle. Self-reliance is about keeping your business open and taking no government help, deregulating, and saying no to socialism.

Further, given its strong evangelical Christian base, the Republican party has often uncomfortably had to take anti-science positions relative to acknowledging the reality of evolution and the need for nondivine, medical intervention to save lives. Mask-use, with its basis in science and professed role in saving lives versus leaving them to kismet, hits against the core of these values.

So, there you have it. Politicians surely helped weaponize the mask into becoming a metaphor for liberal and conservative values. And now that it is, these loyal followers will stick to their brand of values and if need be, die for it.

WORDS OF CAUTION FROM FALLEN ANGELS

Brand vibes can also work against you if you are not careful. If you stuck it out as an investor in L Brands since 2010, you must have had quite a ride. A stock that once quintupled on the heels of the success of its Victoria's Secret brand had, by 2020, plunged right back to earth. It's like it never went up, or worse.

The initial success of Victoria's Secret lay in forging a bond of solidarity with women. It, de facto, championed women's right to be sexy and show it. Before Victoria's Secret, bras were a comfort-and-fit purchase. The Body by Victoria line changed all of that. Its Miracle Bra was heavily padded and strapped with an underwire to accentuate cleavage. Women were looking sexier.

Previously, bras and lingerie were sold in unremarkable boxes in discreet back corners of big box stores. Instead, Victoria's Secret not only decked their stores in racy lingerie and bras from front to end but also put them on a runway show on prime-time television in 1997. It wasn't just that the brand made women feel sexier; rather that it made the new kind of sexiness a part of mainstream sensibilities. Women felt free and empowered and fell head over heels in love with the brand.

Unfortunately, somewhere along the way, Victoria's Secret betrayed that trust. It went from being a champion of women's right to be and show sexy, to trying to be the arbiter of who and what could be sexy. In a *Vogue* interview, its chief marketing officer dissed the idea of body positive women and transgender people modelling on its runway show. "It's a fantasy show," he explained.[14]

Victoria's Secret missed the trend from underwire bras to bralettes, failing to redefine sexiness in a new mold that corresponded to where modern women were headed versus where they had been. Women felt used and disrespected. It was especially painful coming from a friend they had trusted over the years—one that was now judging them. Women simply walked away.

Finally, now in 2021, in a drastic revamp of strategy, Victoria's Secret is showcasing an array of diverse female advocates in its campaigns and boasting inclusive styles and sizes. The ads feature, among others, Megan Rapinoe, the gay and fiery captain of the US National Women's Soccer League. But will consumers be convinced by this moral facelift? Is it enough to fire their old marketing team and trade out the Angels for #GirlBoss influencers and Olympic athletes?

I think not. For a brand seeking such a significant turnaround, there has to be an empathetic connection with its consumer, a brand vibe that goes beyond checking the box by parading a panel of diverse women. To get that right, the brand must reach deep into the angst that modern women feel and touch a nerve somewhere.

Maybe that's through a mea culpa. Let's remember that no brand knows how to let women be and show sexy better than Victoria's Secret. That is nothing to walk away from. But how about acknowledging that they made some mistakes? How about something like "No Judgments *Ever*. Simply the Sexiest Bras for *Every* Body."

Deep vibes with customers do wonders for brands but come with their own risks. Brand vibes are compacts, not fantasies. Brands that betray the confidences they build with their customers can find themselves deep in a hole they cannot climb out of.

KEY TAKEAWAYS

Cognitive brands often connect deeply with the consumer and answer their question, "Does this brand give me good vibes? Can I trust it?"

The idea of including vibes in brands to condition consumers is new. Previously, brand strategies focused narrowly on unpacking their functional or emotional benefits. With the connective tissue of vibes, cognitive brands can do a lot more.

Brand vibes–based strategies mimic our own behaviors as humans and how we relate to and develop social chemistry with others. When brands build that kind of kinship with consumers, choice and preference follow more easily. However, brands that connect with consumers but then betray the trust do so at their own risk.

Good brand vibes may be based on:

- Shared feelings, where the brand says, "I know how you feel" to the consumer

or

- Shared values, where the brand says, "I believe in the same values that you believe in" to the consumer

Now that we have learned how to work with the first element of cognitive brands, namely brand vibes, it's time to dive into the subject of brand sense with System 1 Easers (Chapter 6) and System 2 Deliberators (Chapter 7).

BRAND SENSE

Using System 1 Easers
to Go with the Flow

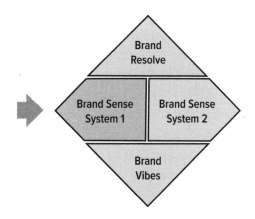

S ome people say it is odd that my dog and I appear to behave similarly at times. That is a bit of a touchy subject with me, and so I feel obliged to call in the big guns to defend myself. Let me start with explaining what this fracas is all about.

Just the other week, I was taking the elevator up to our apartment after walking Kami, our little bichon frise, in the park. Through the corner of my eye, I noticed that two neighbors riding along with us were repeatedly looking at us, eying each other conspiratorially, and then chuckling. When I scowled at them with my best, "Not nice!" look, they explained, "Oh no, it's nothing. But did you know that you and your dog were both yawning together?" I had noticed nothing of the sort but was immediately skeptical of the possibility that the smug cotton-ball puff of a dog could be exercising any level of subconscious control over my physical responses. Never!

When I related the incident to my wife, whose dog Kami really is, she didn't find it as ridiculous as I thought she would. And for good measure, she upped the ante, adding, "You know, I've been meaning to tell you, but the two of you kind of look similar."

Anticipating a spate of vigorous objections from me, to settle matters preemptively, she produced a recent photograph of the two of us, the dog and me, in which we are in my friend Damen's boat, looking at Navy Pier at an oddly similar angle with our mouths slightly open. In the dimming light of the city, against the twinkling stars, there is admittedly a slight resemblance. Very slight, I concede, but in my mind, I am imagining I have landed in the twilight zone. As you may guess, this kind of mortifying event would keep me up at night. I am thinking there must be a *scientific* explanation for this, like when people imagine they have seen a UFO but it really is just a wayward weather balloon.

It turns out that researchers have shown that purebred dogs do look like their owners, much more so than random chance would suggest.[1] This happens because we are subconsciously biased toward liking things that look and seem familiar to us. This theory implies that my wife bought Kami in the first instance because the dog looks like me and (naturally) she likes the way I look. And honestly, I really prefer this explanation a lot. I'm sticking to it.

What about the yawning in sync thing? It so happens that we are also cognitively wired to fit into groups. The sense of belonging makes us feel good. To do so, we may accentuate behaviors that are common to the group, mimicking emotions and facial and body expressions of those around us.

There is in fact a phenomenon known as the *chameleon effect*,[2] whereby people subconsciously imitate gestures, attitudes, and behaviors of those around them in a social setting because of the activation of their so-called mirror neurons.[3] Babies in day care centers cry when they hear other babies doing the same. Smokers light up when they see another person smoking a cigarette. It happens automatically, without much thought. There is limited (but non-zero) research to test this hypothesis across species, but let's go with it.

There are a lot of choices we make and things we do subconsciously. As we will see shortly, familiarity and the feeling of goodness from belonging to a group trigger something called cognitive ease and drive our behavior. In branding, what I call System 1 Easers, are elements of a brand that help the consumer make sense of the brand propositions instinctively, quickly, and without much thought. As we have already discussed, System 1 processes of the brain govern subconscious or low-vigilance human behavior.

MEET THE SYSTEM 1 AUTOPILOT

So, now I bring in the big guns! Daniel Kahneman and Amos Tversky identified two basic processes by which the brain works, namely System 1 and System 2. System 1 makes us able to react to stimuli and to do things in an automatic and instinctive manner. Even though driving a car is an extremely complicated task, we can do it practically in our sleep. Any 18-month-old will inform you that walking and talking simultaneously is not that easy either, but again, once they learn it, it is no longer a problem.

System 1 processes help us do a lot more than walk and talk effortlessly. They account for most of our daily behavior. Some suggest that 95 percent[4] of the choices we make are based on System 1 processes in our brain. From the moment we are born and every minute that we are alive, we are observing and learning things consciously or subconsciously. All of it is processed and continuously encoded into our brains.

The brain uses System 2 processes to create new knowledge only episodically, by applying logic and reasoning. However, System 1 creates knowledge all of the time by recognizing associations across disparate experiences and improving upon our past store of knowledge. Regardless of where it comes from, all knowledge is biochemically stenciled on to the *Learner* subunit of the brain as our personal cache of beliefs and wisdom and thereafter available automatically and instinctively. We use it all the time for making sense of brands.

As consumers, we encode rules and biases about the products we buy every time we experience them. For example, over time, we may come to believe "all organic foods are good and healthy," or "higher horsepower engine means a faster and more expensive car," or "branded products are better in quality than their private label clones." Most of the time, these rules serve us well, and we apply them effortlessly and without thinking across a wide array of choices. The marketer who emblazons "organic" on their packet of mini carrots is counting on that and wants to tap into the neural circuit in our heads that posits "organic = good = buy." That is a classic System 1 play, whereby the marketer successfully plugs his brand into a preexisting mental shortcut that we use and positions it instantly as a sensible choice.

Over time, associations become routine and habitual. Because System 1 rules and wisdom are biochemically "burned" into the neural network in our brain, they function as hard-to-break, very stubborn habits.[5] If you are used to reading your email and texting friends while walking on the street, you will find it difficult to change that behavior, even when the consequences can be grave. Pedestrian injuries due to cell phone use are up 35 percent since 2010.[6] Yet millions of people continue to walk and text because most of the time nothing untoward happens and the brain rules it as generally safe.

So what other rules are wired into people's brains? What can brand marketers use? Well, researchers have documented dozens of common System 1 cognitive biases whereby we have an inbuilt propensity for acting in a particular way in certain situations. Cognitive biases are mental shortcuts for choice. It is like you favoring your forehand in receiving a tennis serve, even though there are times when it is inadvisable. Yet, these mental shortcuts stem from a lifetime of experiences across disparate situations. For most of those, this inlaid wisdom works well for us, but for some, it doesn't. Just like the Ten Commandments. That is why I like to think of these biases as "cognitive wisdom," and like all wisdom, sometimes it is not all that wise, and the more negatively coined term "cognitive bias" may seem more appropriate.

The existence of these known, near universal biases or propensities presents an opportunity for marketers. When they can align their brand propositions with these collective predilections, their brands make a whole lot of sense to consumers everywhere and are preferred reflexively. Recent research by Sam Maglio and Taly Reich has shown that not only do we make choices non-deliberatively, by gut feel, with our System 1 Easers more frequently, but also that those preferences are then more resilient.[6] We believe in these choices more and don't let go of them easily.

BRAND SENSE WITH SYSTEM 1 EASERS

At the heart of our System 1 processes is a cognitive-ease engine. When you feel that a choice is familiar, true, good, or easy, you experience a sense of mental comfort, a processing fluency that is the opposite of stress, and you tend to accept and prefer it. Thus, you experience cognitive ease and will tend to accept a brand when its choice feels: (1) familiar, (2) true, (3) good, or (4) easy—four factors that were identified by Kahneman in his research.[8] You tend to embrace these brand choices without a lot of thought or vigilance. In contrast, when you feel something is foreign, false, bad for you, or requires a lot of time and energy, you experience cognitive stress. You are suspicious and vigilant and will need a lot more convincing before accepting those choices.

Psychologists have researched and documented well over a hundred different cognitive biases that are common to most humans. A number of them are closely related to each other, and so the list of distinct biases is shorter. For our purposes in designing brands, some are more useful than others. In the following sections, I give you a cheat sheet of eight System 1 Easers (see Figure 6.1) that are valuable in building cognitive brands.

	Cheat Sheet 8 Most Useful Cognitive Biases	
	✓ Anchoring Bias	⎫ Feels familiar
	✓ Loss Aversion Bias	⎭
	✓ IKEA Effect	⎫ Feels true/authentic
	✓ Transparency Effect	⎭
	✓ In-Group Bias	⎫ Feels good
	✓ Choice Supportive Bias	⎭
	✓ Occam's Razor Bias	⎫ Feels easy
	✓ Herd Metality/Expert Bias	⎭

Figure 6.1   Common cognitive biases.

1. Brand Sense by Making Choice Feel Familiar

As consumers, we have a tendency to stick with what we have and what we know. It's like Grandpa with his old recliner. He is used to its look and feel. It's what he knows, it's what he has, it's perfect, and it's not going anywhere, even when it is certifiably unsafe for use.

There are two cognitive biases that relate to these all too human tendencies to migrate towards the familiar, namely, the anchoring bias and the loss aversion bias. When brands can align their positioning to these biases, what they say makes sense to consumers instinctively.

Anchoring Bias

We all say "I like this or that" often. The funny thing, though, is that the brain has a hard time telling what it likes or dislikes, unless it can compare it to something else that it is familiar with or knows. That thing is the *anchor*. This is wonderful for marketers because they can suggest to the consumer what that anchor should be as part of their brand proposition. The power of suggestion does the rest subconsciously.

In brand positioning, we use the anchoring bias to enhance the perceived value of our product by providing consumers with a strategically selected, superior anchor. Kraft's campaign for its frozen pizza, "It's not delivery, it's DiGiorno," took the frozen pizza category by storm. Anyone who has ordered takeout pizza knows that it is hard to replicate the brick-oven aroma and charred-crust flavor of delivery pizza with a month-old, thawed-out frozen pizza at home.

However, by anchoring their brand to the experience of delivery pizza, Kraft was able to plant the seed in the consumer's mind that DiGiorno was almost as good. Even if you adjusted for a slight overprom-ise, it was still going to feel better than any other frozen pizza from the competition.

Make no mistake, the brand promise cannot be an illusion; the prod-uct does have to deliver, else over time the *Learner* unit in the brain will figure out that the experience is not measuring up to the expectations and start taking points off the happiness scorecard and repeat purchases will be cancelled or curtailed.

My company Cerenti's client, ConAgra, did the same kind of anchor-ing with its ACT II popcorn in country after country.* Almost from its inception, ACT II promised to deliver theater quality popcorn from your microwave, in the comfort of your home. After all, who can resist the divine feeling you get from watching a great movie while mechanically pouring mindless quantities of buttery popcorn down your mouth. The name itself came from an earlier version of the product called ACT ONE. If you look at the packaging box for ACT II (shown in Figure 6.2), you would think the product itself is an Oscar-worthy hit release from Hollywood. It holds sev-eral visual cues highlighting the connection to movie theaters.

ACT II, the brand name, is enclosed in a Hollywood-style theater sign with incandescent bulbs around it. The name of the flavor, Movie Theater Butter, is splashed across a reel of film. This basic idea worked well not only in the United States, making it the top-selling popcorn in the country, but also made ACT II number one in other countries like Mexico and India.

---

* The events described in the following passages about ConAgra have been fiction-alized and the names disguised to remove any nonpublic information and pre-serve the privacy of the mentioned individuals. The narrative is thus designed to be instructive rather than accurately biographical or historical.

Figure 6.2   Anchoring to the popcorn movie experience.

Yet marketers have to be careful; consumers can also anchor your brand in a manner that you fail to anticipate. Over time, ACT II found that its link to the theater experience was dropping like a lead anchor around its ankles, relegating the brand largely to family movie-watching occasions. That was great when there was just one television that everyone in the house milled around.

Now, with each household member streaming shows to their personal mobile devices, the family television watching moment is going the way of the landline phone. People snack on their own and watch movies alone. Suddenly, ACT II found itself being displaced by brands like SkinnyPop, which as the name implies anchors itself to the idea of being low fat, the opposite of movie theater butter laden popcorn.

Jill Ramsey, the no-nonsense, let's-grow-faster international chief for ConAgra, did not like the look of this and wanted to stop ACT II from being swallowed up by this expanding sinkhole. Together with her country heads for Mexico and India, a brilliant duo, we worked to reposition the brand around a new set of anchors.

The brand was gradually reincarnated as the smarter choice that could "make *any* moment a special moment." The smarter-choice equity *anchored against* potato chips, which by far are the biggest snack category to go after. Popcorn is smarter because it is not fried and thus healthier. With microwaves in every home and office now, and ready-to-eat packaging options, popcorn can be enjoyed anytime and anywhere. Also, microwavable popcorn is a one-of-a-kind snack. When the kernels crackle, pop, and dance out of their steaming bag, there is a drama that turns any moment into a mini fiesta.

Accordingly, the revised strategy in the Indian markets anchored consumers to the everyday moments instead of the rare family movie occasions. How about as a special treat when your 13-year-old daughter returns home from school at three in the afternoon? How about when the boyfriend steals a private moment with his girl? ACT II was also available along with disposable containers that could make sharing easy in offices, turning a frayed afternoon into a moment of respite. The team positioned single-serving size, ready-to-eat popcorn as a healthy snack for hunger-pang moments—a healthier alternative to a bag of potato chips from cross-category competitor Frito Lay.

These anchors to the use occasion are bound to be mirrored by consumers in their own lives. When you see the 13-year-old daughter enjoying a popcorn treat on TV, you are likely to do the same for your daughter when she returns from school. Blame it on the *chameleon effect* we discussed earlier.

Loss Aversion Bias

Kahneman and Tversky are most famous for uncovering the loss aversion bias, which developed into their *prospect theory* and earned Kahneman his Nobel Prize. (Tversky had unfortunately died by then or else would have shared in the prize.) The loss aversion bias says that people tend to view losses and gains differently.

In the near term, people tend to feel losses more acutely than gains. An economist would explain this by telling you that the amount of happiness you get from being given $100 is less than the amount of sadness you feel from having $100 taken away from you. In practice, for example, researchers Tatiana Homonoff[9] and her colleagues, showed that charging a tax of five cents for the use of plastic bags was more effective in curbing their use than offering a reward of five cents for not using them. *People don't like to lose what they already have or own—even when it is just five cents.*

The bias toward losses goes away when the events are remote, that is, in the long term. My own theory is that this bias stems from the lessons of our childhood, forged deeply in our minds *over many generations*. We are taught not to be greedy and to be happy with what we have. Proverbs like "a bird in hand is worth two in the bush," or "the grass only seems greener on the other side," or even "thou shalt not covet thy neighbor's wife," all say the same thing. Stick with what you have. It is sound cognitive wisdom for most real-life situations—even though true economists would take issue with all three and at their own peril.

The loss aversion bias, when it's working well for an incumbent brand, can also help keep competitors at bay. One of Cerenti's pharma clients was able to do exactly that with their drug, which was first to market and pretty good in treating a chronic disease but eventually was facing competition from new entrants with 20 to percent better performance. That meant that the new drugs were able to suppress the symptoms of the patient's disease by about 75 percent versus around 60 percent with our client's drug.

However, we were able to lock out the competition with a brand message that urged the doctors to not rock the boat with their existing patients. We reminded them that they had spent a lot of time and effort in treating their patients with our drug, improving their condition, and so why would they want to take a chance on something new and unknown? In other words, we bet that the docs would be more acutely averse to losing the success they had already achieved with their patients rather than chancing the possibility of gaining more success with some other new drug. That is classic loss aversion bias in play!

For marketers, there are other slightly different but related ways of creating an aversion to a loss. Creating a sense of scarcity, real or otherwise, is a common approach to increasing brand appeal. You can think of FOMO,[10] or "the fear of missing out," as a cousin of the loss aversion bias. In this case, a person experiences a sense of anxiety at the prospect of missing out on opportunities they could avail of now but possibly not later. The "my product is amazing, it's yours only if you buy it now" strategy, even though we all know it for what it is, works and we fall for it all the time.

One of the more spectacular frauds committed in recent memory was the Fyre Music Festival. It was the brainchild of Billy McFarland, now serving time in prison, who had pepped up the festival with spectacular commercials on social media.[11] The spots promised "two transformative weekends" of art, food, and music in the middle of paradise ("a remote island in Exumas," previously owned by the notorious drug baron Pablo Escobar). Festival attendees would experience the "boundaries of the impossible," replete with top bands, the hottest models, crystal-clear aquamarine waters, fast boats, private planes, and luxury accommodations. There was, of course, only "limited availability" for you to "join this quest to push beyond those boundaries."

Thousands of people paid tens of thousands of dollars to attend what turned out to be an unmitigated disaster in a desolate parking lot on a middle-of-nowhere island, with no bands, no accommodation, no food, and no nothing. Customers were so afraid of missing out on the once-in-a-lifetime extravaganza that they did not ask any questions before writing big five-figure checks. But you don't have to be crooked to use the FOMO effect. As a matter of fact, Billy wouldn't be in jail if he had delivered what he promised and not bumbled the execution of an otherwise outstanding idea.

Consumers often don't believe that it is prudent for them to lose what they own or pass on attractive opportunities. Thus the loss aversion bias can provide many good corridors for some cognitive brands to position their propositions as the sensible choice.

2. Brand Sense by Making the Choice Feel True

It shouldn't be a surprise to anyone that consumers tend to favor brands that are seen as honest and authentic. Yet, in today's world of hacks, fakes, and vaporware, it is harder to know what's true. Research that I led while I worked at McKinsey shows that a promising pathway for building trust with consumers is to give them either greater control over shaping the brand or transparency into what is in it.[12] As luck would have it, there are two cognitive biases, namely the IKEA effect and what I call the transparency effect, that can help marketers with this approach.

IKEA Effect

What better way to give consumers control than to let them build your product, or at least a part of it, themselves? That is what the IKEA effect is.[13] It says that people tend to prefer objects that they have put time and effort into building, *even when they turn out to be objectively inferior.*

It's understandable. When you toil for hours to assemble an IKEA dresser, under the skeptical, "we should have hired a professional" watch of your significant other, you are inclined to believe that your creation is immaculate. That despite the fact that you erred in the construction, as evidenced clearly by the several critical-for-structural-stability parts left over from steps 27C at the end of the 35-step irreversible assembly. The IKEA effect is not feasible for all products, but worthy of consideration.

With the advent of innovative technology-based retailers, the IKEA effect is poised to explode with online brands. MTailor, the brainchild of Stanford computer scientists Miles Penn and Rafi Witten, uses nifty technology to deliver made-to-order, custom-fitted jeans without the need for a real tailor.

However, to get the best fit, the customer too has to work at it, making seven different body measurements using their mobile phone. MTailor uses AI technology to help you pull off this feat. You don't take measurements the conventional way with a tape measure. Instead, you put your phone on the floor, leaning it against the wall, and then, with the camera on, do a complete 360-degree turn in front of it. As simply as that, the app magically figures out the seven key custom tailoring measurements. After that short ballet routine, you bet you are going to love that pair of jeans like it is your own baby!

Importantly, IKEA effect researchers caution that for the process to work, the consumer must be able to finish their assigned task with reasonable comfort and success. While you want consumers to put in that labor, it cannot become an exercise in futility, or you will drive them away frustrated. Whether MTailor becomes a billion-dollar brand remains a bit iffy and is likely more dependent on their ability to get the supply chain right than on the brand strategy.

Back in the earthy world of beverages, a Sputnik-era product called Tang long used the IKEA effect to build a loyal fan club. Even as ready-to-drink (RTD) drinks drove away powdered beverages like Tang and Crystal Light from the US markets, the powdered drink pair of brands are loved in much of the rest of the world, delivering well over a billion dollars in sales for Kraft.

When we were working with Kraft's international brand managers, it soon became evident that a big part of Tang's appeal in these countries was that both kids and mothers could get involved in its preparation. It was more than just an affordable, fruity drink; it was a fun bonding moment between a mom and her kids.

A TV commercial that plays in Pakistan shows various vignettes of a mother using her hands to braid her daughter's hair, caress her son to sleep, and lock arms playfully with her children in a dance. The scenes are interspersed cleverly with shots of the same hands also preparing Tang and pouring it into glasses for the family. The voiceover reflectively concludes by observing how everything in the world is more beautiful when it is touched by a mother's hand, with the tagline "Tang, like the love from a mother's hands."[14] The mother-child involvement equity has put the Tang brand on steroids in many developing countries around the world.

It is not always practical to have the customer involved in the creation of the product. In such cases, it helps to acknowledge the role that customers may have played in the creation of the brand itself. For example, pharmaceutical companies often like to say that their drug has been trialed on thousands of patients. In a slight twist, Bristol Myers Squib in its ads for Opdivo chose to thank patients, nurses, and physicians who were involved with the clinical trials, indirectly reminding all three types of customers that the drug, in part, was the end result of efforts of others like them.

Additionally, marketers may do well to remember that brands are more than the product itself. Xerox, for example, provides mailing labels to consumers so they return their printer cartridges and play a role in their safe disposal. Tesla's professed mission is "to accelerate the world's transition to sustainable energy." That is exactly what their customers passionately believe in. By buying Tesla's expensive electric cars, they are playing a role in making their own missions come true.

Transparency Effect or Authenticity

People are wired to trust what they can see with their own eyes. That is why brands that are transparent or authentic make sense to them. Actually, I am hiding something here and I'd better not. There is no cognitive bias called *transparency effect*. It is a term I coined based on prior years of research into what makes for great brands.

Transparency is the idea that you are likely to trust a brand if you can feel that "what you see is what you get." Anyone who has been to a Criss Angel magic show at the Luxor Hotel on the Strip in Las Vegas and been deceived by what their eyes thought was real can see the problems with the "believe what you see with your own eyes" thesis. Nonetheless, in the real world of no magic, brands that are transparent about who they are and say what they mean make perfect sense.

One fascinating newcomer to bet their brand story on transparency is the online retailer Everlane, whose fortunes have been rising like a rocket ship. When I cruise over to their website, their home page starts boldly with the assertion, "We believe we can all make a difference." My eyes glaze over: Isn't that only the millionth company to lay the claim to making a difference? The real head-scratcher is in the smaller letters below that statement, "Our way: Exceptional quality. Ethical factories. Radical Transparency." Again, ignore the first two obvious ones. Who would say average quality and unethical factories? But radical transparency? What is that all about? No company says that because it is not possible. I'm shocked; tell me more.

Further down that page, they explain, "At Everlane, we want the right choice to be as easy as putting on a great T-shirt. That's why we partner with the best, ethical factories around the world. Source only the finest materials. And share those stories with you—down to the true cost of every product we make. It's a new way of doing things. We call it Radical Transparency."

That is crazy. No retailer does that. But Everlane does. I look up their slim-fit jeans in black and they are priced at $68. Below the price is the comparative retail price, which is $155. Click on their $68 price and you see an extremely easy-to-follow graphic that breaks down their cost: materials, $14.93; hardware, $2.15; labor, $7.50; duties, $4.06; and transport, $1.90; for a total cost of $30.54.

In my consulting career of over 20 years, I have worked with or analyzed the businesses of a gazillion retailers. No one shares their true costs with the customer. Does transparency do something for the Everlane brand? You be the judge. In an era where retail brands are struggling to survive, Everlane has gone from a zero to $250 million valuation in just seven years.[15]

In consumer foods, transparency has been the rage in the breakfast and energy bars category. Peter Rahal started a company called RxBar in his mom's kitchen and sold it for $600 million to Kellogg's in just four years. The secret of his success? "Clean Label" protein bars, as shown in Figure 6.3.

Figure 6.3   The transparency effect at work.

Most bars they sell offer 12 grams of protein and list just five ingredients in prominent letters, covering the entire label. Of those, four are foods and the fifth is a statement: "No B.S." For instance, the Chocolate Sea Salt bar contains "3 Egg Whites, 6 Almonds, 4 Cashews, 2 Dates, and No B.S."—and that's it. Totally transparent. End of story. (Actually, I do have one gripe about their branding, which I will cover later in Chapter 13 in a discussion on ethics.)

Brands are proliferating like nobody's business today. On Amazon, so many small businesses from China and other parts of the world are selling products that there are hundreds of brands birthed each day.[16] So much so that many don't even have the time to come up with a good brand name. Whom do you trust? Who is making what and how? What feels true? The transparency effect is about to go mainstream in branding.

3. Brand Sense by Making the Choice Feel Good

Several things make us feel copacetic, satisfied, at peace with the world, and sunny and warm at heart. Research has shown that being in a good mood is correlated to making choices by gut feel, or in other words, more intuitively, creatively, and trustingly.[17] Brands that find ways to make consumers feel good will also find a place in their hearts (brains actually). I discuss here how you can use two cognitive biases, namely the in-group bias and the choice supportive bias, to make brand choice feel good and sensible.

In-Group Bias

It feels good to belong to groups. That human beings are social creatures is not news. It is noteworthy, though, that in our anxiousness to blend we tend to be biased about our brand choices subconsciously. We do this in two ways: (1) by adopting behaviors that make us more like other members in our group, or (2) by doing things that make us distinct from those who are not in our group. That is the us-versus-them syndrome.

One of my favorite recent examples of a brand using the in-group bias in an evocative manner is Diageo, with its Guinness beer campaign.[18] For unfortunate souls who may have lived a life deprived of the taste of this dark Irish stout, perhaps because it bears no resemblance to normal beer, it will suffice to say that Guinness is an ale like no other—with a dark plum interior, a thick and creamy head, and a hard-to-define mild bitter taste. Playing to this differentiation, the Diageo marketers cleverly decided to frame Guinness as the choice of ordinary people with extraordinary attitudes.

In one of their widely acclaimed commercials (see Figure 6.4), we see a team of young men playing full-intensity basketball. It could be just about any community of small-town friends playing at the local YMCA, except . . . in this game, every one of the players is in a wheelchair. OK, so we are witnessing some version of a Special Olympics team, we think. Fine, quite admirable. But when the game ends, all of the players get up and walk away perfectly normally from their wheelchairs. All, except one . . . the one who is actually wheelchair-bound.

Figure 6.4   Guinness appeals to need for group belonging.

The realization hits you in a tsunami of emotions. What kind of friends would play basketball in a wheelchair just to level the playing field for one person? Well, the kind who drink Guinness. In the final scene of the commercial, we see the players in a bar, enjoying their special camaraderie over pints of Guinness, with the tagline, "Guinness. Made of More."

The beauty of the ad lies in the simple premise that Guinness is a different kind of beer, not only in what it is but also in terms of the kind of people who favor it.

Who would not want to belong to a group like that? While not everyone will climb into a wheelchair to play basketball with their disabled friend, it is the kind of thing we would all wish we would do. By drinking Guinness, you can vicariously feel a part of just such a special crew. And in making you want to belong to that group is where the genius of this ad lies, not in its poignancy.

David Buchanan, creative director of the ad agency BBDO, described their brand strategy for another ad in the series in this way:

> Many years ago, Arthur Guinness chose to transcend the ordinary and produce an extraordinary drink, a drink made of more . . . This campaign is about that choice: Do we settle for the way things are or do we take the bold choice to step up and be made of more? Do we settle for an ordinary drink or do we choose one that is made of more?[19]

The challenge with aligning brands to special groups and clubs is that they can be seen as excluding others. As a marketer you have to be ready for the blowback. Augusta National, site of the Master's Tournament and one of the most prestigious golf clubs in the world, managed to hold out as a "men only" zone for years. In today's world, with the risk of becoming a dinosaur looming large, it finally relented and let more women in. The Guinness ad suffers no such problem; it creates a group within which you feel special but whose membership is open to all, with a sip of its delicious beer.

Choice Supportive Bias

Steve Genco, in his book *Intuitive Marketing*, astutely notes that we don't choose what we prefer; rather, *we prefer what we choose.*[20] Choice supportive bias, or post-purchase rationalization, is the tendency of people to justify the choices they have already made, often minimizing the negative information and focusing unreasonably on the positives.

Even if you are not a behavioral psychologist, it makes sense that this defect in our thinking would exist. Without the "I did good" self-congratulatory pat on the back, we would be second-guessing ourselves constantly and feeling depressed about our choices. We don't want to do that, do we? No! We want to feel good about our own choices, *even when they are bad.* Feeling good is what makes sense.

In one of our consulting engagements, my team was fielding focus groups with rheumatologists to understand how they thought about the changes that were taking place in their profession with the advent of modern biologic drugs. One of our ice-breaker opening questions was around how they felt about their choice of rheumatology as a profession.

At the time, the inside joke in the medical profession was that you became a rheumatologist because, well, you stood dead last in your class at med school. There is a mostly unspoken monetary hierarchy in the medical profession, and at the time rheumatologists, who generally earned under $100,000 annually, sat firmly at the bottom of the totem pole.

The main diseases that they treated, namely rheumatoid arthritis, fibromyalgia, and lupus, had subjective symptoms of the pain-and-stiffness variety. The available drugs to treat these symptoms were nothing to write home about, being mainly generic painkiller pills (high-dose Motrin anyone?) and some old systemics, like methotrexate, with one thing in common: none worked particularly well.

Primary care physicians would question the value of referring patients to a rheumatologist, knowing there was not much a rheumatologist would do that the primary care physicians could not prescribe for the patients themselves. Keeping that background in mind, consider their predicament in answering our question, "How do you like being a rheumatologist?" In detailed interviews with 40 rheumatologists, 39 said they loved their profession. "Really, why?" we asked innocently.

Well, they said, in rheumatology, you could be a *true* doctor, spend meaningful time with your patients, and practice medicine the way it was meant to be. The average rheumatologist sees 15 to 20 patients a day, spends 30 minutes or more per patient, listens to their stories about their suffering, and comes to understand their history. They recommend changes in diet and lifestyle, which in all honesty, does help their patients feel better. In contrast, a primary care physician would breeze through 50 to 60 patients in a single day, spending as little as five minutes with each, and make two to three times as much money as a rheumatologist.

But one of the 40 rheumatologists burst out and said, "I made a horrible mistake. I should have done something else." "What else?" we asked. "Anything else!" was the pat reply.

And that's what the choice supportive bias is. Of the 40, only one rheumatologist could bring themself to outwardly regret the choice he had made.[21]

That one person aside, for the rest we felt that it was important to discreetly account for the sense of rationalization that rheumatologists felt about their choice of careers and the way they practice medicine.

Humira was a breakthrough drug that, over time, garnered more than 100 patents. It was one of the few in an entirely new-to-the-world class of drugs and worked astonishingly well compared to the older drugs that were the standard of care. The temptation therefore was to trumpet that fact and say, "Look what Humira can do!"

Instead, the astute marketers at AbbVie, in their early campaigns, elected to say to the doctors, "Look what *you* can do with Humira!" That slight alteration of words was a big deal. We needed to acknowledge the fact that our wonder drug was not a wonder at all without the expert hands of the rheumatologists to guide it to the patients in a manner only they knew. It was a way to subtly support the choices they had made and recognize their part in treating patients effectively.

For marketers, leveraging the choice supportive bias to drive their own brand adoption can be sweet. One way to do this is to position your product as something that customers already love, but something better or more.

In another study that we worked on, we talked to dermatologists who treated eczema. They were in a somewhat similar situation to that the rheumatologists had faced before the advent of biologic drugs. There were no good drugs available for treating eczema specifically. Most of the creams available did not work particularly well, and stronger systemics, like cyclosporin, that were effective had pretty rough side effects.

When finally, Pfizer launched Dupixent, a monoclonal antibody, it was a significant advance and worked for 65 percent of the patients in clinical trials with fewer side effects. Having waited for this miracle for decades, dermatologists were understandably excited and prescribed the drug freely.

Our client was coming out with a better drug, but unfortunately, a few years later. The new drug would work in 80 percent of the cases as compared to the 65 percent claimed for Dupixent, but it did have exceedingly rare, but more serious, side effects.

To our surprise, when we interviewed dermatologists using Dupixent, they swore that the drug was working for 90 to 95 percent of patients in their practice and not 65 percent. This was shocking, as generally drug performance in actual practice is somewhat worse than in a clinical trial, where conditions are tightly controlled and there is persistent follow-up to ensure that the patients stay on the drug for the duration of the trial.

Further, while Dupixent could cause conjunctivitis, a highly irritating eye condition, in one out of 10 patients, the physicians were not concerned at all and claimed they had never seen that in their own practice. On deeper dives into their patient records and chart data, it was clear that the physicians had a rosier view of Dupixent than was the reality in their own practice. We knew we were dealing with choice supportive bias.

Physicians had been using Dupixent for a while, and they were not about to call their baby ugly. One option for a competing brand facing such a dilemma is to say that it offers all of things that they love about their current choice, plus a few other neat tricks. This is the "your brand plus more" positioning that you see by many marketers and in situations like this can work better than a "my brand is new and different" positioning.

Positioning your brand as an affirmation or extension of a choice that a consumer has already made can make powerful brand sense. It plays to the choice supportive bias that is wired into our brains and makes the choice feel good and the brand sensible to the consumer.

4. Brand Sense by Making the Choice Easy

Kahneman points out that System 2 is lazy. If it can get by with System 1 taking care of business with its instinct and intuition, it is happy to let things slide. You experience cognitive ease when the brand choices offered seem simple and effortless. Marketers can make brand choice easy in many ways and thus help brands make sense to consumers.

There is one important point about brand sense by making choice easy. You should note that this is not about providing convenience to make your life easier, as in Instacart delivering groceries to your home so you don't have to go shopping. This is about simplifying the process by which you choose a brand, so you don't have to tax your brain on peeling options. There are two cognitive biases, namely Occam's razor bias and herd-mentality bias, that come in handy in making brand choice feel easy.

Occam's Razor Bias

As humans, we prefer simple answers rather than complicated ones that make our heads hurt. The Occam's razor principle posits that given two solutions to a problem, all else being equal, the simpler answer is better.

Even in the 1300s, when friar William of Ockham noted the existence of a simplification bias, it was not a novel idea.[22] Ages ago, in the fourth century BCE, Aristotle had declared that "We may assume the superiority *ceteris paribus* of the demonstration which derives from fewer postulates or hypotheses."[23] Ironically, if only Aristotle had heeded his own advice and stated the thesis more simply, the bias might have been called "Aristotle's needle" instead of Occam's razor.

Here's the rub, though. There is absolutely no evidence that there is any truth to the Occam's razor principle. In real life, personal or business, complex situations require nuanced answers. If someone did not worry about the little details, we would have airplanes falling out of the sky and the Chicago skyline leaning aside like the Tower of Pisa. Oversimplifying problems can lead to suboptimal or incorrect outcomes. Despite that knowledge, most people are instinctively biased to KISS (Keep it simple stupid!). As marketers, we are not here to judge. We are here to commandeer this behavioral insight for bestowing sense upon cognitive brands.

Staples realized that while it loved office supplies, its customers didn't. Buying them is a tedious chore for people with better things to do. There is a myriad of choices for pens, paper, and pencils from office supply stores.

What if you were to remind people that life was complex and the best answer could be to keep choice simple and buy everything from one place, namely Staples? The company rolled out a major campaign around an outsized "Easy" button. The early spots showed ordinary people in difficult everyday situations. In one, a teacher chalking miles of inscrutable Greek letters on a board abruptly pivots to the clueless little Josh trapped in the front row of class and asks, "So n equals what?" Another features a harried mother changing diapers simultaneously for her twin infants. In the ads, in each case, the bright red "Easy" button from Staples appears magically on scene, and pressing it saves the day. The voiceover observes, "Wouldn't it be nice if there was an easy button for life. Now, there's one for your business. Staples. That was easy."

The idea of not overcomplicating the trivia in life has the hallmark appeal of Occam's razor for our lazy System 2. It knows that the alternative of setting up an Excel spreadsheet, to compare three competing bids for each office supply line item, is about as exciting as sitting by the side of an Arizona interstate, beating rocks. While the spreadsheet might save you some money or get you better products, it is neither simple nor easy.

H-E-B, the popular grocery store chain in Texas, presumably figured out that Staples was on to something. If Occam's razor could help Staples sell disinfectant wipes and hanging file folders, what could it do to help move moderately edible, store-prepared meals?

H-E-B spots feature various situations in which life is getting to be ridiculously out of hand and then remind you that mealtime does not have to be similarly complicated. In one clip, a man driving home from work in heavy traffic looks at his GPS, which estimates the time to destination as "Next Thursday!" The voiceover then pipes in with "When life gets crazy, keep it simple. H-E-B give you hundreds of chef-inspired meals to choose from, all ready within minutes." Works for me.

With the advent of AI, marketers have new opportunities to build brands that make sense with Occam's razor. That is exactly what Stitch Fix is. Since shipping its first box of clothes, Stitch Fix has garnered nearly three million customers and over $1 billion in revenues. For people who like to dress well, but have trouble figuring out what they look good in or plain hate shopping, StichFix provides the simple answer. Its AI engine and a cadre of remote personal human stylists use a series of simple questions and pictures of things that you may like, to figure out your style. Thereafter, it's a standard online subscription service and gets easier and better by the minute, so you can enjoy your own moments of cognitive ease.

Herd Metality/Expert Bias

As discussed before, we feel cognitive ease when making choices that are effortless. What better way to do this than to let someone else do the hard work of figuring out what the right choice is and then do what they do? That is the herd metality/expert bias, and it makes brand choice easier for us. We follow the herd rather than work out an answer for ourselves.

Have you ever found yourself at a cross street, checking messages on your iPhone while waiting for the pedestrian signal to indicate it is safe for you to cross the street? From the corner of your eye, you catch the five other people next to you step off the curb and start to cross. Without taking your eye off the WhatsApp video from Brad of a heartbreaking owl rescue in the tar pits of Venezuela, you too start crossing the street with them.

Now, stop, let's think about this for a second. If you crossed the street without proper inspection of the oncoming traffic, you may get run over by a dump truck and turned promptly into compost. Yet, in crossing without looking, you entrust your life to five strangers who, for all you know, may be fervent disciples of a suicidal cult. That's the wonderful System 1 working the magic of the herd effect.

Online retailers leverage news-flash-type alerts to egg you on to buy their brands by informing you about what the herd is doing. These are the ever-present messages telling you to buy their brands because "six other people are looking at it now" or "ten others bought it today." People are trusting nameless strangers, with whom they have little in common other than the fact that they too are online shoppers, in deciding what brands to buy. That's the power of peer-to-peer System 1 herding in steering people to brands like sheep crossing the road. Not classy, but it gets the job done.

SEEKING WISDOM IN BIASES

I want to take a moment to emphasize again that System 1 Easers are all about tapping into consumers' beliefs and learnings, namely their cognitive wisdom. Too often many experts have equated them with cognitive biases exclusively. Because biases are often slight errors in judgment, this has led them to claim that humans are mostly irrational. This follows from saying, "Wait, if people use System 1 processes 95 percent[24] of the time to make choices, and if System 1 is all cognitive biases, and if cognitive biases are errors in rational judgment, then aren't people irrational 95 percent of the time?" This proof by deduction leads to the inevitable validation of the null hypothesis "The whole world is nuts." It is silly and wrong.

System 1 is the repository of learnings from our past experiences *across a range of events*. It is our collective wisdom on what works and doesn't from our lives, and we use it instinctively. It is true in most circumstances, but sometimes in some specific situations (or within what economists call narrow boundary conditions), it is wrong. What this means is that you as a marketer can build a compelling case for your brand using System 1 Easers *by tapping into any deep-set belief and cognitive wisdom* that consumers have *without relying on known cognitive biases only.*

Building brands by tapping into people's existing beliefs works something like this: The brand makes an argument of the type, "If you believe A is true, then you must believe that so is B." In this case A is something that the brand marketer knows the customer believes already, and B is his brand's proposition. This happens because of what Robert Cialdini identifies as the Consistency Principle.[25] Once you have agreed or committed to an idea, you are inclined to agree with other related ones. Let me show you with an example.

Pfizer, the maker of a pain medication called Celebrex, used this strategy for its consumer campaign. You may not know this yet, but as you grow older, the protective cartilage that cushions the ends of your bones wears down and you develop arthritis. Then with bone rubbing against bone, it becomes painful for you to move around. However, as your doctor will strongly urge, the more you move, the more those bones will grind out the rough edges and spurs, and the less painful it will become. Bottom line, forcing yourself to be active will actually make things better. This is a belief that will be etched in your brain by the time your doctor is done counseling you.

In one version of Pfizer's commercial, you see a man sitting in the front porch of his winter home.[26] In the distance, his son is seen shoveling the snow. The voiceover says, "It's simple physics. A body at rest tends to stay at rest, while a body in motion stays in motion." Well, so far so good. Who's going to argue with simple physics? It is a shared belief.

Then you see the man get up effortlessly from his chair, a mischievous twinkle in his eye, as the voiceover continues, ". . . But if you have arthritis, staying active can be difficult. Prescription Celebrex can ease your pain so that your body can stay in motion."

The man bends down to pick up a handful of snow; he rolls it into a snowball and nails his son with it in a swift arching throw. The ad carefully takes any semblance of blame off you (tells you it knows what arthritis is doing to you silently) and offers Celebrex as the solution for your tendency to be inactive.

It is easy to see why this ad would not have been the same thing if all it said was, "Celebrex is great at easing your pain." By connecting the idea of your inactivity to simple physics, and the advice given to you by your doctor, Pfizer intertwines your beliefs with their brand.

When you have accepted the first premise (that you must stay active to stay healthy), you are more likely to accept the second related idea (that you should take Celebrex to ease your pain and enable your mobility). In cognitive brands built with System 1 Easers, the second idea can be the point, with the first being the connecting vibe . . . a statement reaffirming a shared belief.

Now, biologists and physicists will argue that Pfizer is mixing up apples and oranges by claiming that arthritic joints that are regularly used will behave just like a body in motion in the vacuum of space. They are right, of course, but, who cares? The ad works.

ACCIDENTAL STRAINS

The opposite of cognitive ease is cognitive dissonance or strain, where you ask the consumer to do something that goes against their beliefs. When this happens, customers feel like something is wrong and that they need to focus and think carefully. They use their System 2, which I will discuss in the next chapter.

One of our clients, a manufacturer of a new type of drug for the treatment of persistent skin rash, had toyed with the idea of giving their brand the personality of a "rebel" that was unafraid to go against conventions and take risks. While that was exciting for the marketers, it wasn't so for the dermatologists who treat the disease.

For one, the drug had a black-box warning, which for those not in the industry means that, in rare cases, it has the potential for serious side effects. These side effects could include the risk of inducing a rare form of cancer or hard-to-treat infection. How do you take a drug like that and tell the doctor to prescribe it with rebel-like abandon? Dermatologists we interviewed would tell us, "Look here, no one has died of a persistent rash, but they could die from your drug!" Better sense prevailed, and the client quietly glossed over the "rebel" personality idea and asked for better options.

That is a textbook example of inviting a cognitive dissonance problem. We found that a number of cognitive ease levers were available. We could use the choice supportive bias to say that the choice of our drug was no different than the other choices doctors had made in the past. We could point to a lot of other drugs that dermatologists liked and used routinely that also had black-box warnings, for instance, creams, like topical calcineurin inhibitors, and systemics, like cyclosporin.

In fact, we demonstrated that to diminish concerns around such black-box warnings, the company needed to do three things to create cognitive ease through familiarity, and (1) show that the associated adverse events were very rare as in *other drugs they used frequently*; (2) that indeed if that did occur, the risks were what they were *already familiar* with; and finally, (3) they could be easily managed with *approaches well-known to them*.

We simply said: "Doc, the risks are very similar to the drugs that you already use a lot. In the rare case that something happens, what you have to do is nothing different from what you already do for those other drugs you use." In this way, we were able to ease the concerns that the dermatologists had by saying it was no different than the sensible brand choices they had already made in the past.

KEY TAKEAWAYS

Cognitive brands can create consumer preference by answering their question, "Does this brand make intuitive sense?"

System 1 Easers are all about leading consumers to make sense of the brand proposition instinctively, by going with the flow instead of fighting it. Everyone has their own private repository of biases and wisdom from past brand interactions or even life experiences, whether they were good or bad, and it is just easier to reapply that knowledge rather than make a fresh evaluation. Brands that find a way to tap into that pool of cognitive wisdom will find themselves favored as the sensible choice automatically.

There are four ways to use System 1 Easers to imbue brand sense. You have to make the act of choosing your brand feel effortless by making it:

- Familiar

- More true and authentic

- Good

- Easier

Whether you use a System 1 Easer or not, be aware of them. If your brand accidentally goes against a consumer's deep-set biases and beliefs, it will hit a brick wall.

System 1 Easers are one of the two ways in which consumers make sense of what a brand says. The other way is with System 2 Deliberators, where consumers use reasoning to make sense of brands. I cover those in the next chapter.

CHAPTER 7

BRAND SENSE

Using System 2 Deliberators to Form New Brand Loyalties

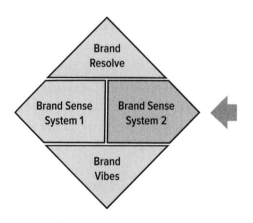

The edge of a precipice is a very merciless school;
over there you either learn to be serious or you die foolishly!
—Mehmet Murat İldan

The *Deliberator* subunit of the brain uses what Daniel Kahneman calls System 2 processes to prevent us from suffering foolish predicaments daily of the type contemplated by İldan. When System 2 perceives there is a risk from making a gut-feel choice that System 1 might advocate, System 2 springs into action.

System 2 can analyze unfamiliar situations, make complicated calculations, solve equations, apply principles, decipher trends, and map out pros and cons of distinct options. It is just the kind of toolkit that comes in handy when shopping for a complicated product, like a home mortgage, which can have a make-or-break impact on your household finances. You compare competitive rates from different banks and read the fine print on fees, prepayment terms, post-lock interest escalation, and other such niceties before deciding what makes the most sense. It is mentally taxing, unpleasant even, but well advised in such situations.

Some people mistakenly believe that System 2 is basically all rational thinking and System 1 all emotional. Just because System 2 is built around reasoning and deliberation, it does not mean that it will not take emotions into account when making sense of brand choices. You may momentarily and logically conclude that it makes no financial sense to buy your wife $45 worth of roses that by definition were dead leaves from the moment they were severed from the mother plant, but you may do so anyway because you figure it will be nice to see her smile on Valentine's Day. There is nothing irrational about that. It is not "just a feeling"; it is a *calculated* feeling.

System 2 Deliberators have other peculiarities. Since they require mental effort, they do not kick in unless necessary. If you can make sense of what a brand says instinctively using the trusty old System 1 Easers, then that is what becomes your preference, almost to a fault.

You may decide that instead of analyzing five different mortgage products and inviting a splitting headache, you'll just go with the one that your neighbor, a certified accountant and financial nerd, went with. All analysis is set aside, and the System 1 Easers make the call using the *authority bias*, a tendency to unduly defer to a so-called expert as decision making shortcut.

However, the *Conator* subunit in the brain, which is the arbiter of all actions, keeps an eye on System 1 Easers and calls for System 2 deliberation when it suspects a problem. For example, System 1 may also volunteer another useful tidbit of related information, namely, that Gordon was recently sighted flinging his green shades off into the neighbor's pool and committing several alcohol-laced indiscretions at the recent block party. That may make you hesitate in blindly following Gordon's choice of a mortgage product.

If the situation warrants deliberation, and you are on the edge of Ildan's precipice, System 2 is dragged in, even though the bar for calling for intervention remains high. Most often things are copacetic and on cruise control, and System 2 deliberation is used only 5 percent of the time.

If your product is innovative or unusual, it may require significant scrutiny or a behavioral shift on the part of the buyer. Your brand will need to awaken the customer's System 2 Deliberators. Even though System 2 is sparingly used, it has one critically important function: it is the source of all the System 1 wisdom wired into the brain.

System 1 can also write rules, but they are corollaries, not new theorems. While System 2 may be the determining process in the initial evaluation period of innovative brands, repeat purchases are routinized by System 1. In other words, brand loyalty flows from the System 1 circuitry.

Oreo grew to be one of the largest cookie brands in the United States by creating a ritual around how the cookies are enjoyed. Rather than munch on them, consumers are advised to "Twist, Lick and Dunk" the cookie, which involves *twisting off* the two sides of the sandwich, *licking* the cream filling inside, and *dunking* the remainder in milk before placing it in your mouth.

When the brand was introduced to markets like India, Pakistan, and China, that choreographed method of consuming a cookie was puzzling for most. But Mondelez, the company that owns Oreo, persisted on promoting the ritual in televised campaigns. The consumers' System 2 Deliberators, which can learn by trial and error, kicked in, and Indians and Chinese alike started taking their first tentative Oreo dunks.

After a few rounds of emerging unscathed and decidedly content from the experience, the "Twist, Lick and Dunk" ritual was in place among these new Oreo consumers. System 2 encoded these findings into the consumers' *Learner* subunit in their brains and they became Oreo fans. In India, after a shaky start, Oreo's share of the cream cookies market jumped remarkably from 1 percent to 30 percent in just five years.[1]

If marketers credit Kahneman for uncovering System 2, they can thank cognitive behavior therapists, like the larger-than-life Dr. David Burns, for perfecting the methods needed for applying it to change consumer behavior. Marketers were the last of psychotherapist Dr. Burns's priorities, unless their minds had wandered away from the true normal. Instead, he was obsessed with figuring out ways to help his patients, some of whom suffered desperately from depression or anxiety disorders. He sought to change their behavior constructively, not just on the rare occasion, but consistently and habitually. The mood-altering drugs that they were taking were just not cutting it.[2] In his book, *Feeling Good*, now a bible for practitioners of cognitive behavior therapy (CBT), Dr. Burns lays out various techniques that patients can use to "untwist their thinking."[3]

Dr. Burns does this by helping his patients deliberate on and break the self-defeating cycle of negative thoughts, feelings, and behaviors they have in response to common situations in life. It is a two-step process. First you diagnose your own problem and then solve it by untwisting your negative thinking.

Let's do an example. Say one day you find you were not invited to an important meeting held by your boss but everyone else was. If you are the kind of person who gets anxious easily, you may feel that you are about to be fired from your job or at the minimum, demoted. Dr. Burns may help you untwist your thinking by encouraging you to think of other reasons why you may not have been included. For instance, it may be the case that you are already overloaded with the two other priority projects that your boss assigned to you earlier in the week, and she doesn't want you to be distracted and set up for failure.

In other words, Dr. Burns gets his patients to channel their System 2 Deliberators to make sense of the situation and diagnose the real issue, when the instinctive System 1 is routinely resulting in regressive thoughts and behaviors. Then the patient can take appropriate corrective action and direct their mind to thinking positively, being less anxious, and not taking a reckless action like firing off an angry email to colleagues. Behavior changed. Problem solved.

CBT methods have been proven to change people's behavior sustainably in controlled clinical trials.[4] Very few marketing methods go through that kind of scrutiny. Dr. Burns has published a rich catalog of methods for untwisting the mind. *If you simply imagine that negative behavior for our purposes is a consumer's rejection of our brand, then these methods are a trail of breadcrumbs for reshaping the consumer mindset.*

Perhaps Dr. Burns would be annoyed that I am hijacking his research, but the truth is his work is very helpful in designing cognitive brands, and oddly enough, no one else has applied it in marketing. In the following, I draw inspiration from his successfully proven methods to present a set of System 2 Deliberators for marketers to apply in helping consumers make sense of their brands.

The good news is that System 2 Deliberators are familiar territory for marketers. In one form or another, they involve selling your brand's value proposition logically to the customer. Value propositions involve four types of strategies (see Figure 7.1): (1) showing them how your brand adds greater (amplified) value relative to other options; (2) lowering the risk of using your brand; (3) making your proposition credible by providing reasons to believe in it; and finally, (4) providing consumers a context for thinking about value or risk of your brand (perception).

However, as I said before, *how* you do branding is just as important and inseparable from what you do with it. And that is precisely where CBT methods are invaluable. In the following sections, I highlight how they can be used to address the four aspects of value propositions: relative value, risk, perception, and credibility.

Cheat Sheet 8 Deliberators for Changing Behaviors	
✓ No-Brainer Method ✓ Pleasure Prediction Method	Amplify the value
✓ Fight-or-Flight Method ✓ Flirting Training Method	Lower the risk
✓ Examine the Evidence Method ✓ Survey Method	Provide reasons to believe
✓ Reframing Method ✓ Reattribution Method	Change the context

Figure 7.1 How System 2 Deliberators change behaviors.

1. SYSTEM 2 DELIBERATORS: AMPLIFY VALUE

In today's hypercompetitive world, to stand out from the crowd you have to offer extreme value. You will catch the mind's eye of System 2, when your brand offers something that is simply too good to pass up or makes the pleasure of consuming it more vivid. We can think of these two approaches as the no-brainer and the pleasure prediction methods respectively.

No-Brainer Method

David Burns calls this the cost-benefit method for changing behavior. He asks his patients to catalog the benefits they feel from their negative thoughts ("What am I getting out of thinking this way?"). Next, he tells them to evaluate the costs of engaging in the same ("What is it costing me to think negatively this way?"). If the costs exceed the benefits, then Dr. Burns asks his patients to confront and alter that unfortunate reality.

To marketers, this is the all-too-familiar value proposition method. It tries to change customer behavior by convincing them of the opposite, namely that the value obtained from using the brand is far greater than its cost.

When I was working as an associate at Booz Allen, this novel concept was exciting. In the consulting world, things like that deserve their own acronym and someone came up with "CONBO." It stands for "cost of next best option."

For any given products, we could catalog all the different ways in which it delivered value for a customer. We could then spring out our Excel spreadsheets and assign a dollar value to each possible source of value. This was A. Then we would go hunting for other competing product options that could do the same thing as our brand and assign dollar values to their cost. This was B. Both letters, A and B, would entail a lot of work and keep us busy for a while. Once all this was nailed down, we could subtract the cost B from the value A and arrive at the consumer surplus C. If the surplus were large enough, the brand had a superior value proposition that could rationally change the consumer's buying behavior, after a mandatory inspection of our spreadsheets.

In the real world, consumers prefer to avoid this way of thinking, but for complex situations they can be persuaded to do so. If you sell hybrid cars, it certainly makes sense for your brand to talk about the benefit of annual savings from the 50-miles-per-gallon fuel economy and $5,000 government tax credit. Still, it is not a natural thing for consumers, and they prefer mental shortcuts instead. A simple way to provide a System 2 shortcut is to amplify the value of the brand so much that a *precise* calculation is unnecessary. A quick top-down check is adequate. It still uses System 2 deliberation, but is less painful.

It took venture capitalists to really take the value proposition method to the no-brainer extreme. They realized that coming up with intricate calculations of consumer surplus was not going to pass muster if they were going to scale up businesses at breakneck speeds. Rather, brands should have smack-in-your-face value. This usually meant selling for a loss for a while and making money later.

Think about Uber. It represented a seismic shift in behavior from how consumers were used to taking cabs. Enter the no-brainer method. Make it so that the consumer goes, "What's there to not like about Uber?"

You don't have to lean precariously into the traffic from a sidewalk to hail a cab. You can order and track it on your phone and not stand in the pouring rain until it arrives. You don't have to negotiate the rate or check if the cabbie is willing to go to your destination. You don't have to present your credit card; it will be charged and a receipt mailed electronically. Oh, and it is often cheaper than taking a cab. That's because it is being offered to you at below-market prices by equity investors who subsidize your Uber ride.

That's smack-in-the-face value. It makes so much sense that it would be crazy to not use Uber. No spreadsheet required. Many famed unicorns (startups reaching $1 billion-plus valuations) like Amazon, Dropbox, Pinterest, Twitter, Facebook, Netflix, Grubhub, and Spotify were born in this manner: offer a phenomenal product, charge little or nothing, spread like wildfire, and worry about making money later.

It also turns out that the brain really likes *free* stuff. There is a huge difference between offering something for nearly free versus completely free in the way the brain's reward centers in the *Conator* respond.

It should then come as no surprise that one common offer with our retail clients is a BOGO, short for buy one, get one free, which often works better than the nearly identical half-off offer. Thus free offers are familiar and instinctively preferred by System 1, while System 2 takes a rest.

When you have a complex product to sell, you can make life a little easier for yourself by first finding something nice to give for free. People use WhatsApp for a lot of different things now to organize their group interactions. But WhatsApp initially gained traction in the market by offering free texting at a time when most telecom companies required you to pay for short message services (SMSs).

With the no-brainer method we also see another important aspect of System 2 deliberation, namely, that it can kick in with low vigilance if needed. When something makes a lot of sense even with a few quick calculations, a full-on evaluation is unnecessary.

Could your brand deliver a "I would be crazy to say no to this" value proposition and worry about making money later? Can you give away free stuff? If not, then read on for other avenues.

Pleasure Prediction Method

The second way in which Dr. Burns helps his patients understand the value of positive behaviors is by making their benefits more vivid. Patients who suffer from depression often underestimate the pleasure they think they would get from engaging in social activities. This causes them to retreat into a shell. By helping them correct that error of perception, a cognitive behavior therapist can get patients to view those activities more positively and pursue them. Similarly, in marketing, we can help consumers see the sense in our brands by letting them imagine their benefits vibrantly.

The Rainforest Alliance uses the pleasure prediction method in its "Follow the Frog" campaign. Its mission is to help multinational companies work responsibly with farming communities around the world. One of the most important tools in their arsenal is the "Rainforest Alliance Certified" seal. When placed on products, it confirms that those brands are produced by companies in cooperation with the farmers under an audited program, which contributes to biodiversity, improved livelihoods, human well-being, and natural resource conservation. However, to make this worthwhile for the companies, the Rainforest Alliance markets the seal to consumers through a consumer campaign.

The campaign is a three-minute spot viewable on YouTube.[5] It features a young family man, maybe you, the viewer, if you have a strong desire to save rainforests, and who at the outset is declared to be "a good person." Proof of the same is provided in the following narrative, "You conserve water while showering, you drive a Prius but use your bike when you can, and you always send a card on Mother's Day." Then the narrator muses that "there is a part of you that does not feel good, because rain forests are being obliterated at the rate of one football field every 72 seconds and all you have done is . . . yoga!"

Disappointed, it continues, "Well, this is what you are not going to do: quit your job, leave your family" and travel to heart of the rain forest. It then shows why and what would have happened if you had done that. In that imaginary voyage, it shows the "good person" suffering through a series of indignities and misadventures, finally breaking down, smoking his first cigarette in four years, and accidentally starting a forest fire. He returns home to find his job gone and wife co-opted by the gym coach. The sponsors then helpfully suggest that he pursue his dreams more practically in his real-life journey and "Follow the Frog" by buying only products that carry the Rainforest Alliance seal.

In its humorous way, the spot helps you visualize how you can help rain forests around the world and be a better person by making small changes in your daily purchases. Now, all of a sudden, you are not just stuffing your face with any bananas but with purposeful Rainforest Alliance–certified Chiquita bananas. This is a clever way to amplify the pleasures from common utilitarian purchases that you may otherwise give no thought to. It drives behavior. No one likes watching advertisements for the most part, but 5.7 million people have watched this three-minute-long commercial on YouTube alone.

Pleasure prediction is not necessarily about attaching teary-eyed emotions to brand messages. The Rainforest Alliance is telling you that there is a practical way for you to engage in sustainability initiatives, providing a functional benefit that is communicated engagingly through humor and storytelling.

The pleasure prediction method has been the go-to approach for many pharma marketers. It goes something like, "Take my drug, and you will not only feel better, but also do all kinds of other amazing things in life that you have not been able to." As we discussed before, this formulaic approach has resulted in a "sea of sameness" across drug categories in how they position their brands. But sometimes you will be pleasantly surprised.

Consider Opdivo,[6] a drug from Bristol Myers Squibb, for the treatment of lung cancer. In our work on terminal lung cancer, we saw that patients and physicians faced difficult choices. About half of the patients die in six to nine months, and there is no cure. We found that in many instances, patients would come to terms with the inevitable and refuse further treatment.

Opdivo can extend patients' lives by about three months. If they do choose to extend their life, they also extend their suffering to some degree. Even though the drug's cost of $150,000[7] is generally covered by

Medicare or private insurance, there are other costs (e.g., hiring a home-care nurse) that suffering patients incur, dipping into the family's savings.

Would they want to extend that life? For many, adding three months to life is neither here nor there, and so the motivation for taking a costly drug is not high. So the marketers of cancer drugs like Opdivo often have to answer the question why three months matter to an older person past their prime.

The answer is that three months can matter if they allow the patient to live long enough to bear witness to certain milestone moments—like the high school graduation day of their grandson or the birth of a grand-daughter.

Opdivo runs a consumer campaign around "Who would not want to live longer?" One version of its commercials features a woman, presumably in her sixties, who is seen with her granddaughter racing toward her, arms outstretched, with the narrator posing the question, "Who would not want another chance for . . .?" (see Figure 7.2). The last phrase is left unspoken, but the two are seen embracing. The scene is followed by the woman standing with her husband, who kisses her on the forehead, as the narrator asks, "Who would say no to another . . .?"

Figure 7.2 Opdivo ad emphasizes pleasure prediction.

You may think of this campaign as an emotional play, but there is nothing impulsive about the decisions a dying person has to make. They deliberate very carefully on what trade-offs they are going to make in terms of their quality of life and family obligations. The Opdivo campaign works. The drug and its rival Keytruda from Merck pulled in an estimated $20 billion in annual sales (the drugs are used in other types of advanced cancers beyond lung cancer) in 2020.

2. SYSTEM 2 DELIBERATORS: LOWER THE RISK

In some cases, even though the value of a brand is understood, consumers are unable to bring themselves to buy the associated products or services because of the "what if something goes wrong" factor. The two approaches to resolving such uncertainty are either to confront it head on, the fight-or-flight method, or to take baby steps to adoption, the "flirting training method," both of which I present next.

Fight-or-Flight Method

In CBT, one method shown to help change behavior is to have the patient safely face his or her fears. The patient may realize that some of their fears are unfounded or discover coping mechanisms for dealing with them.

Marketers may be tempted to find a way to scare customers into buying their product. How about these example pitches: "Put your money in my mutual fund this minute or spend your retirement living on the streets." Or, "Take my arthritis drug now or roll through your old age strapped to a wheelchair." These are surely compelling arguments. They are also risky business.

Marketers jumping onto the face-your-fears train may want to pause and contain their excitement. Research into human emotion sciences has shown that fear stimulus is processed in the amygdala of the brain, which is programmed to act on threats with an instinctive fight-or-flight response. Fear may lead the consumer to either fight your brand off or run away from it. Which one do you choose? I hope you answered "neither" because that is the right answer. While fight-or-flight may be technically a System 1 response, confronting your fears and dealing with them thoughtfully is a System 2 comeback.

Recently, I was testing various brand concepts in a focus group of patients with rheumatoid arthritis. One of the conditioning statements opened with the phrase, "You have but one life to live, make the most of it (by taking our drug to relieve your symptoms)." From some participants, this evoked a stinging rebuke, "I don't like it. You're making it sound like, 'Take my drug or die.'" You handle fight-or-flight methods like you would a stick of dynamite—with steady hands and a little prayer!

There is debate among researchers around whether scare tactics work.[8] The most in-your-face example of such marketing is the anti-smoking campaign in the United States. We have all been subjected to the jarring spots of Terrie, the former chain smoker, who methodically deconstructs her face and larynx, and crackles an instructive warning against smoking through a mechanical mouthpiece.[9]

It is a breathtakingly terrifying commercial. But does it work? There is some evidence to suggest that it does not. Fear ads often show extreme and uncommon situations.[10] We all have friends who smoke, and not many turn out like Terrie. People tend to believe that bad things will happen to others, but not to them. That is why people jaywalk, even though others have been killed doing the exact same thing.

More important, people often cope with fear by tuning it out of their minds. Ironically, scare tactics may trigger the behavior they are designed to prevent. How? Some smokers report getting so stressed out by the anti-smoking ads that they seek relief by doing what they usually do when they feel bad, namely light up!

That said, marketers can try to get away with scare tactics "lite." So how about if we replaced the word "fear" with "concern"? How about if we made the tone less strident and rather than say, "You'd better do this," try a gentler, "Wouldn't it be wise for you to do this?"

In Chapter 1, we talked about how Enbrel, a drug for patients of rheumatoid arthritis, uses a child to voice her mother's fears of becoming disabled.[11] Instead of the brand marketers asking, "Hey, Mom, you sure you will be able to stay Mom when you get older?" they have the cute little daughter pop that very question. After all, we are OK with children innocently asking inappropriate questions. It is clever, but it is risky as the impact on the amygdala of the brain could still be the same, namely fight-or-flight, or total shutdown.

Xarelto, a drug by Janssen, is a blood thinner that can treat and prevent blood clots. It helps lower the risk of stroke, deep vein thrombosis, and pulmonary embolism. Unless you are actually having a stroke, you are really not going to be feeling anything in your heart or veins. Xarelto has no choice but to talk about the horrible things that could happen to you if you don't take the drug.

In a slight twist, Xarelto's commercials speak instead about how wonderful it is that all kinds of awful things that could have happened did not happen, because you presciently took their drug.[12] They do this in their commercials by showing a battery of emergency workers from various walks of life who profess their delight at not having had to come to your rescue. The lifeguard on the beach declares, "I didn't have to run for help"; the waitress at the restaurant says, "I didn't have to call 911"; the hospital helicopter pilot muses, "I didn't have to come and get you"; and the nurse closes with, "... because you didn't have a heart attack, not today." All that, because you took the advice of your cardiologist to take Xarelto to heart (yes, the pun is also in the commercial and lightens it up a bit).

While we are talking about a System 2 Deliberator here, it might also be noted that there is also a System 1 play. Xarelto plays to the *loss aversion bias* by reminding you that you could *lose* the good life you're enjoying in a heartbeat (my pun, not Janssen's this time). Likewise, Amgen, with the Enbrel ad, sort of under the breath whispers to the patient that she is a good mom now, but could *lose* the privilege in the future.

Another interesting attempt at modulating the tone of a fear message comes from Australia, by marketers for the Melbourne Metro[13] who wanted to produce a train safety message. They produced an animated mini-movie and song about all the dumb ways to die.[14] The song starts perkily, enumerating all the stupid stuff you can do to kill yourself—for example, set fire to your hair, poke a stick at a grizzly bear, use your private parts as piranha bait, or eat a tube of super glue (yes, it is a regular bucket of Aussie humor).

Toward the end, the characters switch the catchy little ditty to list the stupid things you could do to guarantee annihilation by one of their trains: by, for instance, standing on the edge of a train station platform, driving around the barrier at a railroad crossing, or running across the tracks between the platforms. Those latter few are the ones they would rather that you avoid doing and are the point.

However, by attaching their message to a long list of dumb ways to die, they make their message seem less shrill and more commonsensical and memorable. Does it work? Who knows! However, it did generate a lot of positive press for the campaign, with the likes of Daisy Dumas of the *Sydney Morning Herald* describing the narrative as "darkly cute—and irksomely catchy" and the chorus as "instant earworm material."[15] For that free commentary alone, I'd say it is worth every penny.

So should you frighten your customer into buying your products? Here are a few words from those of us who enlighten ourselves with street-sign wisdom: "Proceed with caution." I showed you how marketers have done it with some success—by not making grim consequences vivid, and instead about calamities avoided, using friendly faces to deliver the message, and finally, preceding the heavier message with lighter ones.

Flirting Training Method

Sometimes, letting wary customers flirt a little with your brand is a great way to begin a relationship. While flirting may not be the foundation of your brand, it may be part of the scaffolding. For a number of online brands, flirting was the key to breaking out into billion-dollar brands.

Warby Parker, an online retailer of prescription glasses, disrupted the $140 billion[16] eyewear industry dominated by the industry giant EssilorLuxottica,[17] It's easy to see that shopping for prescription glasses online is risky. How do you know what the frames will look like on your face? Initially, the company tried all kinds of advanced visual simulation software that could allow people to upload pictures of their faces and superimpose the frames on them, but it just wasn't doing the trick.

To get around this problem—of buying online and being stuck with the glasses you hate—Warby Parker launched its "home try on" program, whereby a customer receives not one but five frames by mail before buying anything at all. You can also post a picture of yourself in the frames on the #warbyhometryon hashtag and have strangers with time on their hands, and some Warby Parker staff members, give you their opinion on your spectacled mug shot. By 2019, 56,000 videos had been uploaded, and 50 percent of the shoppers who had done so went on to make a purchase. This flirting training method has now become an essential feature of the Warby Parker brand experience.

StitchFix is another online apparel retailer that uses the same approach. Once you have answered a few basic questions about your preferences, their AI engine-based virtual stylist and human personal shoppers mail you a set of clothes to try. You keep what you love and send the rest back for free. StitchFix then sends you sets of new clothes periodically, so you can change your status from just flirting to devastatingly hooked.

Incidentally, flirting approaches also draw on a known System 1 cognitive bias called the *endowment effect*, which is closely related to the loss aversion bias we learned about in Chapter 5.[18] It states that people are more likely to retain an object that they own rather than acquire a new identical one they do not own. Something that you hold in your hands, even briefly, can make you feel like you own it. In India, family jewelers understand this well.

On one of my not-so recent trips to Jaipur, the city where I grew up, my wife and I wandered unsuspectingly into exactly one such store, ostensibly just to browse the latest local trinkets. Next thing I know, my wife is seated comfortably on a chair, with one store executive dedicated to helping her try on all kinds of necklaces, each with the power to burn a sizzling hole in my wallet. Dozens of necklaces later, she had three potential candidates in the race. At this point, get this, the owner, who has vaguely known my family as long-term residents of the town, suggests, "Why worry? Take all three home and call me at the end of the week, and I will have them picked back up."

Over the next several days, my wife flirted with all three, amassing an encyclopedia of compliments from friends, who as you might guess were financially uninvolved in the transaction and hence, objectively unmindful of its consequences on my finances. Amid reasoned protests from me, at the end of the week, she kept two and returned one.

Warby Parker may have hashtagged flirting now, but the old man in the jewelry store has been playing this game for years. As this example illustrates, System 1 and System 2 don't have to work at the exclusion of each other; rather, they can complement each other seamlessly. With System 2 Deliberators, the flirting training method, the crafty jeweler lowered the risk of my wife buying something that people would think didn't look good on her, and with the System 1 endowment effect, he made it her own even before she had paid a penny.

3. SYSTEM 2 DELIBERATORS: PROVIDE REASONS TO BELIEVE

Sometimes consumers run into a brick wall when they believe that a brand is too good to be true and promises more than it can deliver. In these cases, the marketer needs to provide pointed evidence to refute the beliefs with the "examine the evidence" method, or a path for the consumer to discover the truth for themselves with the survey method.

Examine the Evidence Method

In Dr. Burns's handbook for cognitive behavior therapy, he describes a method called *examine the evidence*, in which a patient seeking help with his condition is encouraged to assess the facts and to prove or disprove his beliefs. For example, to an overly anxious patient who believes that no one likes him, Dr. Burns would say "Why don't you invite some people to go out for coffee with you and see what happens?"

It is important that the facts gathered be those that "put a lie," as he says, to the beliefs that the patient holds dear. When that happens, Dr. Burns found that he could successfully change the person's behavior. In marketing too, if people believe that your product sucks (and it doesn't), you may have to hit them between the eyes with directed facts. When

System 1 is faced with severe contradictions to its own deeply held beliefs, it refers the matter over to System 2 for deliberation.

In recent years, the market for frozen foods has been under pressure as consumers seek out healthy, fresh foods. When we think about frozen foods, our minds are flooded with unpleasant thoughts like, "Gee! What eon is it from? Is it real or synthetic? What toxic chemicals is it laced in? Is it for human consumption?"

One UK manufacturer has taken on the challenge unapologetically by promoting the healthiness of frozen foods. Birds Eye, a producer of frozen vegetables, informs you that flash freezing has many advantages over fresh foods. Really! For instance, it locks in vitamins and minerals, whereas fresh foods lose them in storage; it uses no preservatives; it lets you eat the many healthy vegetables that are seasonal and only available frozen; and you waste less by using what you need and refreezing the rest. All of that makes sense. This battery of new facts can stir the System 2 neural net into a reevaluation of the instinctive bias against frozen foods.

This is what Dr. Burns means when he reminds us to examine the evidence.

One of the more recent brands to score with the evidence method is Chipotle. Until 2015, Chipotle was a high-flyer in the fast-casual dining market segment. In that year, Chipotle suffered a series of stumbles, starting with an outbreak of E. coli that sickened hundreds of customers across 11 states in the United States. E. coli infections are serious and can kill people. Customers abandoned their beloved Mexican bites in droves. Brian Niccol, the new CEO hired to breathe life into the dying brand, knew he had an uphill task in regaining the trust of his customers.

Brian and his team came up with a strategy of rejuvenating the Chipotle brand with a campaign around "Food with Integrity" at a time when no one believed the brand had any. Their campaign "Behind the Foil" lifted the veil off what goes on behind the scenes at a Chipotle restaurant. And what you saw there is real food and real people. In the fast-casual dining world of processed food and robot chefs, this stands in stark contrast.

One commercial features a woman chef at a Chipotle location talking about the difference there as compared to the other restaurants where she had previously worked, where guacamole is squeezed out of factory packaged bags and not made by hand from real avocados as she is seen doing on camera. In another commercial, a young male employee talks about how they have no can openers at Chipotle restaurants because nothing comes out of a can. The ads close with the tagline, "The Difference is Real. Chipotle for Real."

Chipotle's strategy of "we're fresh and real, and they're not" is working like dynamite. If you owned their shares, you would know. Since the calamitous decline in 2015, Chipotle share price has quadrupled by 2021.

The examine the evidence method works best when you can find product attributes that put a lie to customers' unfounded beliefs.

Survey Method

When using the survey method, Dr. Burns encourages patients to go check if their (misguided) beliefs are true by asking others. For example, if Rhonda suffers from deep anxiety about public speaking, she can go ask other people if they feel similarly so. In her survey, she may discover that she is not alone in feeling nervous and then deal with her anxiety constructively. After all, we have all had our "Oh! I thought I was the only one doing this wrong" moments. Dr. Burns does not simply tell patients to go conduct a survey; rather, he coaches them on how to do it to ensure a positive outcome.

The survey method is commonly used by marketers of consumer financial products. An added bonus to the approach is that the marketer can appear more objective and the customer can own the solution. A wonderful example of this approach comes from a campaign launched by Prudential Financial to encourage consumers to be more realistic in their retirement planning.

The commercials[19] feature Harvard psychologist Dan Gilbert using the survey method to dispel the rosy outlook we may have about our future. Gilbert's academic research shows that people forecast future happiness very poorly and unduly optimistically.

In one version of the commercials (see Figure 7.3), Gilbert surveys a group of people, asking them to note down the good and bad things that had happened to them on yellow- and blue-colored magnetic pads

Figure 7.3   Survey method approach.

respectively, and to place them on a large board labelled "Past." Next, he asks them to note down some of the good and bad things that could possibly happen to them on another set of yellow and blue magnetic pads and place them on a board called "Future." When looked at from a distance, the board for the past has a checkered mix of yellow and blue, indicating that life has actually had a pretty even share of ups and downs. On the other side, the board for the future looks mainly yellow, or mostly rosy! Gilbert then turns to the participants and asks this question, "What does this mean to you?"

The somber realization from one volunteer is that "We all want to think about positive stuff . . . but realistically there will be downsides too." That cues Gilbert to muse, "It's good to think optimistically, but let's plan for whatever the future brings." This is followed by the brand's tagline, "Prudential, Bring Your Challenges." And it could just as well be added, bring us your money to manage.

In other versions of the commercial, Gilbert poses questions like, "How long do you think your savings will last?" or (directed to a group of young people), "When do you think you should start saving for your retirement?" In each case, the questions were followed by clever surveys and visuals to show how woefully inadequate most peoples' plans were. These ads are an example of the using the survey method to trigger System 2 Deliberators into correcting for the "*hakuna matata*, be happy" bias of System 1.

A key piece of the puzzle is for the marketer to provide the questions to ask to ensure a desirable outcome. It is often a question that the consumer is not asking, but should be. In other cases, the consumer may be asking the question but not answering it in the way the brand would like it to be answered. In these cases, the marketer may pose the question and answer it themselves. That's not really a survey, you say. I know, but this pseudo-survey technique can seem real to the brain because of the Q&A format.

De Beers is a master at telling consumers how to think about what diamonds to buy and when, as shown in Figure 7.4. A key question for any couple is how much to spend on a diamond engagement ring. The marketers at De Beers wanted to take no chance that people (men) may lowball

Figure 7.4   A marketer's artful question.

the answer. So they went ahead and framed the survey question implicitly for the unsuspecting consumer in full-page print ads that shouted out, "How can you make two months' salary last forever?" Below that is a picture of an engagement ring with a massive diamond. How is that for brilliance? A question with the answer embedded into the question itself.

Other taglines for the campaign provided the same answer to the implicit question: "Two months' salary showed the future Mrs. Smith what the future is like." The beauty of the campaign lies in the mathematical fact that it allows people with more money to part with more of it and for those with less to also not be spared the pain. As a side note, the two months' salary campaign also leverages a System 1 lever, namely the anchoring bias, whereby the consumer now subconsciously uses that as the starting point for determining their budget.

4. SYSTEM 2 DELIBERATORS: CHANGE THE CONTEXT

Sometimes consumers don't see the value in your brand unless you help them think about it in the right context. This may mean giving them a new way to think about your brand with the reframing method. Or at other times you may need to use the reattribution method to clear up matters when consumers blame your brand for something that it isn't really responsible for.

Reframing Method

If you have ever convinced someone to come over to your point of view in a discussion and they finally relented with, "Now that you put it this way, I get it," then you know what we are talking about. The reframing method aims to change the way a customer thinks about your brand by putting it in a way he or she understands it.

Patek Philippe, arguably one of the world's most expensive traditional watch brands, has been a master of this method. I want you to think about the following for a moment. Why would anyone want to buy a traditional mechanical watch in today's age? If you are like everyone else—the garden-variety non-Neanderthal—you own a smartphone, which will tell you the time more accurately than any hand-crafted Swiss watch at no additional cost. It will throw in a few extra tricks for good measure, like unlimited alarm settings, global clock, stopwatch, timer, and a sleep monitor. So why would anyone shell out a whopping $40,000 to $100,000 for a conventional watch from Patek Philippe?

The challenge from the likes of a smartphone is not new for this stalwart. Even when the company first introduced its watches, there were plenty of other ways to buy timekeepers for a cost that did not entail selling a large chunk of front lawn.

Patek Philippe addressed this challenge with a metaphysical brand strategy. It goes something like this: Well, it is not a watch really; it is a piece of art. You are not spending any money really; you are making an investment. It is not yours really; it is a legacy for your next generation.

This ontological reframing of a Patek Philippe watch—as "what you think it is, is what it isn't"—has been the secret sauce that allowed this Stern family enterprise to rise from the ashes of the 1929 Great Depression and prosper to this day.

So where did this all start?

In the 1990s, it was common for high-end watch companies to feature celebrities donning their products, in the hope that consumers would buy their products for the vicarious thrills of being seen like those celebrities. Think of Cindy Crawford on all of those "Omega! My Choice!" advertisements.

At the time, Tim Delaney, the principal at Leagas Delaney, a London-based agency, was conducting focus groups with well-heeled purveyors of fine watches. And what he heard made him stop and rethink the conventional wisdom of routinely selecting celebrities for jewelry commercials.

The consumers were saying, "Hey, wait a minute, I am a pretty accomplished person. Why do I have to look like someone else to feel special? Where is my story?" On the flight back to London from San Francisco, Delaney wrote four words, "Begin your own tradition"—a line that would become an epic campaign lasting many decades.[20]

The first print ads that were launched featured photographs of people wearing no watches. The words below the photos put the brand's strategy in plain sight, "Begin your own tradition. Each Patek Philippe watch is crafted by hand. Each one is subtly different from the next one. This is what makes it uniquely personal for each owner."

It was not any watch; it was the owner's personal story. "The ladies' Golden Ellipse ref. 4831 has 180 carats set in 18 carat solid gold" reminded you that it was not a watch, it was jewelry. "Any woman who owns one will treasure it. And this will be its true value to the one that wears it next" made it clear that it was not a watch, it was a legacy.

Slovenian philosopher Slavoj Žižek, who said "Beyond the fiction of reality, there is the reality of the fiction,"[21] would have happily given a nod to this campaign. In 1997, the tagline was tweaked a bit and became the iconic, "You never truly own a Patek Philippe, you merely look after it for the next generation," as shown in Figure 7.5.

Many observers feel that the power of the campaign lay in its emotional appeal, and they are wrong. There are plenty of ads depicting women thrilled to tears when gifted a piece of jewelry. This cam-

Figure 7.5   One line that became a decades-long campaign.

paign was about reframing the issue for consumers: spending on a Patek Phillipe was not an expense; rather it was like buying and holding a valuable asset.

The reframing method can also be a great way for brands to not just differentiate themselves but also to grow by giving consumers new occasions for consumption. The grandmaster of System 2 strategies of this variety is De Beers, the diamond company that has held that crown for nearly a hundred years.[22] De Beers was conceived by British businessmen as a cartel based out of South Africa and continues to this day to be a dominant player. So how do you grow a business if you already own practically the whole pie? Simple, you tell everyone to eat more pies!

Diamonds are not particularly rare in nature, which is why De Beers became a cartel in the first place. And for a long time, diamonds were not considered particularly desirable in the United States and in many other parts of the world.

Specifically, the concept of a diamond ring as an indispensable proof of an engagement was largely nonexistent. Working with N. W. Ayer, a leading advertising agency at the time in 1938, De Beers created the "A Diamond Is Forever" campaign to change this mindset and create a mental association of diamonds with lasting matrimony. This part of the strategy was a System 1 play that subconsciously associated the diamond's well-known physical property of being one of the hardest[23] and most indestructible substances in nature to the desired property of making wedding vows long-lasting (and hard?). Over time, the solitaire ring became the unshakable standard for commemorating engagements, with the measure of your love reflected conveniently in the size of the diamond.

But again, if you are a monopoly and you have already captured most of the addressable market for outsized rocks, what do you do next? Well, you come up with something else to celebrate, like "Your Past, Present and the Future" with, of course, a three-diamond ring. And next, perhaps a life beyond this life? That would be the "Eternity" ring, with a string of diamonds wrapped around your finger. That should cover everything, right? Yes, it certainly should. Everything, except for the right hand! Enter the "Women of the World, Raise Your Right Hand" campaign, serendipitously in time for the women's rights movement. Now, women can liberate their beings from the clutches (and wallets) of men by (wait for it) buying a ring for themselves. That is the picture-perfect example of the System 2 reframing method. And nobody does it better.

Reattribution Method

Psychotherapists use reattribution techniques to help patients with depression who unduly believe that they alone are the cause of all their problems. They do so by helping the patients see other reasons why things may be awry. Sometimes, brands face a similar dilemma when they are boxed into a corner due to factors beyond their control or due to the unwise choices by their marketers. The latter's job then becomes to set things right so that the brand can continue to prosper.

In pharma marketing, there is a cardinal rule of not positioning your brand as being so good that it works for even the hardest-to-treat patients. Any pharma marketer will tell you that that risks making your brand the preferred choice of "train wrecks"—an insensitive but descriptive term heard in the back halls of pharma companies to make the point unambiguously. It brackets your brand as the reserve choice for patients in the worst possible condition.

This is the saddest thing you could do to a great drug because the most severe patients constitute a small segment of the market and treating them can be hard, dooming your drug to lots of public failures. Physicians like to always have multiple prescription options in hand. If you position your drug as the nuclear option, you will be siloed until World War III breaks.

Krystexxa, a drug for patients of gout, found itself in exactly such a predicament. It was developed by a small, financially shaky company called Savient. The US FDA rewards companies that develop drugs for neglected (orphan) diseases that impact only small populations of patients with faster approval times. Thus Savient went ahead and positioned itself as the drug of choice for refractory patients with chronic tophaceous gout, meaning those with the worst of the worst disease.

This tactic succeeded in getting the drug approved in a shorter period of time, but for the doctors it became the brand of last resort, to be prescribed only to patients who had exhausted all other options. In 2013, Savient was astutely purchased by GTCR, a private equity firm, out of bankruptcy for $120 million and nursed back into health.

In 2015, Horizon Therapeutics saw a golden opportunity to buy the company from GTCR and reposition the brand. The CEO of Horizon, Tim Walbert, is a seasoned marketer and immediately recognized that there was a great opportunity to redefine Krystexxa as a drug for not just chronic refractory patients, but for those whose gout was uncontrolled by other drugs. What's the difference?

There are only about 40,000 or so chronic refractory gout patients. There are nearly three million gout patients treated with other drugs! Of those, at least 30 percent or one million are not receiving sufficient control of their condition with the treatments they use. Tim bought the drug from GTCR for $510 million, at what most thought was an outrageous premium. Working diligently with his team of crack marketers and us, over the following three years he fundamentally shifted the trajectory of the drug and tripled sales, much of this by strategically reattributing the drug as the recourse for not just patients with tophaceous gout—but also for the million or so whose condition was inadequately controlled by other drugs.

One word of caution for marketers eying System 2 Deliberators for growing their brands. When you awaken System 2, you need to be aware that the consumer is going to look at your brand value propositions critically. So while you may want the consumer to read your lips and look at only the positives of the brand, the consumer may also consider the negatives. They will wonder, "What's the catch? What's in the fine print?" Maintaining a keen awareness of that fact can help marketers avoid nasty surprises. Be careful what you wish for.

Cognitive brands can create preference among consumers by answering their question, "Does this brand make reasoned sense?"

System 2 Deliberators are the second type of process by which the brain makes sense of what the brands say. In contrast to System 1 Easers, which make sense of choice by going with the flow, comparing options against prior wisdom, Deliberators do so by changing it and giving consumers a new religion or new brand loyalties. This must be done when the biases and beliefs that sit in the consumer's brain are unhelpful to the brand, either because they are contrary to what the brand stands for or because the brand is new and unfamiliar. Thus we have to convince the consumer to use their System 2 Deliberators to recode their brains and lay down new wiring. They are used if Easers alone won't do the job of making good sense of the brand.

System 2 Deliberators are familiar territory for marketers used to selling brands based on their value propositions. However, instead of just listing the *what* of the brand, namely its benefits, System 2 Deliberators also provide the *how* of the brand. They do so in four different ways by:

- Amplifying the value of the brand

- Lowering the risk of choosing the brand

- Providing reasons to make consumers believe in the brand

- Framing the brand choice favorably

Of course, even when a brand choice makes sense, consumers may not be motivated enough to buy its products or services. In the next chapter, we will figure out how to get the consumer off the fence of indecision or inaction, and make them go buy what's offered by our brands instead of waiting. Easers and Deliberators can make the consumers like our brand and perceive it as the sensible choice. But we need brand resolve, the third component of cognitive brands, to make them really want and buy what it offers.

CHAPTER 8

BRAND RESOLVE

A Mantra for Happiness

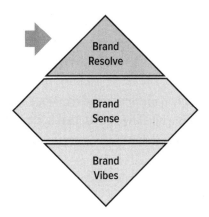

f System 1 and System 2 were all there was to brand choice, we could call it a day with the previous chapter. But there is a problem. It's called indecision.

Without indecision, you might have married your great-after-all high school sweetheart sooner, opened your own bacon gourmand store in the West Loop rather than stick it out as grade 13 shift supervisor at the piñata factory, and not eaten both the mushroom ravioli and the cheeseburger for lunch.

The consumer sitting on the fence of indecision is often a challenge for brands that entail bigger purchases like a car, home mortgage, or furniture. But indecision can also take the form of indifference where smaller purchases are concerned. With such detachment, you buy your morning black coffee from whatever tienda you happen to be near rather than making that small detour to the Starbuck's on Hubbard for a Grande Pike.

Even when consumers trust a brand and what it says makes sense to them, they may hesitate to buy it or truly make it their own, especially after the this-week-only sales discount is gone and the sweet sales lady who sold it to them is a wispy memory. That is where brand resolve comes into play. Marketers need to tap into the brain's conative energy to break these impasses.

In the cognitive world, the motivation to buy or attach yourself to something is a function of two things, namely, how happy we expect to be with the brand choice and our inner zeal to pursue such happiness. All of this happy talk sounds a bit New Age at first, but it isn't. Before we delve deeper into it, let me offer a summary of the thesis:

- All consumers pursue happiness as a conscious or subconscious goal.

- It is the pursuit of happiness that gets people off the fence of indecision or indifference.

- Brands that find a way to be of help to the consumer in this pursuit are preferred and loved longer by consumers.

- Brands can align with consumers' goals for happiness by addressing any of the three known universal needs or intrinsic motivations.

- The conative energy with which consumers pursue these universal needs is different from person to person and hence across customer segments.

These principles are inspired by the research of many psychologists but reflect the adaptations I have made to make their work useful in branding.[1] With that caveat out of the way, let's get started.

THE PURSUIT OF HAPPINESS

It is in the DNA of all humans to pursue happiness. This idea was so obvious to the founding fathers of the United States that they enshrined "life, liberty and the pursuit of happiness" as the three "unalienable rights" of all humanity in the Declaration of Independence.

If you are academically unimpressed with the founding fathers' pitch, then for you there are three ideas in psychology that will get you to the same place. The first is that personal goals are ubiquitous, and humans are wired for "goal pursuit."[2] The second is that all aspects of goal pursuit—making goals, pursuing them, and making progress on them—make us happy.[3] The third is that we pursue goals consciously and subconsciously, and mostly the latter.[4] There is a truckload of research on the topic, but if you are a marketer you will want to take my word for it: your consumers, whether they realize it or not, are hardwired for one goal, to constantly pursue happiness and well-being. Consequently, and ultimately, all brands are about making the consumer happier.

In brain sciences, happiness is not an abstraction; it's science. There are specific structures in the brain, referred to as reward systems, which serve as hedonic hotspots and neuronal pleasure networks that help us calibrate which stimuli we want more or less of.[5] There are four actual chemicals in the brain that create this sensation of happiness—namely, dopamine, oxytocin, serotonin, and endorphins (DOSE).[6, 7] They are triggered by everything, from the experience of sex and drugs to eating and exercising. We feel good when these chemicals are released and tend to do more of the things that trigger them.[8] When we experience brands, we feel this neurochemical reaction induced happiness in one shape or form.

Here's the rub. You don't have to experience the brand to feel such happiness. You can sort of feel it even when you *imagine* experiencing the brand. Your brain can use its circuitry to forecast roughly how happy you would feel if you were to have a certain brand experience without having it yet. For example, it can imagine how happy you would feel licking melting dollops of Ben & Jerry's Cherry Garcia ice cream off a hand-rolled waffle cone without requiring you to stick your face into a tub full of it.

The brain can simulate make-believe happiness by recalling what it may have experienced in the past, called consummatory pleasures (if you've had Cherry Garcia before), or in other cases by dreaming about experiencing them in the future, called anticipatory pleasures (if you've never had Cherry Garcia ever).[9] *A brand promise of happiness is just that—an invitation to let you relive memories of past pleasures or fantasize about possible future ones as mental sensations.*

So it comes down to this, when we are promised a certain experience by a brand, the release of DOSE chemicals to one degree or another allows us to simulate how nice it might be to go for it. If it is enticing enough, we do.

Can it be that simple? Brands are there to make people happier. Check! But wait. There's more!

BRANDS AS THE KEYS
TO UNIVERSAL HAPPINESS

What kind of happiness are we talking about? Two psychologists from the University of Rochester, Edward Deci and Richard Ryan, gave a pretty good answer to that question with their self-determination theory (SDT).[10, 11] They found that, beyond the obvious physiological needs that we all have, there are psychological needs (or wants) that we all pursue as part of our goals. They called the latter intrinsic motivations and these account for activities we pursue for their own sake even when there are no physical rewards for doing so.

The wonderful news about brands that tap into intrinsic motivations is that we tend to want to stick with them of our own volition. There are three universal needs or intrinsic motivations:

- **Need for autonomy.** We want to be free to make our own choices and shape our destiny. Consumers must feel like they chose their brand and were not manipulated into choosing it. In US companies, it is common to have annual charity drives with the United Way, a nonprofit that raises funds through company-sanctioned campaigns, where the employer solicits contributions from their employees. Well, the employees often hate it! They feel pressured to sign up because their bosses have "suggested" a level of giving that is appropriately fattened to align with their position in the company and conveniently deducted from their pay. Needless to say, most of those generous donors stop writing checks to the United Way as soon as they leave those companies. Autonomy, matters.

- **Need for competence.** We want to be better at doing stuff and feel good about ourselves for it. This can make us aspire to master the art of mixing the perfect Ramos Gin Fizz or train for excellence on the intricate path of Nuido, the Japanese way of embroidery. We may buy things that help us be better than our peers and revered in our work or social circles. We may experiment with the unknown to enhance our talents and learn more.

- **Need for relatedness.** We want to be socially networked with other people and a part of something bigger than ourselves. We do like to make the world a better place for others because that helps us connect with them more. That is why we may buy brands committed to social good and in doing so belong to the vaunted circle of enlightened consumers. For instance, if you live in Japan, you may ship Grandpa's old choppers to the Japan Denture Recycling Association so they can retrieve the $17 worth of silver and palladium and donate the proceeds to UNICEF[12] ($80,000 donated in total in 2007). It takes a bit work, but people do it to be part of a bigger whole socially.

The common element here is that research has shown that these needs and wants are super motivational and resilient; we will act on and pursue them over a lifetime. In self-determination theory, these three needs are not just nice to have but innate, essential, and universal and lead to a psychological sense of well-being.[13]

We started with the question, what is it that is going to prompt consumers to get off the fence of indecision and go buy our brands purposefully? The answer to that is that *marketers must make their brand* the *key to unlocking happiness for the consumer by helping them in their quest to fulfill one or more of these intrinsic needs.*

If you are selling a cure for headaches (and you might well have one by now), what could you do beyond saying my pill "kills pain fast" and christening the brand *Pronto!*? Well, you could link it to the need for autonomy by talking about "*Pronto!*" being the elixir that helps a stricken consumer take back control of her day. You could link it to the need for competence by talking about *Pronto!* as the magic eraser for her headache so she can go back to displaying her mastery of Nuido to her Japanese embroidery class. You could link it to the need for relatedness by talking about *Pronto!* being Artemis, the Greek goddess, that slays Antaura, the migraine demon, transforming her monster mama persona to normal, lovable mom, allowing her to rejoin the human race. This making of your brand the key to or necessary vehicle for happiness is the path to engaging consumers, so they reach for "*Pronto!*" over a lifetime of headaches and not the cheap generic ibuprofen proffered by your insurance company.

"*Pronto!*" is not an actual brand of headache medicine. Not yet anyway. But there are real-world brands that make us happy. Let's take a look at how some marketers have made their brands the key to the three universal needs we discussed.

BRAND RESOLVE THROUGH AUTONOMY

National Car Rental's recent "Go Like a Pro"[14] campaign was a clever example of a brand that targeted frequent business travelers, tapping into their need for control. As a consultant, I was a road warrior for a long time. Every Monday morning, I was flying off to some city to work with my clients, and everywhere I went, I rented a car for the week. All I

Figure 8.1   National Car Rental's "Go Like a Pro" campaign ad.

wanted was for the universe to march to my tune so I could get to work fast and easy, and do my job.

In one of National's many hilarious executions of the campaign (see Figure 8.1), we see the somewhat obnoxious and overly confident protagonist, Patrick Warburton, turn to the screen and inform the world, "I've been called a control freak, but I like to think of myself as more of a control enthusiast."

He cuts straight to the front of the line at the coffee shop, snares the cup of coffee being served, and pauses a moment to enjoy a sip of the steaming beverage, as the woman whose order it was supposed to be glares at him aghast. "Hmmm, a perfect 177 degrees!" he murmurs unapologetically.

He turns his attention back to us and explains why he rents from National: "Because I can skip the counter and go straight to my car, without talking to any human, unless I want to, . . . and I don't! At National, I can pick any car from the aisle . . . Control! . . . Hmmm. What's the word? So sexy!" At this point the voiceover comes on with "National! Go Like a Pro!"

The campaign works like a charm on frequent business travelers. Rob Connors, the vice president of brand marketing at National Car Rental, told *Marketing Daily*:

The ads use humor to address the lack of control frequently felt by these travelers at the airport, so they relate to Warburton and overwhelmingly enjoy his portrayal of the ultimate "control enthusiast." As a result, Warburton has become a recognized brand cue for National and helped drive home the message that National offers unparalleled autonomy over the rental experience.

The brand campaign increased communications awareness by 4 percentage points and grew National's airport market share by 5 percent.[15]

With pharma brands, the promise of self-control or independence is among the more powerful ways to position drugs with patients. For many, the disease takes a life of its own, preventing patients from doing things that that they should be able to do, from unhooking their own bras to spending an hour in peace, without needing to go to the bathroom. Brand resolve for many drugs follows from the promise of delivering on this universal need for autonomy.

BRAND RESOLVE THROUGH COMPETENCE

In 2006, my company was working with a hot biotech startup, NeoPharm, on launching an innovative drug code-named CB (after its biologic molecule cintredekin besudotox) for treating advanced brain cancer. CB was among the early wave of biologic smart bombs that worked by affixing itself to a cancer cell and releasing a toxin into it.

However, CB was a large-molecule drug that was hard to administer, as the brain is sheathed in what is called the blood-brain barrier, which prevents drugs released into the bloodstream from penetrating the brain. Hence, a new type of pump with the ability to deliver the macromolecular drug in a controlled flow over 36 hours was paired with the drug. Yes, the patient would be sitting in a hospital bed with a small part of his brain exposed as the drug slowly infused into it over a day and a half!

Selling a complicated new drug like that to doctors is hard enough. Now, we also had to convince the super busy neurosurgeons to learn to use this newfangled pump as well. We thought it was all building up to be a royal mess. But guess what? It wasn't.

Much to our surprise we discovered quite the opposite; the doctors were just as excited about getting their hands on the CED (convection enhanced delivery) pump as they were about having access to the groundbreaking drug. The neurosurgeons we interviewed, from those at Duke University to the ones at the University Medical Center Hamburg-Eppendorf, confessed, "Oh, this is the first drug that will allow us to use CED in practice. That experience will be invaluable for many other drugs in the pipeline that hold greater promise."

Without realizing it, we had stumbled upon the conative energy of the brain surgeons, namely, their obsession with advancing the mastery of their own art. While CB itself, ultimately and sadly for the patients, failed to work in its Phase III clinical trials and never came to market, we learned an important lesson: brands could influence physician resolve to buy by showing them how they could enhance their competence.

BRAND RESOLVE THROUGH RELATEDNESS

One of the best examples of the principle of achieving brand resolve by providing opportunities for consumers to enhance their relationships with others was Mastercard's iconic "Priceless" campaign. In multiple vignettes on television, Mastercard showed how you could achieve your own personal nirvana by using their card to spend your money.

The first television spot, which was designed by McCann Erickson, aired in 1997. It showed a father taking his son to his first ball game.[16, 17] In what has now become a familiar refrain, the narrator of the scene itemizes the day's expenses as two tickets for $46; hot dogs, popcorn, and sodas for $27; and an autographed baseball for $50. But the "real conversation, with your 11-year-old son? Priceless!" The ad closes cleverly with the iconic line "There are some things money can't buy. For everything else, there's Mastercard."

In this way, the marketers at Mastercard shrewdly positioned their card as the key that allowed their cardholders to unlock a quotient of happiness well above any pain of the spend, and increase their relatedness or connections with the beneficiaries of their largesse. And that results in the resolve to use the Mastercard brand over and over.

This might be a good place to make a note about the idea of the three universal dimensions of happiness. You could ask "Hey, if I won the $200 million prize on Mega-Millions lottery, wouldn't I be on seventh heaven? How does that fit with the three dimensions of happiness?" Only a moment of reflection is needed to realize that the happiness from money flows from what you imagine you will do with it. Mastercard's campaign showed exactly that: it was not about the card; it was about what you would do with it to increase your connectedness with those around you.

I cannot emphasize enough that the brand must implicitly be the key for unlocking more happiness. Practicing marketers often forget this. They make the mistake of showing people dancing in parties or frolicking through hills in their ads without clarifying how their brand was the key to unlocking that happiness. Those ads create emotional stories for their own sake, without ever selling anything.

As a brand marketer, you have a product to sell. Show how your brand is the instrument for getting consumers from point A to point B on the happiness scale.

LUCKILY, HAPPINESS DECAYS

In her book *Delirium*, Lauren Oliver writes, "You can't be happy unless you're unhappy sometimes. You know that, right?"

Think of humans as hardwired to constantly pursue happiness and well-being, but without ever managing to stay perfectly happy. This unfortunate truth about the inaccessibility of lasting happiness is so much a part of the human DNA that it has plagued generations of philosophers for as long as philosophy has existed.[18] What most philosophers don't know, but some marketers do, is that this is a very good thing.

Let's do a little exercise here. On a scale from 1 to 10, think of the number that represents your overall happiness with life at this exact moment. A score of 10 would mean perfect happiness and fulfillment. A score of 1 would mean you are clinically depressed and need to see somebody. Ready? Close your eyes, think, and trace out the number with your finger in the palm of your hand.

OK, now here's my guess. Odds are that you wrote the number seven in your palm. Now ask yourself, "How come he guessed my number or was pretty darn close?" After all, the readers for this book come from all walks and stages of life, make less money or more, and have different highs and lows with friends and families at this moment in life.

The reason for this convergence is that most healthy human beings are wired for a level of happiness 20 to 30 percent below the perfect score of 10. Even making a lot more money does not change the score that much.[19] The gap between perfect and actual happiness creates a healthy desire among individuals to not be satisfied with what they have and to strive for more. This quest for greater happiness is what gives rise to wants. And where would brands be without wants?

Happiness decays because people anticipate happiness narrowly but experience it broadly. This means that after the initial thrill of getting what you want from a brand, you go back to where you started. Consider this: Are you going to be happy eating a cup of delicious Ben & Jerry's chocolate chip cookie dough ice cream? Yeah! Make that a 9! That is anticipated happiness. As the ice cream melts and streams down your throat, you will briefly be a 10 on happiness.

Then the door swings open and in walks your wife. Does she think you made a mess of the kitchen and forgot to pick up dinner? Yeah! Bring that back to a 7! That is the diffusion of experienced happiness. But that is OK if you are the brand marketer at Ben & Jerry's, because people will want to eat your ice cream again and again to try to stay happy.[20]

THE CONATIVE ENERGY TO PURSUE HAPPINESS IS DIFFERENT ACROSS CONSUMERS

Think of happiness as resting on three coiled springs within each of us. Each represents one of the three universal needs. When a brand promises you something that could make you incredibly happy, the spring is stretched wide apart. Now, how tightly wound that spring is depends on your genes; everybody's spring has a different amount of tension. If yours is tightly wound and profound happiness is in sight, you are going to snap and go for it. You have a high tendency to pursue that particular need to achieve happiness.

Your friend, with a lower tension spring, may be a lot more laid back and disinclined to pursue whatever it is that sent you marching off. That intuitively makes sense. For some people, autonomy is way more important than being master at their crafts. For others, having social bonds and relationships is more important than just pursuing their own will. Different people pursue different goals in the same situation.

When I was writing this in 2020, the streets of Chicago were overrun by protesters. A few weeks earlier, a Black man, George Floyd, was choked to death by a white police officer, who was suppressing him during an arrest. Marches and rallies were taking place in cities across the country. Most of us felt the deep angst of the people in the Black community who have been subjected to repeated injustices by the members of the police force. People understood why, for so many, pouring out into the streets and protesting was the only way to pressure the government into doing something. It made total sense.

Yet not everybody rushed out to join the protestors. Some of us lit candles in solidarity, others wrote angry letters to newspapers, and still others did nothing more than vent their distress with neighbors. While everyone wants the world to be a happier place, our conative energies are different, and we act in different ways and sometimes not at all. When that happens with brands, we call it brand resolve, and it is different from person to person.

Because people are different, a brand may never make everyone happy. That is why we have customer segmentation as an important tool in marketing. We only have to position our brands for resolve with the customers we want to target.

What marketers should pay attention to more is to include the right tendencies or universal needs as dimensions in their segmentation. At Cerenti, we dubbed this method of targeting consumers as a tendencies-based consumer segmentation. In the following chapter, I illustrate this in an in-depth case study.

KEY TAKEAWAYS

This chapter introduced the final piece of the puzzle in designing great brands, namely, brand resolve. If you get this right, your brand will fly. Mess it up, and you will scratch your head till it hurts trying to figure out why it is stuck in the mud. Remember the lessons:

- With good vibes, consumers trust your brand. With good sense, consumers believe what your brand says. With good resolve, consumer want your brand and buy it.

- This happens because consumers want brands they believe will make them happier.

- Brands build resolve when they become a key to helping consumers move up on the happiness scale by addressing one of the three known universal psychological needs.

- Each consumer's tendency to pursue happiness is different and based on his or her own DNA, and thus a brand must determine who it wants to target.

If it feels like you have taken a drink from a fire hose, don't sweat it. It is not that the four parts of cognitive brands that we have discussed so far in this book are complicated, it is just that they are new and different. So take your time to let it sink in.

In the next chapter, we'll do a case study. We will apply all that we have learned so far to a brand close to my heart, PediaSure, a children's nutritional supplement.

CHAPTER 9

FOR THE LOVE OF KIDS

t was the waning end of a bleak Friday afternoon in a windowless conference hall in an entirely forgettable hotel in Florida. There I was, giving a routine speech on branding to a sea of nodding heads. There were as many faces staring at my slides as there were glancing at their flight departure times on their iPhones.

All except for one man, who appeared a little restless. Barely had I ended my spiel when he jumped up and cornered me as I stepped off the podium. "That was great! I loved it! I'm gonna hire you!" he said, by way of introduction, pressing his business card in my hands. That's how I met Tripp Chenoweth, the head of Abbott's sprawling international nutrition business. And minutes later, he did hire me, right on the spot.

What I couldn't tell at the time was whether he really needed help with branding his products or getting some monkey off his back. It turned out to be both. Tripp had a flourishing nutrition business, selling infant

The events described in the following passages have been fictionalized and the names of individuals disguised to remove any nonpublic information and preserve the privacy of the mentioned individuals. The narrative is thus designed to be instructive rather than accurately biographical or historical.

formula and children's nutrition supplements. It was a well-oiled machine chugging along nicely, making plenty of money every year for Abbott and growing modestly. Despite that, two of his deputies had been haranguing him to make a push to grow the business faster. It involved making a seismic change in his business model, and Tripp was not the kind of guy to light a match in a forest without knowing what it was he was going to set on fire. He liked ideas, but he loved money more.

Later that week, I found myself seated at one end of a long conference table in Abbott's headquarters on the north edge of the Chicago suburbs, across from Mel Fisker and Walt Perman, two dynamos at the helm of Tripp's marketing department. Mel Fisker was a seasoned street-smart manager. He had been in the nutrition business for many years, knew more about it than just about anyone else in the industry, and had an instinctive sense for what worked. Walt Perman was his energetic young deputy, brimming with new ideas for taking over the world.

What they had on their hands was PediaSure, a decades-old brand introduced in the late 1980s as a nutritional substitute for sick, hospitalized children who were too weak to take table foods on their own. PediaSure was a milkshake-like drink, which when taken three times a day, could meet *all* of the nutritional needs of a child. This was not in a manner of speaking but literally true: PediaSure was medically formulated to provide balanced and complete nutrition so that a sick child could survive for days on it with nothing else.

I'm going to tell the story of PediaSure in detail, and not just because it's a story that's close to my heart. It will show you exactly how the concepts we discussed in the previous chapters can be used as a new framework to design cognitive brands, really nice ones. With PediaSure, we'll see how good vibes, sense, and resolve can work perfectly together to create stupendous brands.

It turned out that "kids too weak to eat" constituted a tiny hospital market segment, and PediaSure was locked up in pharmacies that saw it as medicinal product. As a result, it was trudging along in most countries, with low single-digit growth from one year to the next. Mel and Walt had a much bigger dream. They asked, "Why can't all kids drink PediaSure instead of only those in hospitals?"

Taken aback a little, I looked questioningly at Walt. "Really?" I asked, with more than a hint of skepticism.

"I drink it myself all the time," Walt responded, pulling out a can stashed in the depths of his desk drawer and helpfully proceeding to consume the contents.

"That's a sample of one, Walt," I pointed out.

"I give it to all of my kids, too," he said, pointing to a picture of three beautiful siblings in a frame teetering at the edge of a crowded corner of his desk. Great! Now, we were up to a sample of four; I had to give in.

Understand my initial skepticism. PediaSure faced an uphill battle crawling out of grungy hospitals and into peoples' homes. After all, when was the last time you saw a sick person in a hospital and said to yourself, "I want to have what she's having?"

Also, its price point of about $3 per serving was seriously high compared to the glass of milk—which is pretty much what PediaSure looked like. In developing countries, a month's worth of supply could resemble the loan payment for a secondhand motor bike.

Perhaps most important, most mothers believed that the best way for children to get nutrition was from normal table foods, not a medication. Think about it. If I told you that you don't need to eat regular meals anymore, and should instead just take this tablet that doctors at the Cook County Hospital give to their sickest patients, would you go for it? How in the world would we ever change anybody's mind?

"That is exactly my question," piped in Tripp, who had slipped into the room, adding gravely, "Welcome to the team!" Then he shook my hands and left the room as abruptly as he had snuck in.

Not everything was quite so grim, though. Mel noticed that sales of PediaSure in Indonesia were surging. Its price there was astronomical compared to local income levels, and yet the product was flying off the shelves. The country head, Vic Monk, was an entrepreneurial hotshot who preferred to say little and only when prompted. Instead, he let his numbers do the talking—and his were off the charts. PediaSure was growing at a double-digit clip year after year even as other country managers struggled.

Vic had done something very different in Indonesia. We heard that he had decided to put PediaSure on TV, where it was promoted by a hugely popular child prodigy singer called Sherina. But Walt was concerned that a sponsorship-type strategy would be hard to replicate in the 30 plus other small and large countries where they sold PediaSure.

"Sherina is not known outside of Bahasa land. What happens in Mexico?" he asked. "What happens in Vietnam? Even in Indonesia, Sherina won't stay a child forever. What then?"

Mel and Walt wanted one playbook for PediaSure that could make the brand sizzle not just on the islands of Indonesia but everywhere in the world.

BORROWING FROM THE WHITE COATS

In 2004, cognitive branding was in its early days and we hadn't quite worked out everything. We needed a new framework for getting inside peoples' heads and find a door in for PediaSure. We wanted something that was proven to work. Tripp was into known quantities and firm answers, and not so much into classroom-type experiments with his business.

Just then, someone on the team had an epiphany. Since it was consumer psychology we were interested in, why not take a peek at what the mind doctors were using, instead of scraping the empty bottom of the marketer's toolbox. It turned out that psychotherapists had been using a recent diagnostic tool called *cognitive schemas* to map thought patterns of their patients. They had done it with millions of patients successfully and the evidence on how well it worked had piled up high.

Psychotherapists use cognitive schemas to decipher what they call "automatic thought distortions" of their patients. These are sort of the first thoughts that come to your mind in reaction to an event. For people with psychological issues, these thoughts are generally negative and unhelpful. They make them feel worse and act in a manner that is unconstructive, leading to a downward spiral of mood, temperament, and dysfunctionality. The therapist's goal is to break that cycle and train the patient to think positively instead. As we discussed in Chapter 7 on System 2 Deliberators, over time psychotherapists have developed a library of such methods for repro-gramming the thought patterns of such patients and turning them around.

We figured that we could think of consumers' automatic thought distortions as beliefs and behaviors that would prevent them from using PediaSure. Like a psychotherapist, our job was to untwist such thinking, banish these thoughts, and to plant new ones with a happier disposition toward PediaSure in their place. But first, we had to map out the thought distortions.

BRAND VIBES: CONNECTING WITH THE ANGST OF THE JAKARTA MOMS

To unravel the mystery of why PediaSure was selling like hotcakes in Indonesia, I jumped on a plane to Jakarta with my team of Cerenti con-sultants to search for answers.

From mornings thick with the haze of humidity to nights with unre-lenting, torrential rain, we herded dozens of Jakarta moms into dark rooms for focus group research. They all had one thing in common; they were all dishing out dollops of PediaSure instead of butternut squash to their kids. We wanted to know why they'd see child pop star Sherina on TV and think: "I want what she's having for my kids."

In Figure 9.1, I show the cognitive schema we mapped out after lis-tening to the Jakarta mothers. We found that in home after home, meal-times were traumatic prime-time spectacles between moms and kids. Mum after mum told us the same story: their kids were not eating well. They didn't eat what they were supposed to, when they were supposed to, or how much they were supposed to.

The mealtime stalemate would lead to several automatic mind distor-tions for the moms. Many thought that there was something wrong with their kids. Most had had them checked for at least the presence of stom-ach worms and found none. Many concluded that it was they themselves who were the problem: "I'm a bad mom. I'm such a klutz. I can't cook to save my life." These thoughts would then create a swirl of emotions in them, that would leave them depleted and in despair.

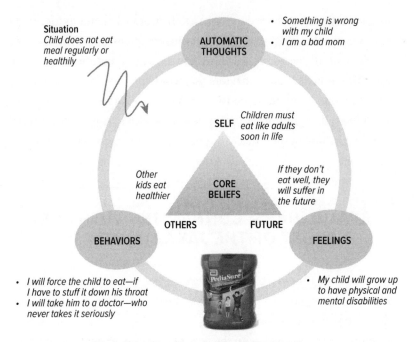

Figure 9.1   Cognitive schema of Jakarta mothers.
(*Courtesy:* Cerenti Marketing Group, LLC)

In cognitive schemas, you can map core beliefs relative to yourself, others, or your expectations of the future. Moms had issues on all three fronts:

1. Some moms compared their child to Greta, the one outlier kid in the neighborhood, who consumed a steady diet of toasted pecans and artichokes. These not-so-great moms would then feel distinctly unnerved.

2. Other moms believed that their kids should eat adult food, like leafy bok choy and Nantes carrots. Instead, the kids preferred gooey chocolate-chip cookies with sprinkles or jumbo franks with double ketchup and no bun.

3. Yet other moms thought that poor nutrition now would spell certain doom in the future. Their kids would grow up with grotesque physical or mental debilities. These thoughts would bubble unchecked like a boiling goulash of worries in their brains.

Mealtimes turned into a battle of wits and will, with determined mothers shoveling kale or some other nutritious food down their kids' throats and the latter faithfully puking it back out in steely resistance with all of the attendant drama of a gagging cat.

Frustrated, many of the moms bundled their kids into the car and headed off to their pediatricians to demand on-the-spot answers: "What's wrong with the brat? Tell me!" At some point, the harangued pediatricians realized that they were not going to be able to fob off the moms by informing them that their kids were normal, just like millions of other kids. They had tried it and it was deemed unacceptable.

Vic told us about one clever old pediatrician in Surabaya who had come up with an idea. He started telling moms that their kids had a "condition"—they were "picky eaters." To get the them off his back, he would then make a big production of drawing out his prescription pad slowly and with a flourish, write them a script for PediaSure.

You didn't really need a script; PediaSure was not a drug. But he did it anyway for effect. The relief that the moms felt upon finally having an answer was palpable. Other harried pediatricians also caught on to the practice and soon everyone was "prescribing" PediaSure. The universe was at peace!

The wily doctors had found a way to connect with the angst that moms everywhere in Indonesia felt. No, there was nothing wrong with mom herself. She was a good mother. She did the right thing in bringing the little tyke to their attention. Yes, there was a little something wrong with the kid. A disease called "picky eater." Nothing too serious, really. It was easily remedied by a glass or two of PediaSure every day.

Armed with this discovery, we checked back in with the moms in our focus groups. After several conversations with them, it became apparent that it was not so much the popular Sherina who was driving the sales, although she was surely a factor. It was more that Sherina was a beautiful and talented girl. Every parent wanted to make sure that their kid was not undernourished and would not grow up unhealthy—the diametric opposite of a Sherina. They all nodded vigorously when we offered that maybe their kids were picky eaters. And sure enough, Vic's TV commercial also said something about "picky eater" kids, even though the star of the ads was Sherina.

We and the Abbott team subsequently conducted focus groups in culturally disparate Asian countries from Vietnam to Philippines and Malaysia to Taiwan. The cognitive schema mapped out in Indonesia played out to a tee. Mel and Walt were super excited. The fact that the Indonesian market was on fire not because of Sherina, but because of this universal angst, was terrific news. It meant that PediaSure could be a global brand and not just a nontransmittable Indonesian aberration.

The insight that most kids are picky eaters, or rather that their moms universally believed so, gave us the vibes that we needed to make moms receptive to PediaSure. Remember, in Chapter 5, I had said that one way to give a brand good vibes was by connecting with the consumer by telling them "I know how you feel."

The PediaSure brand campaigns in the future would typically begin with a sentence like "We know that kids can be picky eaters. That's because they are kids!" This critically allowed the marketers at Abbott to let moms know that they understood their anguish and that neither they, the moms, nor their kids were to blame for the latter not eating nutritious food regularly. Once they had established that connection, the moms were ready to hear the rest of the PediaSure brand story.

Notice that with this statement, we were not yet talking about what PediaSure was. We were just building an unspoken bond and common chemistry between the moms and the brand. The statement "for picky eaters" should also not be confused with what is a framing statement in a traditional brand positioning, which attempts to answer the question who the product is for. The latter might say something like, "For new moms between the ages of 25 and 35, PediaSure is . . ." Nope, brand vibes are about connections—not clarifications.

I should point out here that for the purposes of understanding thought patterns and mapping them in cognitive schemas, it is useful to think that a brand stimulus triggers automatic thoughts, which spark certain emotions—and then the emotions subsequently congeal into behaviors, linearly. However, as I have shown before, the brain does not work in sequence like that. Once particular thought patterns are encoded into the brain as wisdom, the right cognitive threads will directly trigger buying behaviors and attendant thoughts and emotions reflexively. Cognitive schemas are thus useful tools for understanding reality but are not reality itself.

BRAND SENSE WITH SYSTEM 1 EASERS: PEDIASURE AS OCCAM'S RAZOR

Back in Chicago, when we sat down with Tripp and Mel, the verdict was that we needed to go deeper. Getting doctors to prescribe PediaSure was great and it worked, but it was very slow. The mom had to go to the doctor, who had to write a prescription, which led the mom to the pharmacist, who had to dispense PediaSure. There were simply too many opportunities for things to go wrong.

We needed to be on TV with our message and have moms see us and rush to the supermarket to buy PediaSure. Mel was adamant that the brand needed to be on supermarket shelves, ripe for the picking, and not hidden behind counters in pharmacies. "Remember, the *s* at the end of the word *brands* is really a $ sign. Make it big or go home," offered Tripp poetically, if somewhat somberly, after yet once again appearing magically in the group.

We set aside a day to lock ourselves up in a room with Mel and Walt. Now, remember I said earlier that the brain makes sense of choices using the *Associator* subunit 95 percent[1] of the time? We rolled up our sleeves and went through the list of cognitive biases, which we had presented earlier with the intent of developing one brand concept against each. Walt wanted many different ideas to take to research. Forcing ourselves to work with one cognitive bias at a time, we generated eight distinct concepts (see Table 9.1).

The team bundled back into a plane and headed off to do more research in Taiwan, the Philippines, Malaysia, Indonesia, and Vietnam. It was time for the brand ideas to face moms.

We had thought that the concept of using the anchoring bias to tag PediaSure to "all the goodness of" real food had promise, but Walt

Table 9.1   PediaSure System 1 Options

	SYSTEM 1 EASERS	DEFINITION	POSSIBLE BRAND CONCEPT
FEELS FAMILIAR	Anchoring Bias	Tag brand to familiar anchors—showing comparability or superiority	PediaSure provides kids all the goodness of real food and more
	Loss Aversion Bias	Position brand as helping to avoid losses to what consumers have today	PediaSure ensures that kids don't lose their chance for proper physical and mental growth in formative years
FEELS TRUE	IKEA Effect	Position brand as something that consumer plays a role in making	Not a viable concept
	Transparency Effect	Position brand as trusted because you know what goes in it	PediaSure has every one of the 26 nutrients that kids need for proper growth and development
FEELS GOOD	In-Group Bias	Position brand as the way to show the special group you belong to	PediaSure puts kids in the "Super Stars"club who have their own secret developmental advantage
	Choice Supportive Bias	Position brand as affirming the consumer's own choice	PediaSure comes in a taste that kids already love
FEELS EASIER	Occam's Razor Bias	Position your brand as the simpler and therefore correct choice	PediaSure makes any meal a perfect meal with the addition of just one glass of the nutrition kids need
	Herd Metality/Expert Bias	Position your brand as the choice of the herd or expert	PediaSure is recommended by doctors for children that are picky eaters

warned us that moms considered table food to be an unapproachable gold standard and would be unreceptive to any suggestion that it could be replaced. He was proven right.

How about saying "recommended by doctors" to exploit the *authority bias*? That would get us around the problem of finding a Sherina-like child star in every country. That tested well with moms, but Mel worried that it would again limit the market by locking the product back in its medical roots as something to take only when the kid is sick.

We ended up using two System 1 Easers in our brand strategy. We used the "Occam's razor bias" to position PediaSure as the choice simplifier. Add a glass of PediaSure to any meal and the job of nutrition was done. No need to worry about finding foods with the precise quantity of vitamin E or choline or zinc and magnesium. PediaSure had them all and more. With table foods, you virtually need a degree in nutritional science to orchestrate a cadence of balanced and complete meals for the week. Compiling that is stressful for young mothers whose cooking skills may not be up to the task.

The moms in the focus groups also loved the idea that PediaSure was available in flavors, like vanilla, strawberry, and chocolate, that kids loved. It was the kid's choice, not Mom's, and it put mealtime skirmishes at bay. That was the choice supportive bias at work, the second of our two System 1 choice drivers, and the kids would prefer what they chose themselves more and more.

Our brand concept was coming along nicely. We now had brand vibes and System 1 choice drivers working for us to make sense of the brand. PediaSure was evolving into: "For moms whose kids are picky eaters, PediaSure provides the nutrition they need, in a taste that kids love."

BRAND SENSE WITH SYSTEM 2 DELIBERATORS: EXAMINING THE EVIDENCE

We knew that for many moms the idea of not worrying about what their child was eating and giving them a nutritional supplement instead was going to be a new religion. We needed to break old habits and shatter beliefs around "real food or nothing." That calls for using System 2 choice drivers to make brand sense. So we used our frameworks to generate eight System 2 options for testing, as shown in Table 9.2, which are the same set that we introduce Chapter 7 on brand sense with System 2 Deliberators.

Table 9.2   PediaSure System 2 Options

	SYSTEM 2 EASERS	DEFINITION	POSSIBLE BRAND CONCEPT
AMPLIFY VALUE	No-Brainer	Position brand as far superior value versus its cost	PediaSure is the best of the best for the one thing that matters most in your life— your kids
	Pleasure Prediction	Amplify ultimate impact of brand on consumer vividly	With PediaSure, you can imagine their potential—at the top of the corporate ladder or dancing with the stars
LOWER RISK	Fight-or-Flight	Position brand as consumer's ally in the face of adversity	PediaSure is the nutritional shield that ensures no harm comes to your child
	Flirting Training	Make initial trial or ownership a key part of the brand promise	PediaSure is so good that we guarantee that your child will love it—or your money back
FIND RTBs	Examine the Evidence	Position brand as the right answer given the weight of available evidence	PediaSure is balanced and complete nutrition—100% of what my child needs, nothing less and nothing more
	Survey	Position brand as the preferred choice in consumer orchestrated surveys	More mothers everywhere choose PediaSure over any other brand for kids who are picky eaters
CHANGE CONTEXT	Reframing	Position brand as the answer to a much bigger problem than the obvious one	PediaSure is not just nutrition; it is an investment in your child's health and future
	Reattribution	Position brand as the agent for getting to the real cause of the problem	It's not you Mom; its just that kids are kids. Let PediaSure help.

PediaSure's main System 2 benefit was that it was "balanced and complete" nutrition. In fact, given its origins as a medical product, PediaSure had been proven to be exactly that in clinical trials. We didn't want to get technical with the consumers, but this was a claim that PediaSure alone could make.

We leveraged the examine the evidence method to string together this cognitive thread. The evidence itself appeared not only as a long list of nutrients on every PediaSure box, but also in other campaigns across various channels in stores and magazines. Ultimately, in various executions around the world, the promotions highlighted the "25 essential nutrients" or "triple benefit" of increased immunity, accelerated growth, and improved appetite, with kid-friendly images of teddy bears (suggestive of pleasant looks) and giraffes (cuing healthy growth).

The System 2 options used in the brand strategy were adopted after we carefully tested them using survey and focus group research to confirm that the cognitive keys we had uncovered were the right ones for unlocking consumer minds. Other credible threads around "PediaSure as best for the one that matters most in your life" and "PediaSure as an investment in your kid's future" were tested and dropped for lack of resonance. The moms had heard it all before. With the System 2 information added, the PediaSure positioning was fortified to: "For moms whose kids are picky eaters, PediaSure provides balanced and complete nutrition in a taste that kids love."

BRAND RESOLVE: PEDIASURE AS THE KEY TO BLISS

Recalling Tripp's mantra that brands needed to come with a $ sign appended to the end, we wanted to be certain that moms were not just going to prefer PediaSure but also that they would go out and resolve to buy it. Ultimately, all moms wanted their kids to grow up to be their best and turn out like Sherina in Indonesia—beautiful, talented, and competent in their craft. As mothers, that was their goal and it provided us the opportunity to tie the brand positioning to the intrinsic motivation for competence.

As I explained in Chapter 8, when you tie your brands to consumers' intrinsic goals, you set them on a path to greater happiness and spur them into action. Thus, the final PediaSure positioning morphed into: "For mom's whose kids are picky eaters, PediaSure provides balanced and complete nutrition in a taste that kid's love, so they can grow up to be all they can be, physically and mentally."

By then, Mel, Walt, and my Cerenti team had done a ton of work. We felt good with where we were and headed off to Tripp with our recommendation. After reviewing our work, Tripp suddenly turned around to us and asked: "You know what the proof of the pudding is?" As Walt and I looked on warily, he proceeded to answer his own question: "Go make this work in Mexico and then I'll believe it." Without skipping a beat, Mel leaned forward and countered with, "Then give me a Blue Plan."

A Blue Plan at Abbott is brilliant tool for spurring innovation and supporting breakthrough strategies. It means you get extra money, over and above any budget you have, to invest in your idea. Remember, I told you, Mel was a street-smart cookie. This wasn't his first rodeo. We got the money. The show was on.

A CONATIVE SEGMENTATION OF PEDIASURE MOMS

We never expected every mum to become a PediaSure mom. One of the first things we did in Mexico was to segment the market to find the moms most likely to become one.

It is common for marketers to start with an attitudinal segmentation, grouping people who generally think about things the same way, for this purpose. However, marketers have long struggled with this approach, as attitudinal segmentation does not correlate well with consumer brand purchases. Even groups of people who think about, say, nutrition in the same way will have wildly different favorite foods. So we went instead for the two known psychological drivers of resolve, happiness and tendency (conation).

We developed a simple 2 by 2 matrix. The horizontal axis was "Tendency" and vertical axis was "Happiness." As noted earlier, people are naturally wired to increase their happiness quotient. Yet customers differ in their tendency to act on a given stimulus. *Thus when marketers can promise a bit of happiness to a segment of customers that have more of an inclination to act, they can carve a lucrative place for themselves.*

Tendencies are not attitudes. Your attitude may be that the healthcare system in America stinks, but that does not mean that you will leave the country. The latter would happen only if you had a high tendency to seek healthcare happiness elsewhere. A very small number of people have left the United States and moved to France, for instance, for that reason, but most are unwilling to take such a dramatic step.

We used a consumer segment where a tendency can be positive, inert, or negative. A positive tendency will predispose you toward certain actions, and a negative tendency may incline you to do the opposite. An inert tendency would leave you indifferent to the brand stimulus, which might pique your interest, but you are unlikely to do anything about it. In Figure 9.2, we show the output of such a conative segmentation in the children's nutrition market in Mexico. We found four kinds of moms:

1. **Business moms** who were generally working women who approached child-rearing like a job-to-be-done project. They had a conative, or innate, tendency to institute order into their lives by getting on top of problems as soon as they spotted them. If her child was a picky eater, she might gather the facts on a spreadsheet and perform multivariate analytics so to speak, or at least

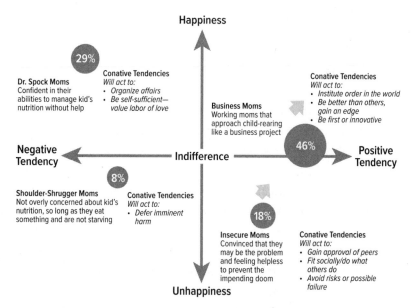

Figure 9.2 Conative map of children's nutrition market in Mexico. (*Courtesy:* Cerenti Marketing Group, LLC)

keep track of what the kid liked and didn't like. Outsourcing nutritional needs to PediaSure was an appealing path to happiness for this mom.

2. **Shoulder-shrugger moms** who didn't feel their children's nutrition was such a big deal. So long as the little tykes were munching on beef jerky and ice cream, they would live. Shoulder-shrugger moms would have a conative, or natural, tendency to act only if things were getting out of hand, but not otherwise. Trying to counteract this tendency would have been hard for PediaSure. It would have been like trying to sell vitamins for the indestructible baby Pubert of *The Addams Family* to his mother, Morticia.

3. **Dr. Spock moms** were another segment that was hard to crack for PediaSure. These moms, whom we named after the eponymous Dr. Benjamin Spock who wrote the once-pervasive US child-rearing practices bible, also had a conative tendency to organize their lives, but not with anyone's help. They liked to get their hands dirty and solve problems. They tended to make perfect nutritional meals for their kids and derive happiness from their own labor of love. PediaSure, if anything, would have taken away from that happiness.

4. **Insecure moms** were miserable and felt unfit for reporting to motherhood duty. They had a conative tendency to avoid risks, overcompensate, and make attempts to not be seen as incompetent. They would take help, any help from anywhere and anyone. PediaSure was that extra help and their ticket to happiness.

Business moms and insecure moms constituted nearly two-thirds of the Mexican market. We could live with that.

In 2005, when Walt, and I arrived in the haze-filled Valle de México with the Blue Plan money burning in our pockets, PediaSure was growing at just 1 percent per year in the country, as it had done for the preceding five years or so. We spent a year there with our teams prepping the market. We went to the supermarkets like Walmart and Chedraui to convince merchandisers to shift PediaSure out of the in-store pharmacies and onto the shelves. We hired an army of in-store samplers to intercept moms and kids as they walked into the stores and greet them with chilled cups of chocolate PediaSure.

We went on TV, but with no Sherina-like child star to promote the product as had been the case in Indonesia. We teamed up with a brilliant ad man, Ricardo Ferraris, who at the time led Grey's agency office in Mexico. His team developed a memorable commercial that would go on to win many awards.

It opened with a mother and son in an everyday mealtime standoff. Mom's there, kid's staring back, dinner plate's there, chicken and broccoli are in place. But Mom makes a fatal mistake. She looks away for one half of a second. As she turns back around the chicken is gone, only traces of the broccoli remain, and the plate is clean.

As she is about to declare victory, the overhead fan turns gently in the breeze, and a drumstick casts a long pale shadow across the table. It is a delightful moment that captures the interplay between a desperately caring mother and a mischievous, but obviously intelligent, child. Mom gives in and gives her son PediaSure. Both are happy. Problem solved.

In the following three years, sales of PediaSure in Mexico grew a whopping 1,000 percent. Tripp had nailed his $ sign to the end of the word *brands*. Working with us, Abbott turned the PediaSure story into a global branding playbook for the company. The legend of Mexico was told and replicated in many other countries. Today, PediaSure is a multibillion-dollar brand in Abbott's nutrition portfolio, one of the largest and most profitable anywhere in the world.

The things we do for the love of kids!

EPILOGUE

The three-part cognitive brand model is not just a fancy theory; it has been applied and seen to work fabulously with real-world brands. PediaSure was a good proof of concept in my work. As a matter of fact, my firm, Cerenti, has used these methods successfully, over and over, with clients in industries as disparate as consumer products, financial services, and pharmaceuticals.

The eight specific System 1 Easers and System 2 Deliberators that I describe in the earlier chapters are more than enough for designing most brands. But for marketers who feel like they need more, there are over 100 different cognitive biases that have been documented by psychologists, and Dr. David Burns offers over 50 System 2 methods to "untwist your thinking." With a little bit of web research, these lists are easy to find, but hard to use. Using the Occam's Razor principle, I suggest starting simple with the eight Easers and Deliberators described in these pages.

CHAPTER 10

BRANDS WITH PURPOSE

The venture capital (VC) industry is great at finding and betting on winning formulas for building businesses. They work until they don't.

The formula du jour is adding a dash of purpose to companies targeting millennials. If you are that kind of a consumer products startup, you must check off the "brand purpose" box.

Consider Harry's, an insurgent brand launched by Jeff Raider and Andy Katz-Mayfield in 2013. It quickly captured a 4 percent share of the men's razor blades market and was almost acquired by Edgewell (which makes razors under the Schick brand) for $1.4 billion in 2019, until regulators scuttled that deal.

How did they create this billion-dollar market cap rock star in just five years? Answer, they found a way to sell and mail decent quality razor blades, direct to you at your home, for a cheaper price. But wait, there's more!

Harry's worked with Mythology, a marketing studio on Lafayette Street in New York that specializes in working with "brands of the new economy." It works with up-and-coming companies to ensure that their brands have a memorable story and a good-for-the-world purpose.

For Harry's, the brand narrative is around how the company was born from the frustration that the founders felt at running around from store to store to find the right blades for their razors, standing in long lines at the CVS, and then overpaying for the blades from Gillette and Schick. Not particularly original, after all, that *is* what all online products offer, but quite sensible nevertheless.

But Mythology wanted more. They believe that "the feeling of belonging to something positive is the most influential marketing." Thus to give Harry's more of an oomph, make it more than just cheap blades, Mythology also added a larger-than-life purpose to the brand: it would donate 1 percent of its revenue to charities, like Crisis Text Line, that serve as a resource for men with mental health issues. That 1 percent with every purchase could be a reason to keep buying Harry's blades.[1] Given the billion-dollar valuation milestone cracked by Harry's, every other VC-backed consumer brand of the new economy has been busy replicating some version of this strategy. But does it work?

If you are going to build a brand with purpose, there is a right way and a wrong way. Harry's is the wrong way. I could argue that all they are doing is charging me 1 percent more than they need to and donating that money to a charity. Now, remind me why I am giving Harry's money to donate to a charity when I could Zelle[2] it myself in my own name instead of theirs?

Don't get me wrong. Brands that do good add to the consumer's resolve to buy the product by appealing to their intrinsic motivation to increase relatedness via a desire to make the world a better place for others. But are all acts of doing good equal? I showed earlier in Chapter 7 on System 2 Deliberators that the Rainforest Alliance amplifies your pleasure of buying everyday consumer products certified by them. Their seal signals that those products were manufactured by farming communities that use sustainable cultivation methods.

I have also argued that conative motivations are key to getting people off the fence of indecision. People are highly motivated to buy brands that let them express their identity in a way that makes the world a better place. So you may well ask, what's my beef? Isn't Harry's making the world a better place with their mission to help 500,000 people with mental healthcare needs?

OK, I owe you an answer. And here it is. Brands with purpose must meet the following three criteria to be successful:

- They support causes that mesh with what the brand is.

- They do good in a way their consumers cannot on their own.

- They are seen to be authentic.

Let's check this out.

SUPPORT WHAT YOUR BRAND IS ABOUT

Ask yourself this, what if Harry's gave 1 percent of its revenues to Toys for Tots, which distributes playthings to needy families, or The Humane Society, which works to stop animal cruelty? Would you feel better about that? There are plenty of worthy causes around the world. You can write checks all day long. Which is the one that makes sense for your brand?

So rule number one is to work with a charity that fits with what your brand is about. In Harry's case, yes, it is a men's grooming product, and yes, it is giving money for an issue that relates to men, although not exclusively so. Yet wouldn't Harry's be better off with some charity that helps men be better and affordably groomed? Not everyone can afford an expensive razor, but being better dressed and shaved could help such a person get a better job. Maybe Harry's could work with young kids who can't afford to get a haircut and are made fun of at school? After all the brand is also about affordability.

Mental healthcare for men is undoubtedly a great cause, but as a consumer I am hard pressed to see its connection to grooming or cheap razors, the stuff that Harry's is about. And that's the link consumers need to see. If you do that right, the charitable organization will enrich your brand through what in psychology is known as the evaluative conditioning effect we discussed in Chapter 4 on brand vibes.

In contrast, Warby Parker, another new economy rocket that sells prescription eyeglasses, gets this exactly right. Through their buy-a-pair, give-a-pair charity program, the company makes monthly donations to their nonprofit partner, VisionSpring, which provides free eyewear to people in developing countries. The company has distributed more than four million pairs of glasses since its start in 2010.[3] From a branding lens (!), it is easy to see how a company that wants to be the leader in affordable, quality prescription wear would also want to bring the gift of better sight to those most in need. It is a cause that mirrors the brand itself.

This is not just for startups. Pfizer is one of largest manufacturer of anti-infectives in the world. Currently, 700,000 people die each year from infections from drug-resistant microbes, and that number could well rise to millions by 2050.[4]

The problem is getting worse because superbugs are proliferating dangerously in different parts of the world. Pfizer has launched several initiatives to educate people about the seriousness of the threat and how they can play a role in mitigating it through better daily hygiene.

In the United Kingdom, they work with organizations that educate children in schools and through public exhibitions in science museums. They have also set up surveillance programs to allow healthcare workers to rapidly report the emergence of evolving new strains across the world.

Arguably, some of these programs will slow down the evolution of new microbes and reduce the size of the market for Pfizer. They will have fewer anti-infectives to sell than if they do nothing. But it is the right purpose for the brand. It helps Pfizer stand out as a brand for public good, and not one interested in making a quick buck with its drugs. And it is not all public service. Some of these programs will surface opportunities for developing and introducing new anti-infectives.

DO WHAT YOUR CONSUMERS CAN'T

Brands with purpose need to do more than just write a check. Tim Brown, the ex-vice-captain of New Zealand's 2010 FIFA soccer team, totally gets this. After retiring from the game in 2012, he founded Allbirds, a sneakers company, out of his annoyance with all the fancy shoes from Nike and Adidas that he wore when he played.

All he wanted was a good, comfortable pair of sneakers made without loud colors and logos or nondegradable, engineered plastics. It turns out that so did a lot of other people, and Allbirds became a $1.4 billion sneaker company overnight.[5] But what made the brand great was not a mushy shoe to plant your feet in; it was the singular purpose that the Allbirds, the brand, pursued.

The company is committed to manufacturing and marketing shoes made entirely of planet friendly or recycled materials. This was not easy. Allbirds invested a lot of time and money into research and engineering to make shoes from natural merino wool, eucalyptus tree fibers, and shoelaces out of recycled plastic bottles. Most of us want to recycle, but all we can do is to separate our trash into two bins, or three if we are really good. But by buying Allbirds, we can do something that otherwise is out of reach for us. It is not just another slap-on-a-dollar donation to the next green charity. That is why Allbirds is so special for many of its customers. It is a way for them to do more than they can on their own.

BE AUTHENTIC

A few months back I was talking to business buddy, Henrique (not his real name), who is a senior partner in a 100-plus person placement agency. He had seen my recent blog "Brands with Purpose" on LinkedIn and was commiserating about his own experience. In his company, there was a fist-pounding debate about what the company ought to do to give back to the community.

If you have ever worked in a partnership-based firm, you already know that internally they are often completely dysfunctional. Because many partners have a nearly equal share in the business, there are de facto many masters running the company. Most are highly accomplished and thus have strong and quirky opinions about all topics, even trivial ones.

Not that giving is a minor topic, but it is certainly one to elicit more ideas than you can sort through. Henrique felt like they were stuck. Maybe the best option was to let each partner do their own thing.

As we talked some more, Henrique shared with me his own personal story. His son, Dion, unfortunately, had gotten into drugs and been fired from a string of jobs. He had completely hosed his career.

After years of struggle and multiple recovery programs, Dion finally broke the spell. With Henrique's hand-holding and coaching, he was finally able to return to work and keep a job. But it has not been easy, and Henrique has to keep working with Dion on the side, in the evenings or weekends at home, to keep him on track.

As it turned out, Henrique was not the only one with this problem. Slowly, there were other parents, friends of friends, who wanted advice for their own children. As a professional in the placement industry, helping people with their careers was what Henrique did for a living. He advised them on how to be seen at work and handle pressure. Clients paid him big bucks for exactly that. In fact, his firm was full of professionals like him with those skills and training.

One thing led to another, and with Henrique's strong support, the firm decided its new purpose: helping recovering drug addicts return to productive careers and counseling them on keeping their jobs. It made the firm a brand with purpose.

You would guess that I like this story because it meets my first two criteria for successful brands with purpose. The nature of the charity, free career management advice, fits hand in glove with a placement firm's brand DNA, and the company is providing a service that draws on its unique talents and resources. Check and check.

Actually, I like it a lot for another reason, and that is, authenticity. Recall my distaste for people just writing checks. For one, what Henrique's firm did was born out of something that was deeply inspirational for him. It was something that had touched one of their own and many in their community personally. It helped the company understand why they were doing what they were doing. Just as important or even more so, the senior leadership of the company was involved intimately in the cause, dedicating to it their own blood, sweat, and tears. Those two things together are what make brands with purpose authentic.

In large companies, where giving can become a two-page calligraphic list of charities supported, that connection to the brand and authenticity is often lost. At Allbirds, too, one of the cofounders, Joey Zwillinger, is personally the lead for finding new earth-friendly materials to work with and developing new engineering methods to make them suitable for great shoes. How C-suite executives get involved with the charities they support says a lot about the authenticity of brands with purpose.

KEY TAKEAWAYS

Brands with purpose are a great idea. They work well because they tap into the innate conative energy for relatedness among consumers, whereby they want to make the world a better place for themselves and others. Thus many people are drawn to brands with purpose and buy more of them.

However, check-the-box giving does not create a brand with purpose. Is yours a real brand with purpose? Try this pop quiz:

- Do the activities of the charity fit with what your brand does?

- Does your giving draw on the unique talents and resources of your company?

- Do the company leaders put their heart and soul into the cause?

If you answered "yes" to all, you've got it!

In the next chapter, I turn my attention to brand execution. Cognitive brands are designed to work the way the brain does. And brand execution, too, must follow the same principles.

PART

THREE

COGNITIVE
BRANDS:
EXECUTION

CHAPTER 11

TALES FROM THE TRENCHES—BRAND EXECUTION

B rand execution is the fun part of branding, isn't it? This is when you get to go to the island of Kauai to shoot television commercials. It is your chance to pretend play Martin Scorsese. There is the setting sun against aquamarine waters of the Pacific, beautiful models and actors sunning on the beach, and you pensively downing the requisite mango coconut daiquiri. It's all strictly business; you can expense it. Yeah! Brand execution is the doing part of branding versus the thinking part. Or is it?

Well, consider this. Consumer brains don't see most of what you want them to see in your commercials. They hear a different brand story from the one you are telling. And they don't necessarily pay attention to your ad when it plays; instead, they sleep on it. Say what? Need another daiquiri? A double, perhaps?

Traditionally, brand execution or activation has been a straightforward exercise. Write the three things (equities) that your brand is about on the left side of a sheet of paper. Then move over to the right and list all of the places where a customer runs into your brand (customer touchpoints). The latter can include a wide range, namely, television and magazines, billboards, retail stores, customer service calls, online video channels, sports sponsorships, T-shirts and hats, streamed audio channels, you name it. Decide what customer touchpoints will display or activate which of the three equities of the brand.

Add it all up and put it together. That is how consumers come into contact with your brand. It is your brand experience. Or at least the one you envision. Between that and what consumers actually experience is space in which their prodigious brain sits. And there's plenty that's lost in translation.

With the latest advances in brain sciences, we are understanding a lot more about how the brain learns and remembers things. For marketers, understanding what the brain latches onto and what it recalls about your brand is so important. To ensure that important stuff is not mislaid, let's take a look at what brain science tells us about the following four questions:

- What makes for a brand impression? Do all parts of the brand experience matter equally to consumers?

- Which brand experiences are more likely to be noticed by consumers?

- How should brand experiences unfold so that consumers internalize them deeply?

- How much can you say about your brand? Is there such a thing as an information overload?

Let's dig into these questions a bit.

1. BRAND IMPRESSIONS ARE BASED ON THE CLIMAX AND CONCLUSION OF AN EXPERIENCE

Lesson number one is that the brain does not look at everything it is presented. It focuses on a few odds and ends and makes up the rest. This is kind of like hallucinations, which are defined as "sensations that appear to be real but are created within the mind. Examples include seeing things that are not there, hearing voices or other sounds, experiencing body sensations like crawling feelings on the skin, or smelling odors that are not there."[1]

Paul Fletcher, a professor of neurosciences at Cambridge University, in his lecture entitled, "Psychosis: Bending Reality to See Around the Corners,"[2] argues that we, all of us and not just those suffering from mental diseases, routinely hallucinate reality. What is he talking about?

Ever been in a situation where a work colleague was so ponderously explaining an obvious business point that you jumped up and cut him off with, "I got it! I got it! OK?" or "You can go faster." Well, it turns out our brain does that all of the time. After all, it is flooded with data from the senses every second that we are alive. So it deals with the barrage by taking shortcuts. It picks up a few fragments, connects the dots, jumps up, and says, "I got it!" Well, OK, it does not jump up or anything, but you get the idea.

Here's a fact. When you look out of your window, the part that the brain perceives in full color and high definition is limited to the size of your thumbnail with your arm outstretched in front.[3] All else is peripheral vision with imagined details. All of your senses sort of operate like that, in "sound bites."

When you step outside in the morning to take your kids to the school bus, your brain takes only rough notes; a large yellow vehicle arrived and your kids got on it. Other details like the yellow body paint with the black stripe, Jenny the driver in her blue uniform, screaming kids ripping each other's heads off are automatically retrieved from prior memories and populated into the experience.[4] This is why witness accounts of the same scene of crime often differ.[5] You would swear that Jenny was driving the bus even when it was Gertie, a substitute.

The consumer's brain focuses only on bits and pieces of your exquisitely crafted brand experience. It does not ignore the rest; it cooks it up with guesses. It does that even when it hasn't quite got it; which means what the consumer's brain thinks it is, is not what it may be. This is also why people may confuse your ad for another brand's! Ouch! *Hence, marketers designing brand experiences should note that only selected elements of what they present will register with consumers. Understanding what those are is key.*

Lesson number two follows from the work done by Kahneman, who makes a distinction between what he calls the "remembering self," what we recall of an experience, and the "experiencing self," what we actually experienced. He argues that your recall of an experience is heavily influenced by just two things, its peak and ending, which is known as his "peak-end rule."[6, 7] So, marketers must pay attention to not only the content of the message, but its cadence.

In the summer of 2019, I found myself travelling in business class on a flight from Chicago to Zurich on Swiss Air. After trying their selection of wines, I loved the French for my dinner course. When the flight attendant came around to ask if I wanted to buy anything from the duty-free catalog, on an impulse, I said, "No. But I would like to buy a bottle of the wine you served." Instead of saying "That's not in the catalog, dude," she smiled and said "Sure."

In a few minutes she came back with a bottle packed nicely in a "Swiss Shop" duty-free bag. As I handed her my American Express card, she said "With our compliments, sir."

That high point is the only thing I recall about that eight-hour-thirty-five-minute flight. I don't remember anything about how comfortable my lie-flat seat was or how delicious my Bircher muesli breakfast was or even the perfectly perked faces of the crew members. When we landed in Zurich, I used the showers in the Senator Lounge, which were drop-dead, drown-in-luxury gorgeous. And that was the ending to my flight experience as I boarded my connection to Vienna. If you asked me how Swiss Air was, I would say they were fabulous. The high point and finish were the sum total of my brand experience, and all else, the remaining nine hours of a ten-hour period, a mere blur.

At restaurants, servers have figured out that what translates into bigger tips is how well the meal ends. A waitress who leaves a check with a pleasant smile earns better tips than those who quietly slide it across. Waitresses who draw a smiley face on the check, and write "Thank You, Mr. Smith (get the last name from the credit card)" earn even bigger tips.[8] And it is not a coincidence that many come and ask you how you like the special or the "favorite dish you were dying to eat" while you are eating it, as that is the high point of the meal and they want that to be the defining moment in your memory.

In pharma marketing in the United States this can be irksome. All advertisements are required by laws around "fair balance" to not only speak to the benefits of the drug but also to itemize its risks. The ads usually open with a titillating story about how life with the drug is awesome and ends with a laundry list of heart-stopping side effects of the "may result in genital warts and suicidal thoughts" variety. The side effects are detailed in a monotone with calming elevator music in the background in the hope that it won't alarm prospective patients and inadvertently become the highlight, the "remembering self," of the brand message.

Yet, the ending, it turns out, is important. In focus groups, we often hear patients talk about how scary those ad tails are. That may be exactly what the FDA intends, but it makes life not fun for both the marketers and patients. A better strategy is thus to shift the fair balance statements in between the climax and the end, ensuring that the conclusion of an advertisement is sufficiently positive versus merely an obligatory and unremarkable suggestion to talk to the doctor about the drug.

2. DOING WHAT CUSTOMERS EXPECT ISN'T WHAT'S NOTICED; DOING THE UNEXPECTED IS

What does the brain gloss over? For one, it is wired to ignore sameness and note differences. For some reason, if the school bus you loaded your kid on was green, your brain will stop and take notes.

In a series of experiments, researchers at Johns Hopkins[9] showed that babies learn by focusing their attention on the unexpected. When something unanticipated occurs, they try to learn more about it and resolve the mystery. In one test, when the babies saw a ball apparently pass through a wall, they checked the ball by banging it on a table. When they saw the ball seemingly hover in the air, they tested it by letting it drop. Moral of the story: If your brand experience is what the consumers expect, they are less likely to notice it! If it is the same old same old, they will gloss over it. If it is new but nothing to write home about and still sort of the expected, same thing. This is why you can drive from work to home over a thirty-minute commute and remember absolutely nothing about it.

Our client Sagent Pharmaceuticals, which sells generic injectable drugs, found a clever way to differentiate its products. Think about this for a minute. Generic drugs are certified by the FDA to be chemically identical to each other. Propofol is propofol. Ibuprofen is ibuprofen. So how do you differentiate?

Sagent marketers noted that there are 1.4 million medication administration errors annually, where a nurse or doctor accidently injects a patient with the wrong drug or dose. Often that happens because all drug vials sit in a tray and look terribly similar. A tired nurse, in the midst of a 16-hour double shift, may only look for a few cues to delineate one drug from another and crucial details maybe assumed.

Sagent Pharma thus changed the packaging of its drugs so that each type had a unique carton, bottle label, size, and color under a program called "PreventIV Measures."[10] Different doses were also demarcated by fonts or bottle shapes and sizes, as shown in Figure 11.1. In a market

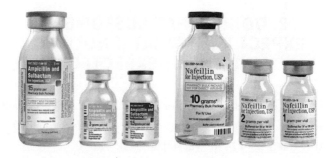

Figure 11.1   Sagent Pharma distinctive packaging reduced chances of accidents.
(*Courtesy:* Sagent Pharmaceuticals)

where drugs are sold by their chemical name and not their brand, Sagent made its generics stand out and lowered chances of accidents. The nurses and pharmacists at hospitals just loved it.

In retrospect, it seems to make so much sense to do what Sagent has done, but competing marketers continue to produce vials that look like vials have looked for 50 years. Their products disappear into the "sea of sameness."

Brands that show their differentiating features in a surprising way do better. John West, which markets canned salmon, wanted to differentiate itself by claiming it uses high quality fish. Its television commercials[11] (see Figure 11.2) start serenely enough at a scenic bend in the river, where a sleuth of bears are shown peacefully catching the salmon springing out from the water. A *National Geographic*-like deep male voice soothingly murmurs, "At the river mouth, the bears catch only the tastiest, most tender salmon." This placid calm is interrupted by a crazed man in an

Figure 11.2   John West uses the unexpected to create a memorable ad.

orange jumpsuit, who rushes out of the forest, directly at a bear, with an "aaaaahgh" war cry. The voiceover continues unperturbed, ". . . and that (fish) is exactly what we at John West want."

A comical fistfight ensues between the bear and the man, with the latter ultimately nailing the grizzly with a kick to its crotch and making off with its catch. The voiceover concludes the scene with, "John West endures the worst to bring you the best." The brilliance of this ad is in communicating a fairly common quality claim in an unexpected and hence memorable manner.

So next time you think about meeting customer expectations; don't. Surprise and delight them instead.

3. BRANDS MUST TELL STORIES AND NOT RECITE LISTS OF BENEFITS

In 1981, an Indian man, Rajan Mahadevan, recalled 31,811 digits of the math constant *pi* (π) from memory. Eight years later, Japan's Hideaki Tomoyori topped that with 40,000 digits.[12] The current Guinness World Record is held by Rajveer Meena of VIT University, Vellore, India, who, in 2015, rattled off 70,000 digits over a 10-hour period, while wearing a blindfold.[13]

If you think there's room for improvement, that could be something to kick at on your next Easter break. But hold on. There are thousands of kids, schooling in madrassas around Pakistan, who can recite the Koran by rote, all 77,449 words, consisting of 320,015 letters, in the right order, accomplishing a feat nearly five times as great as that of the record break-ing, memory savant Meena by sheer volume. How?

The answer lies in stories. The decimals in the constant *pi* constitute a disconnected list. The Koran is a story. *The* Learner *subunit in our brain is wired to remember stories better than random lists.* It checks for how things relate to each other, and the more they do, the better it remembers them. Stories by their very nature have many associations built into them, in how each part of the story connects to another and perhaps in elements of the story that may relate to the consumers' own experiences.

Brands, if they are to be remembered, need to become great storytellers. Some brands do that quite literally. You have many examples of brands that have built stories around their formation. It's almost obligatory for every wine maker to spin a yarn about how generations of the family carefully tilled the soil and nurtured the grapes. *However, storytelling for brands is not just about forcing a story around its origins, though it sometimes works. It is about letting consumers imagine their own stories around your brands.*

We, as consumers, not only like to listen to stories but also to tell our own. This creates an opportunity for marketers to create brands that can become a part of the consumer's stories. Think about it. Every product that you sell is used by consumers in their own lives, and, in a very real way, becomes a part of their lives. When consumers can better visualize how your brand will be a part of their story, they are more inclined to buy it.

So when you are buying groceries, you may think about the meal you would cook for that special someone and how they might react. When you are buying a bison jerky doggie treat, you may envision how "Ralph" will toy with it. When you are buying a bottle of wine, you might want to imagine what you will say about why you picked that bottle for the occasion. Giving consumers the breadcrumbs around the stories they could tell about your product is a fabulous way to engage them with your brand.

The way to insert your brand into your customer's stories is to understand their routines, rituals, or even special moments in their lives. These are already alive and kicking in their memories. All you have to do is to place your brand in those narratives.

TANK GARAGE WINERY: MAKING YOUR BRAND'S STORY THEIR STORY

Tank Garage Winery takes storytelling to heart. Each one of their bottles has a story, in which they invite you to see yours. Now, selling wines is not easy. In the United States over 700 million bottles are sold each year by the 9,600 or so wineries. You might imagine yourself as an oenophile that mentally savors the terroir, vintage, and varietal of each bottle you plan to buy, but truth be told, most people buy wine by just considering its label.

Tank Garages wines are inspired by special moments in the lives of the winemakers, James Harder and Jim Regusci. "Lords of the Boulevard,"[14] their Napa red, recalls the "nostalgic exuberance and naiveté" of the fifties and sixties era. The label dons a famous Joseph Sterling photograph of two youths in starch white tees leaning casually out of the windows of their car at a drive-in. The winemakers capture that spirit by introducing the wine with the byline "We were young, broke, and reckless, but we ruled this town." It is a story of adolescence that perhaps you too can relate to from a more carefree time in your life, and more fondly today, now that you can afford a $65 bottle of wine.

The one brand that wins the grand prize in masterfully executing this strategy is Google in India. With a three-minute long commercial called "Reunion" that debuted in 2013 on YouTube,[15] they captured the hearts and minds of the local citizenry. The ad fictionalizes what was the true story of many when India and Pakistan were partitioned by the British, at the end of the colonial era, leading to many friendships and families being ripped apart overnight as masses of people migrated from one country to the other.

It opens with the elderly Baldev, a Hindu, showing to his granddaughter, Suman, a faded sepia picture of himself and his closest friend, Yusuf, a Muslim, from when they were little kids living as neighbors in Lahore, Pakistan. The picture remains the sole vestige of a happier time and of a bond that at the time must have seemed inseparable. Recalling those fond memories, he tells her of the park that was next to his home. It had an ancient gate, from times immemorial of "Baba Azam," where he and Yusuf would fly kites and eat *jhajariyas* from Yusuf's family's confectionary shop.

Suman's brow furrows pensively as a sudden thought crosses her mind. She turns into an amateur sleuth flipping open her computer and cruising to Google search. A quick search of "park in Lahore with ancient gate" uncovers Mochi Gate. "What is *jhajariya*" reveals it is a local dessert made of caramelized milk. "Oldest sweet shop near Mochi Gate" lists Fazal Sweet along with their telephone number. One search leads to another until she finally locates "Yusuf," still alive and well, living in Pakistan.

In what follows, and as the story unfolds, she is on her way to pick up the long-lost Yusuf at the Delhi airport, checking flight arrival times along the way on Google search, and a touching reunion takes place between Baldev and Yusuf on his birthday.

The ad, which has been viewed nearly 16 million times on YouTube to date and also featured on Indian TV, is simply brilliant on multiple levels. It tells a story that is cleverly woven around what Google is. The search engine is invoked six different times during the vignette for everything from finding phone numbers to checking India's visa requirements for Pakistani tourists. Compare that to having an ad that just lists all the things you can do on Google Search. The story touches us, and we know emotional memories last longer. In Chapter 2, I caution against overly emotional ads in which the brand may be lost. Not in this case, not with six well-placed pieces of "life-with-Google" in the story.

But that's not all. I said earlier that recall will be even stronger if you can associate your brand's story with other knowledge and beliefs that the consumer holds deeply. By building the Google story around the events of Partition, a moment set deeply in the Indian consumer psyche, the brand ensured that it would never be unnoticed or forgotten. Further, the way that the search engine is used in the story portrays use occasions that we as consumers can easily relate to.

Yes, the ad is three minutes long, but it does check every box I can think of in getting cognitive brand execution right. Don't get me wrong. Not all brand executions need to have beautiful stories like this, but they do need something, even if it is simple.

A final technical point on this topic. We now know that stories make your brands easier to recall. Why is that important?

Because *things that are easier to recall by the brain, seem more important to it*. In psychology, this phenomenon is called *availability heuristic*.[16] If your brand benefits are easier to recall, those features, the strengths of your brand presumably, will seem more important to the consumer in making their choices. When presented with competing choices, they will assess them against the standard set by your brand.

4. BRAND STORIES CAN BE LONG OR SHORT, BUT MUST BE STORIES

The good news is that brand stories can be short or long. The real point is to tell a good story. Again, marketers wrestle with this idea a lot in branding. Should your brand have a single compelling idea that hits the customer in as little time as possible? But what if they were inattentive, thinking about something else, when you pitched your one-liner at them? And what should you do when your brand has three or four great features to talk about? Shouldn't you then turn your brand into a "mixto" burrito with everything on it?

The answer is that those are the wrong questions. *The number of brand equities you put in your brand positioning is not the problem. The real question is whether you can tie them into a coherent story that connects with your customers.*

Remember what we talked about. Most people cannot memorize even a shopping list with just seven items, but just about everyone can follow the storyline of the 142-minute movie *Forrest Gump*. Length does not matter, stories do. Consumers don't need to commit every word of your brand proposition to memory, but they do need to follow the story. So make sure your brand has one.

And while you are at it, tell a coherent story that consumers can follow. Marketers often trip over this. They show ads with multiple vignettes of consumers relishing their brand. This happens because the market research department tells the marketers that they need to target three different consumer segments or use occasions. So they say to themselves, "Why choose? Let's put all of them in!"

So a commercial may feature a Black man slipping a protein bar in his pocket as he rushes off to work, a white mom enjoying it as a snack after the morning Zumba class, and Grandpa partaking of one during his morning walk in the park. Those are three different stories. Further confusing matters, all of this is also accompanied by a voiceover detailing the ingredients in the bar and their salient benefits. Guess what? Now, they're lost. Make it easy. Tell one coherent story and you'll thank me.

Here's why. Most people think they can multitask. But research has shown they can't; especially when it comes to doing two things that require deliberation (System 2). You can do a System 2 task together with a System 1 task. For example, most people can drive and think at the same time. But two System 2 tasks are a no-go.

Psychologists Christopher Chabris and Daniel Simons demonstrated people's inability to multitask in a hilarious experiment described in their book *The Invisible Gorilla*.[17] The authors made a film of two teams passing two basketballs.[18] One team is dressed in white shirts and the other in black. They are running around each other passing the balls.

The viewer's task is to count the number of times the white team passes the ball to its own members. This is a little complicated because the players are mixed together, and thus the task requires the viewer to focus. Somewhere in the middle of this, a woman dressed in a gorilla suit saunters across through the players, pauses to thump her chest, and then walks back out of the frame.

At the end of the video, the viewer is asked how many times the white team passed the ball. They are then asked if they noticed the gorilla! Of the thousands of people who have taken this test, roughly half didn't! *When System 2 is busy, it can miss some obvious activities that it is not focused on. If you have too many stories that your brand is trying to tell, all at the same time, they will be missed like the chest-thumping gorilla.*

Abbott's recent television spot "We're Changing Parkinson's Tune" succeeds in relating relatively complicated information about treating Parkinson's disease through a coherent commercial. It opens with a scene showing endless rows of artists performing in a string orchestra, shown in Figure 11.3. The picture is a bit unusual because instead of the usual 60-odd performers that you would normally see in an orchestra, this one has millions, so many that they disappear into the horizon.

The unexpectedness of the imagery catches your eye. Over the reassuring symphonic notes, the voiceover says, "In the human brain, (there are)

Figure 11.3   Abbott ad relates an orchestra to its medical technology.

billions of neurons playing in harmony." As the music builds to a crescendo, the narrator, walking down the aisle, explains, "For people with Parkinson's, some neurons change their tune, causing uncontrollable tremors." On cue, one of the performers goes off-track, playing his own tune. The obvious disharmony of this draws in the viewers, who wonder, "What's going on here?" It compels them to absorb the message around what goes wrong with people who have Parkinson's. At that time, the narrator chimes in with, "Now Abbott technology can target those exact neurons and restore control and harmony once thought to be lost forever." This is a well-executed ad where the visual analog of the string orchestra to Abbott's medical technology relates a coherent story. And that's what the game is all about.

Let's turn our attention now to another important subject. How much brand information can you toss at the consumer? How much can they really absorb in a short amount of time?

Marketers believe that consumers have fleeting attention spans. Hence, they often condense brand messages into terse one-liners in hopes of sneaking them into the consumer's consciousness. Kind of reminds you of moms who fool their kids into opening their mouths and then quickly slide in a tablespoon of thick distasteful tonic with a "See that wasn't so bad" assurance.

If your customers are slow to tune into you, then your pithy brand proposition will appear and disappear in the blink of an eye before anyone takes note. But there's good news. *The brain does not just process dumbed-down brand storylines. It can and does internalize more complicated stuff over time, and marketers can take advantage of those background processes.*

In the introductory chapter, I described dreams as a time when the *Learner* subunit in the brain can kick back and ruminate over events of the day. But dreams are not the only occasion for doing so; our brains are constantly thinking, pondering, and ruminating when they are not focused on complex mental tasks. To tap into residual dreams and thoughts, marketers need to find ways to keep consumers thinking about their brands.

One way to do this is by presenting brand messages in an enigmatic manner, using anachronisms, hyperbole, surreal imagery, and mental riddles. The brain sleeps over those conundrums to make sense of them; it can't help it. When it encounters the unexpected, it not only notices it, but tries to resolve it. I have coined the term *residual thoughts method* for when a brand strategically embeds its proposition in exactly such an enigmatic message and subconsciously triggers the brain into discovering it.

This is the route the drug Skyrizi took in the eczema market. The AbbVie marketers wanted to communicate the idea that once you use their drug to clear those unseemly splotches on your skin, you could feel freed of the disease and enjoy life to the fullest. But the problem was that they were late to the party, and other entrants had already done pretty much the same messaging.

Otezla, from Amgen, had blanketed the airwaves with their campaign "Your spontaneity is showing!" In the ad, we see a woman swinging from a rope like a monkey and flopping into the lake. Stelara, by Johnson and Johnson, had an ad of a guy running around the beach with his surfboard in a campaign that said, "That's 361 days to focus on life, . . . and not psoriasis!" That was a reference to taking the drug just four times a year and the rest of the time being free to do whatever.

Of course, all the ads had to be in swimming gear so you could see lots of clean skin. That was a given. With all these ads already cramming the airwaves, you can see the problem AbbVie had. Free as a monkey swinging from a rope? How much freer and more limitless could you show people being? Fire them off on top of a rocket to the moon in a bikini?

Len Spears,* who was AbbVie's point man for Skyrizi in global markets, was not happy with his options. Rarely sticking to the agenda at any meetings and obsessive about his business, Len was a rare and creative strategist. Those two words, "creative" and "strategic," don't generally go together, but in Len's case, they exactly do. He asked his agency to develop eight different brand concepts, which they did. Except, he didn't like any of them. He had sent them back to drawing board so many times that I thought they might just pack up and leave.

"Look at Skyrizi! It has the best clinical data of any drug in the market! We have almost no side effects. Nothing! Zero!" he exclaimed, drawing a big circle on the nearby white board. "We get a hundred percent skin clearance for more patients than anyone else," he said writing a "1" above the original "0" and a second "0" below it, to now show a "100" on the board. *"You see? No more patches! No more blotches! Everything's gone! Zippo! It's perfect!"* he went on in a how's-this-happening-to-me tone.

Somewhere in the midst of these inspirational outbursts, something clicked with one of the creative wonks at the agency. Nothing but everything? Say what? And that ultimately led to a dazzling campaign around "Nothing is Everything," that finally pleased Len. The tagline presents a paradox: How can nothing be everything? How does zero equal infinity?

The incongruity of the message, which is laced into a sprightly sing-along worthy ditty in the television commercials, triggers residual thoughts in the audience. The answer to the riddle lies in unraveling the brand message, namely that Skyrizi has virtually no side effects and leaves *nothing* of the psoriasis on the skin. And is that not the whole point for the patient? Isn't that *everything*? Yeah! And he scores!

---

* The events described in the following passages have been fictionalized and the names of individuals disguised to remove any nonpublic information and preserve the privacy of the mentioned individuals. The narrative is thus designed to be instructive rather than accurately biographical or historical.

OLD SPICE AND THE RESIDUAL THOUGHTS METHOD

The residual thoughts method is used more widely than you might think in markets as diverse as pharma, consumer, and retail.

The trend may have been revived by Old Spice. In 2010, Old Spice was a 75-year-old, tired brand, struggling to be noticed by an entirely new generation of consumers. Seven years back, Old Spice had introduced bodywashes for men, but the products battled in vain to gain traction in the market. The brand's legacy as "the after-shave that most reminded you of what your grandpa smelled like," was locked around its ankles like an iron ball and chain.

Old Spice also faced competition from industry goliath Unilever, which was launching its Dove for Men bodywash products on the backs of the monumental success of its "Real Beauty" campaign with women, with heavy investments planned for Super Bowl 2010.

Old Spice came up with a campaign that still mystifies marketing experts as to why it worked. A not particularly original, but eminently forgivable, approach would have been to simply splash images of a beautiful woman fawning over her Old Spice lathered man. But that was not at all what they did. They did something better: a fantastical campaign that made the viewer stop and go, "Whoa! What the heck was that?"

The TV commercials[19] featured former NFL wide receiver Isaiah Mustafa as "the man your man could smell like" in a range of clever vignettes. In the first one, the super sexy Isaiah finds himself magically transported to a nice yacht. Then hard-to-find tickets to an exclusive show prance out from an oyster in his hands and turn into a pile of plump diamonds, after which Old Spice appears in the midst of the heap. Thus explains the narrator, "Anything Is Possible When Your Man Smells Like Old Spice."

To erase any doubts as to the premise, in the next moment, Isaiah finds himself bare-chested on a paper-white horse, observing

"I'm on a horse" leaving unsaid "how about you?" The commercial finishes off with the tagline "Smell Like Man, Man." Pretty crazy, huh? (See Figure 11.4.)

Figure 11.4   The Old Spice ad makes sense once the consumer uncovers the brand's message in the enigmatic cues.

Despite the fantastical visuals, the brand stays true to the idea that anything is possible when your special lady is charmed by the smell of Old Spice on you. The key is not just to show incongruous audiovisuals, but also to weave the brand narrative into the ad for latent thought processing. But it does take time to get it. You may have to watch the ad a couple of times before it sinks in.

In the aftermath of the campaign, Old Spice sales lit on fire and doubled. Social media engagement of the ads leapt to 40 million plus viewers across a range of sites including Facebook, Twitter, and YouTube.[20] The best form of flattery, as they say is mimicry, and many different brands have latched onto the idea of "Anything is possible" with actors portraying unnatural acts empowered by their brands.

The residual thoughts method does not have to be complicated. It just has to inspire consumers to think. A simple example is an iconic billboard that appears a mile before Exit 24 on Interstate-95 between New York and New Haven. All it says is "Your Wife is HOT!" with the letters HOT in fiery red, a picture of a swimming pool, and a suggestion to take the exit and visit "Fairfield Pool." You are at Exit 24 by the time you process this out and smile sheepishly to yourself. The play on the word "HOT" causes the reader to pause and make the connection that putting in a swimming pool in the backyard could be a great way for the wife and kids to cool off in the *hot* summer.

I should note here that not everyone living in Fairfield County took a liberating view of the poster. In fact, there was a petition[20] signed by concerned citizens on the appropriateness of objectifying women in this manner. Would you have said "Your Husband is HOT?" they asked.

Notwithstanding the intricate gender equivalence issues in play, the method for latent introspection is what marketers should be after. Thinking taxes the human brain. Thus, having a humorous payoff certainly does not hurt.

The residual thoughts method is a different idea from the notion of surprising customers. The *bizarreness effect* tells us that wacky images, sounds, language, and events stand out more and are remembered by the brain better.[22] This, as we saw, is because our brain is wired to focus on differences or changes from the expected. Unfortunately, these two strategies have prompted some ad agencies to create zany spots that at times make no sense. It is not enough to be weird; the ad has to relate to and unfold the story of your brand.

KEY TAKEAWAYS

In this chapter, we learned how to be smart about executing our brand strategies in the way the brain works. The following principles should guide your designs:

- Brand impressions are based on only a small part of the total brand experience, namely, the climax and the end.

- Brands that deliver only what the customer expects are noticed less; it is the unexpected experiences that stand out.

- The brain tends to remember your brand better and longer if you relate its benefits in the form of a story rather than as an itemized list.

- Brands need not limit the number of things they are about; but what they are about needs to tie into a coherent storyline.

- Brand stories that connect and associate with the consumer's other experiences and stories can be indelible.

- Brand stories and experiences do not have to be oversimplified or dumbed down; consumer continue to process information long after having seen the ad.

One thing I have said a number of times is that the more associations you create between your brand and the consumer's other experiences, the stronger your brand will be in their minds. One way for some brands to create stronger associations is by commissioning all five senses into the experience.

In the next chapter, we take a look at the role of our five senses in designing brands. After all, we see, hear, taste, feel, and smell our brands through our senses. Your strategy for designing brand experiences thus need a plan for each.

CHAPTER 12

BRAND SENSATIONS

66 ❙ felt enraged. I felt flabbergasted. I felt confused," fumed Chinyere Ezie, a staff attorney at the Center for Constitutional Rights, on Twitter.

It wasn't anything that anybody had said to her. It was what she saw in the Prada store window in the SoHo neighborhood of lower Manhattan that left her shaking to her core in anger. And that was a $550 Pradamalia character, the latest in the line of keychain figurines, that looked like a black monkey with outsized red lips.

She took a picture, posted it on her Twitter feed and Facebook page, and lit up a firestorm. Her post went viral, building a tsunami of outrage as people around the world saw in the fantasy charm, an obvious resemblance to "blackface," an odious image from a racist past. It sent executives at the Prada HQ scurrying for cover and apologizing profusely with:

The Pradamalia are fantasy charms composed of elements of the Prada oeuvre. They are imaginary creatures not intended to have any reference to the real world and certainly not blackface.

Prada Group never had the intention of offending anyone and we abhor all forms of racism and racist imagery.

To be fair, the entire Pradamalia collection did offer several other characters, most of whom looked nothing like monkeys and some even resembled aliens and spaceships.[1] But the damage was done.

This unfortunate incident offers an important lesson for cognitive brand marketers. *Our senses, comprising vision, hearing, smell, touch, and taste, are the gateway to our brain. They consciously and subconsciously awaken past experiences, the good and bad, and intertwine them with the present.*

Earlier in the week, Chinyere had returned from a visit to the National Museum of African American History and Culture in Washington and been deeply moved by the exhibits. And that day in New York, no one had tried to sell her a Pradamalia. Nor did she step into the store. It was only what she saw through the store window that enflamed what were still raw emotions from her visit to the museum in Washington.

Brands, in what they show, tell, feel, smell, and taste like, say a lot. *When designing and executing brand experiences, it is important to think of a plan for each sense,* or at least consider its impact on them, rather than have to make one as a by-product of an unforeseen crisis.

Most real-world brands have a theater of operations and ambassadors. They go to market through retail stores and/or a salesforce.

Sergio Zyman was Coke's chief marketing officer when they sponsored the Summer Olympics in Atlanta in 1996. Years later, I was Sergio's chief marketing officer in his consulting company. Sergio told me that when he ran the sponsorship for the Olympics, he had his teams build a thick binder called the Red Book, which was a detailed playbook for everything that Coke would do at the games. How and where Coke would be seen, who would do and say what and when, what it all meant, and how it all fit together in a single brand mosaic. The Olympics would be Coke's theater of operation. Anyone with the red Coke shirt would be a brand ambassador, and every moment would be choreographed according to the Red Book.

When consumers step into a brand's theater of operations or inter-act with its brand ambassadors, there is an opportunity to build immersive experiences for them by engaging their five senses. The strongest brand experiences, as we learned before, are those associated with multiple prior experiences. They are recalled easier and better, last longer, and feel more important to the brain. When marketers weave their brands with the human senses, they layer multiple associations in the experience that do exactly that, make it easier to recall and preferred. That's why *immersive sensory experiences make deep impressions on our brains and lure us to the brand.*[2]

If you walk down the Magnificent Mile in Chicago, even if you have never done that before, you can recognize the Burberry store with its trademark black and brown tartan crosshatches from blocks away with no help at all. The store design itself makes a visual statement about the brand. As you step inside, you can smell it.

During spring and summer, Zaluti scent machines diffuse the spring crocus scent, and during autumn and winter, a special autumn scent.[3] You look around and see that the wall colors are neutral with darker accents and furniture. That is deliberately orchestrated to bring to mind Burberry's classic trench coat or tartan pattern.[4]

The personal shopper who greets you leaves an impression with how they look and sound, and how they gently direct you to where you want to go in the store. Every one of those sensations adds a veneer to the unmistakably Burberry brand experience.

The brand theater of operations does not end with the store. Burberry also livestreams its runway shows, to share the excitement of decloaking new fashions as they happen with its fans worldwide, and lets them buy select new fashions online with its "see now, buy now" strategy.

Even brands like Away, Glossier, Farmer's Dog, Made In cookware, Lively Intimates, and Everlane that started out as pure play online brands, have opened exciting stores on Lafayette Street in New York. They realized that bringing people into a brick-and-mortar store was the best way to create immersive experiences—which is what many consumers want. Virtual companies like Facebook and Google have opportunities to expand their brand theater of operations into the real world with events and sponsorships.

In this chapter, I will lightly stray into the topic of how brain sciences can help brand ambassadors and brand theaters of operations engage the human senses. The truth is, cognitive selling can be the subject of a whole different book. We flirt with it here because salespeople are the torchbearers of the brands, and how they come across is how the brand comes across.

Now, when we discuss engaging the senses, you should know that the brain can mix up the signals it picks up.[5] This happens because sensory inputs are processed by shared neural circuits in the brain and separated by interpretation, considering the context and other cues. Most of the time, this works pretty well, but not always.

In the extreme, people who have synesthesia mix up their senses routinely because the brain messes up the contextually appropriate interpretation. So, for example, when they hear the sound of a trumpet, they may see the color orange or smell a lemon tartlike scent. You don't have to go to the extremes, or be a synesthete, to experience a bias called the *misattribution of arousal*.

As the theory goes, a number of stimuli elicit the same physiological response, for example, shortness of breath or racing heartbeats, which can confuse the brain into mixing one emotion with another. Exercising can cause your heart to beat faster. Meeting a person you are attracted to might do the same. Since the physiological response is the same and triggered by the same parts of the brain, cognitively you can confuse the two to some degree.

In this example, if you were to go jogging with this person you are attracted to, your hearts would race, the endorphins would flow (from the exercising), and you may feel a tad bit more attracted to each other than if you had only met and not run.[6] Yes, really! Yes, use it! Broadly, this means that in truly immersive experiences, when many senses are activated together, it all gets whisked into a single fantastic feeling and association about the brand. In the future, if even a few of those individual associations are missing, the brain can fill in the blanks from its memory.

With that, let's start peeling the onion a bit, one sense at a time, recognizing that every brand has to make its own calls on what senses to play with.

A PICTURE PAINTS
A THOUSAND WORDS

People believe that "what you see is what you get." You trust your own eyes. Yet many experts advise you against that; from the street magician who made your $20 bill disappear up his sleeve to ancient Indian philosophers who warned that the entire world was a *maya jaal*, a perverse illusion of our senses. Despite these warnings, we trust what we can see.

This gets the gears turning inside the heads of marketers, who ask, "What do people need to see to believe that my brand is really quite wonderful?" Visual selling is a System 1 tactic. As we know, System 2 is lazy. So if a picture looks good based on familiar patterns from the past or makes the choice seem easier, System 2 may take a pass saying, "If it looks good to you, System 1, it looks good to me." No further evaluation is necessary.

That is the direction Prudential Finance decided to take. Retirement planning is complicated, known to involve scrutinizing often depressing spreadsheets, and most people, especially the younger crowd, are not highly motivated to plan for a distant future. Prudential commissioned Harvard psychologist Dan Gilbert to help them find a way to get the message across simply.

Gilbert figured out that the one question most working professionals worry about is "Am I saving enough for retirement?" The challenge is how do you tell them "probably not" without getting mired in mind-bending spreadsheets? When you overload people with convoluted math models or make them feel anxious about their situations, they can shut down, stop listening to you, and run away. It is the "flight" part of a fight-or-flight response. So Gilbert took the show-them-a-picture route.

He helped design a series of commercials with games that end with the "probably not saving enough" answer in a visually memorable and tonally cheerful manner. In the Walkways Experiment,[7] the narrator asks several randomly intercepted young couples, "How much money do you think you will need in retirement?" The couples take a guess at a savings number that seems suitably large to them.

Next, they are lined up against what look like lanes in a bowling alley (see Figure 12.1). The foul line at the approach is day one of retirement

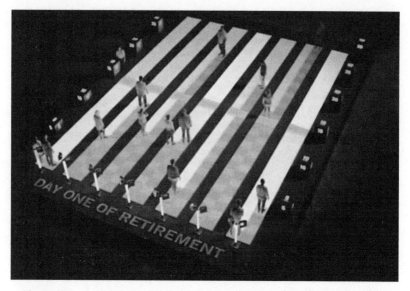

Figure 12.1   Prudential's ad gently pushes consumers to prepare for retirement.

and the back end of the lane is presumably the day they die. I say presumably because they don't spell that out so as not to darken the moment.

As each couple starts walking down the lane, like a bowling ball hurling slowly toward the pins, the tiles behind them light up blue signaling the passage of time in years. They can keep walking so long as they have money in the bank. When it turns orange, sorry, they just depleted their savings and have to stop.

The camera then pans to show that most couples are only partway down the bowling lanes and have a disconcertingly long way to go till the end in retirement with no money left. Picture shown, message sent.

The point of it all is that most people grossly underestimate the money they would need after retirement and therefore must talk to a Prudential planner immediately. The visual is light, but memorable, and without making you feel terrible, makes you wonder which lane you would be in. After all, there is only one person in the game in the commercial that makes it all the way to the end. The rest suffer an unspecified, but surely, disagreeable fate.

But what does all this do for Prudential, the brand? It tells consumers that Prudential can be a brand they can look to for helping them understand their retirement needs in a simple manner. That is not the only thing that Prudential the brand is about, but yes, that is one of the core brand equities.

In pharma marketing, visualization is a particularly effective way of communicating how drugs work. And that is quite a trick because pharma marketers themselves often don't know exactly how their drug works.

If you read the product label of many leading, multibillion-dollar medication brands, you will see an incomprehensible description of how certain proteins or cytokines work in the body, which then ends with a caveat like, "However, the relevance of specific JAK combinations (their drug!) to therapeutic effectiveness is not known." In plain English, that says, "Our drug does work, but we're not sure how." So if you don't exactly know how your own drug works, how do you explain to patients how it does. The answer? With a suggestive picture!

In focus groups with patients suffering from joint diseases, we discovered that there was a strong desire to get a medication that went straight to the root cause of the disease and worked from the inside of the body to fix what was wrong. The ad agencies went to work and came back with mockups of x-rayed human bodies showing glowing or flashing joints where patients usually report pain.

The concept boards tested well in research with patients, convincing them that the medication was going to work on the pain where the patients wished it would, namely, deep inside their bones at its root cause. No further explanation was necessary. Communicating how the drug works is a core part of the brand sense proposition and particularly important in convincing patients that the treatment is the right choice. All of this by the way is not intended to mislead patients—the scientists that designed the drug do completely believe that it gets at the root cause of the disease, and without that conviction, would not portray this.

While visualizations like these can be incredibly helpful, marketers still need to present impactful images unique to their brands. In the market for drugs addressing joint pain, most leading manufacturers have discovered that the glow-in-the-dark skeleton images test well with patients. So now, most competing drugs feature similar pictures in their television commercials. Even though the drugs are vastly different in some cases, the skeleton serves as a cue that makes them all look like they do the same thing.

Hence, in cognitive selling, it is important to own the visualization, like Burberry's signature tartan stripes, and associate it uniquely with your brand—or else it might help the category grow but not necessarily your brand differentially.

IF I CAN FEEL IT, TOUCH IT, IT'S REAL!

Even as scientists puzzle over the psychological connections between the sense of touch and behavior, it is not news for waiters and waitresses, the brand ambassadors, in the countless restaurants around the country. They have known that a slight, natural brush of arm with a customer creates an instant personal connect and—wait for this—bigger tips!

To be sure, April Crusco and Christopher Wetzel[8] studied the phenomenon and emerged with some interesting findings. It turns out, that a touch on the arm by a waitress increased customer tips anywhere between 10 and 40 percent. It could be anywhere on the arm, with the customer being male or female, at many different types of restaurant. "No touch" yielded a 12 percent tip on the average. A touch on the shoulder resulted in a 14 percent tip, while a touch on the palm a 17 percent tip.[9] Pretty impressive, isn't it? It happens subconsciously. The customer is not calculating, "Oh! if she touches my arm, I'm doing a bigger tip," but they do.

So what is it about a human-to-human gentle tap that is so reassuring and rewarding? Dr. Jane Gruber[10] of Yale University points out that an interpersonal touch (light handshake, pat on the back or arm) triggers reward centers in the brain of the person who is touched, making them more likely to cooperate (be receptive). Simply speaking, "touchers" make "touchees" feel more connected and aligned with you.

If you are a brand ambassador, field sales rep, or working with a customer in any way, you can use this information. It will help your cause if you gently touch the person on the arm or shoulder and increase their confidence in your brand.

Of course, make sure you are not creepy about it. In this instance, the brand ambassador is using the sense of touch to build a friendly and empathetic vibe with the customer so that the following brand proposition is more warmly received.

All of this may leave you wondering what a brand, like Coke, could do with touch other than serve up a nicely chilled can of the soda. Turns out, a lot! Fifty years ago, ad agency McCann Erickson designed one of the most iconic brand campaigns of all time for the Coca-Cola Company with the tagline, "I'd like to buy the world a Coke." The brand transformed itself to being the "real thing" that stood for uniting people of the world with a refreshing drink that everybody, no matter from where, could enjoy in a shared moment of happiness.[11]

Fast-forward 40 years to 2013 and hop over to the other side of the planet to India. Coke and its ad agency, Leo Burnett, unveiled an ingenious brand event "aimed at breaking down barriers and creating a simple moment of happiness between two nations at odds—India and Pakistan.[12]

If you read the Google search example in the prior chapter, you know that the two countries, which were once a single family, were sheared in two along religious lines by the British when they left India in 1947, and have since fought four wars among themselves and been bitter enemies. The clouds of suspicion linger, often fanned by politicians and religious cults.

Coke, with its initiative called "Small World Machines," installed vending kiosks in a mall in India with corresponding, connected ones in Pakistan. The machines were fitted with full-length, touch-sensitive, interactive screens that served as virtual portals between the two countries. If you were on the Indian side, you could walk up to it and put your palm on the screen and a person in the mall in Pakistan could do the same and put their palm against yours.

Over the three days, thousands across the two countries joined hands virtually and drew out peace signs in unison on both sides of the portal screens. Ten thousand chilled cans of Cokes were dispensed from the machines along with the warmth and happiness of two countries united virtually as one, if just for a moment. Andy DiLallo, the chief creative officer of Leo Burnett Sydney said:

Being on the ground in India during the Small World Machines experience is probably the highlight of my career so far. To be able to take two countries that have been divided and to unite them through the world's most iconic brand, and see the purity of the experience was amazing.

And DiLallo was Australian. Can you imagine how it felt for the Indian and Pakistani consumers?

Even though the touch was only virtual and momentary, the brain knows what a touch is supposed to feel like and is able to simulate emotions and sensations mentally without anyone touching anyone. The campaign commercial documenting the event has been seen on YouTube almost four million times.[13]

This was not just a feel-good gimmick with no benefit for the brand. As I mentioned earlier, the phenomenon of misattribution of arousal, where the brain confounds two stimuli with each other when they happen together, is at the root of the ad. The ad leads consumers to merge the elation from the experience of the event with the refreshing feelings from drinking the dispensed can of Coke. It goes to show that for determined and creative marketer there is always a way.

In the context of branding, when we think of touch, let me be clear that I am not talking about a consumer feeling a product to test its integrity. You may very well pull a sweater off the shelf in a store and yank it around from side to side to see if it tears and so be it. I am talking about touching the consumer in ways that say something more about your brand and build a greater sense of connectedness and alignment.

Another surprising truth about touching a product is that a touch of one object can trigger the purchase of an unrelated object.[14] There are a number of weird experiments that show this. In one, people who were asked to hold a warm therapeutic pad versus a cold one subsequently invested 43 percent more money with an investment planner. The feeling of warmth was misattributed by the brain for a sense of overall trust and safety.

Likewise, in another test, people sitting on hard chairs negotiated harder on prices than people sitting on soft cushioned chairs. When I worked with Dexter, a company that manufactured automotive coatings, we found that cheap plastic parts commonly used for the interior dashboard of a car when coated with tactile paints formulated to feel soft would communicate a sense of luxury in cars and make people more willing to pay a higher price for them. Touch is felt as texture, temperature, vibrations, pressure, weight, and humidity. It is good idea to think those elements through for your brand and marketing collateral.

SOUND ADVICE

Hearing is a sense that is "always on" and thus associated with every experience that we as humans have. It is always on because it is the first line of defense when we are asleep. For the prehistoric man, the best hope of detecting a threat while asleep, before he saw, felt, tasted, or even smelt it, was to *hear* it, wake up, and hide. Scientists tell us that even when we are in deep delta-wave sleep, neurons in the reticular activation system at the base of the brain stay active, listening to everything like a built-in alert system.[15]

Because the brain is associative, sounds can trigger recall of the experiences and emotions connected to them. We feel fear when we hear a blood-curdling scream and pure joy when we hear a young child crackle with laughter. If you have watched the movie *Jaws*, the music accompanying the arrival of the great white shark is undoubtedly burnt into your brain's circuitry. You only have to play the two-note sequence twice, as in "thumph-thumph, thumph-thumph," and people will look around and laugh nervously. Yes, try it at your next party. Without the movie experience, that sound would mean nothing, much less a great white on the prowl.

Music has always been a big part of the brand theater of operations, in retail stores and in both online and offline commercials. The brain's relationship with music is particularly intimate and mysterious. Music has its own persona. It can make us happy or sad just as another person can. When we hear music, we tap our feet, clap our hands, sway from side-to-side, and bob our heads. Who knows why, but we just do. No one is untouched by music. It is how our brain works.

The key to "sound selling" lies in the *Jaws* strategy. You can use sound to:

- Heighten brand experiences

- Create your own brand signature

- Even influence the pace of activity

As an example of the latter, research[16] shows that supermarket sales can be influenced by the tempo and type of the background music. Sales went up when slower music was piped through in a minor mode (a major scale had no impact). The slower music subconsciously caused customers to relax and slow down so that they browsed and bought more. Conversely, in a fast-food restaurant, music with a faster tempo will keep the lines moving along at a good clip and reinforce the brand impression of speed and efficiency. People tend to align their behavior with the background music.

Aren't you likely to get fewer irate customers in a store with tranquil music? Against the murmur of Beethoven's "Moonlight Sonata," wouldn't you rather whisper your complaints than blare them out at the top of your lungs?

If you are going to make sounds a part of your core brand experience, make them distinctive so they are part of your brand signature. Joel Beckerman, in his book *The Sonic Boom: How Sound Affects the Way We Think, Feel, and Buy*[17] gives some great examples of companies that have created iconic sounds enmeshed with their brand experiences. He tells us how Disney spaces out the different fantasy lands within the park with "fake quiet" sounds that kill extraneous noise. This is done to ensure that your experience of being in the Magic Kingdom is not dissected into bits by planes flying overhead or a passing semitrailer blasting its horn. Yes, they use sound to kill sound!

The restaurant chain Chili's amped up the sound of sizzling fajitas in its commercials to get the audience salivating and wanting to jump in their cars and go get one.[18] Since Nokia, every cell phone company has hunted for its own perfect ring tone to demarcate their brand signature to millions of users daily.

Man Made Music, a company founded by Beckerman, has mapped the emotions that connect to the sounds of different instruments, so you know what feelings to work into your brands:

- Strings—warmth, scale, or scope; passionate, uplifting

- Horns—power, elegance, impact, importance, strength, honor, bravery, and heroism

- Synthesizer—modern, forward-thinking, evolutionary

- Piano/percussion—heartfelt, emotive, personal, driving energy, velocity, or anxiety

- Drums—driving, motivating, primal, communal

- Electric guitar—power, youthful energy, rebellion

So there you have it. Next time, you want to sound off your brand, make it your own, make it add to the experience, and pace it to your desired experience.

IF IT SMELLS

The sense of smell is also another always-on sense and thus accompanies every brand experience.

Even while you sleep, the smell of smoke may alert you to a fire in the house. We can't possibly underestimate the power of smell. From scientists to budding Casanovas, there has been a high interest in locating and using pheromones to attract the opposite sex.[19] Unfortunately, no joyous news so far, unless you happen to be a fruit fly—and even then, there are detractors.[20]

However, smells can by design or inadvertently become a part of the brand experience; they can turn you on or turn you off.

Singapore Airlines has branded its own curated scent and proudly informs customers that "Stefan Floridian Waters fragrance is a signature aroma of Singapore Airlines.[21] It is used in the flight attendants' perfume, the airplane interiors, and infused into the hot towels given out on take-off." It is described as silky, feminine, and exotic by those with a discerning olfactory apparatus.

The strategy of using smell to enhance your brand is not just for rarefied brands like Singapore Airlines and Burberry. For the longest time, the scent of Procter & Gamble's (P&G) Tide has been the secret of its 70-year reign over the laundry detergent market. In 2018, Tide was the number one liquid laundry detergent in the United States, controlling over one-fifth of market sales[22] while commanding one of the highest price points of any brand.

Smell started as a necessity for P&G but became something much more. At the beginning, P&G added a fragrance to its detergent to hide the smell of the ingredients, alkyl sulfate and sodium triphosphate. Over time, the Tide scent evolved to a citrus, floral, and fruity combination, with hints of lemon, orange, lily, rose, and apple. Each scent has been market-tested to trigger specific associations for consumers. The smell of citrus relates to a sense of cleanliness. The sweet, fruity scents result in a feeling of comfort and well-being. The floral scents evoke maternal love and care. The scent of Tide recalls childhood memories of how the clothes smelled spilling out of Mom's laundry basket. It has kept millions of consumers across generations hooked to the brand, with its projected feelings of cleanliness and general happiness.

The brain science behind smells is quite extraordinary. Genes in the olfactory bulb of the brain can process and sense nearly a trillion different smells. Compare that to the 170,000 words in the English language; that is way more smells than there are words.

The smell receptors of the brain are connected directly to the emotional centers (amygdala and piriform cortex) in the brain. This simply means two things: (1) smells are connected to long-term emotional memories, and (2) people can be influenced by smell without being conscious of it.

This is why Singapore Airlines creates a lasting and subconscious brand impression with its Floridian Waters fragrance. If you are a retail store, you have to be thinking about the smell of your brand experience.

JUST FOR THE TASTE OF IT

The senses of smell and taste go together because the processing circuits in the brain are the same. If you hold your nose, you will find it hard to distinguish between the taste of chocolate and vanilla ice cream.

Instinctively, it feels like bringing food into a brand experience is a great idea. The idea of breaking bread with someone to build a relationship and engender cooperation is as old as time.[23] So, finally, let's take a look at the sense of taste.

Foods are associated with different experiences and occasions and tickle more than just your taste buds. Think about champagne. Comité Champagne of France reminds us that it hits every one of your five senses: "the soft sigh and hiss" of a correctly popped bottle; "the spectacle of the bubbles as they rise irrepressibly to the surface, collecting in a jostling ring to form the cordon" in your glass; and the scent of white flowers with a hint of orange peel. And then the taste, according to Louis Bohre, an early twentieth-century champagne explorer:

> The palate should be surprisingly but pleasantly sparkling, instantly seductive and velvety. The taste should have an underlying fruitiness, with a lingering fragrance that causes you to meditate silently and at length on the wine's aromatic qualities—long after you put down your glass.[24]

For me, the taste of champagne equates to an intense celebration in the mouth. It feels like a reward for an accomplishment. No wonder that most airlines will serve you champagne the minute you settle into their business class cabin. It feels like they are overjoyed to see you and celebrating your arrival. Hopefully, that starts you off happy on your long flight.

So how should you think about food and taste if you are a brand? If you are Chanel and you invite your best customers to a preview of the fall collection at the Oak Street store in Chicago, what should you serve as hors d'oeuvres? If you are a pharma rep calling on physicians, what is the best food or beverage to bring in for office "lunch and learns"?

Unfortunately, there is not a lot of research out there to help marketers layer their brand experience with taste! However, the basic rules still apply, namely that the sense of taste is linked to our emotional memories, and taste and emotions can influence each other.

It is hard to know whether specific tastes can put people in certain moods. There are six basic tastes: sweet, sour, salty, bitter, savory (umami in Japanese), and fatty. Generally, sweet, savory, and salty foods will influence moods, emotions and memories positively. Bitter tastes are a signal to the brain of things you should not be eating, like poisons, and are acquired over time. They are obviously riskier to incorporate into your brand experience than chocolates and caramel ice cream. Sweet flavors are generally winners and make people feel rewarded and celebratory.[25] Comfort foods (fats) convey a sense of security and well-being. Coffee improves moods, energy, and alertness during the day so long as you don't overdo it.

KEY TAKEAWAYS

In this chapter, we learned that both online and offline brands have an opportunity to create immersive and memorable experiences by engaging the five senses thoughtfully in the brand theater through their ambassadors.

- All brand experiences involve one or more of our senses.

- These sensory responses are woven into our emotional memories and can last for an awfully long time.

- Marketers must think about a plan for involving each sense to enhance the brand experience.

- Sensory experiences should be unique and act like a brand signature.

For marketers thirsting to learn more about sensory branding, the "go-to" encyclopedia of these methods is undoubtedly Martin Lindstrom's book *Brand Sense*.[26] It is chock-full of real-world examples and practical advice on making these approaches work.

With knowledge about how the brain works comes the power to control consumer behavior. That can tempt marketers to manipulate consumers and steer them to brand choices that are not beneficial for them. In the next chapter, we march on to take a look at the ethics of cognitive branding.

CHAPTER 13

MINDING YOUR MANNERS

You would think that I would be in love with RxBar.

It represents the heartwarming story of entrepreneur Peter Rahal, who parlayed a $10,000 investment in energy bars into a company that sold for $600 million to Kellogg's just four years after its launch. Rahal's success is fascinating for more than one reason. He is a lifelong dyslexic, which he says makes him a poor linear thinker, but gives him a superpower, namely, that of making out patterns and connections where others see just dirt and muck.[1]

In the hypercompetitive breakfast snack market, Rahal could see a gaping hole, an unmet need for a portable and nutritious energy bar targeted at the on-the-go, health-conscious consumer. His branding for the bars was equally brilliant. Each one typically consists of just five simple ingredients, all boldly spelled out on every pouch he sells as egg whites, dried fruit, nuts, and dates. And the fifth ingredient?

Oh! That is "No B.S."

That last item was in fact the brand. It leveraged the *transparency effect* (as we discussed in Chapter 6) to a tee to play up RxBar's clean-label positioning, turning millions of consumers into overnight devotees. So what's wrong with this pretty picture?

BRAND CUES THAT MAKE IT WHAT IT ISN'T

My issue with RxBar is its name. In the United States, *Rx* is a term commonly associated with something that is prescribed or recommended by a physician. Don't take my word for that. Here's what Merriam-Webster the dictionary says about *Rx*: "a doctor's prescription, also, something resembling a doctor's prescription in being an advisable or corrective course of action."[2]

Is RxBar prescribed or advised by a doctor? No. Would a doctor advise it? Maybe, given its healthy ingredients. Has a doctor actually advised people to take RxBar? Nope. Maybe the recipe is created by a doctor? No, Rahal concocted the ingredients in his mother's kitchen. For an energy bar that promises "No B.S." on every label, that is a lot of B.S.

The term *Rx* is a brand cue. The brain associates it with "doctor recommended" subconsciously given all of the past history and general use of the word. Thus, RxBar subconsciously cues its customers to believe that it is physician endorsed, which it isn't. The association with medical science triggers that in your brain without you being aware of it. Is that OK? On one hand you might argue that it is not like anyone is going to die from this. The bar is after all healthy and good for people. So no one is harmed.

However, there is a fine point of ethics here. When you use psychology—in this case, a *primed* association—to attract consumers to your brand, it is good practice to use it to convey what your brand is and not what it isn't.

On the other hand, White Claw, a hard seltzer that has become an overnight sensation with millennials in the United States, uses tall thin cans to hold its delicious alcohol-spiked beverages. The package cues the fact that the brand is low calorie. This is an example of a good cognitive branding practice, where you use subconscious cues to communicate something that your brand truly is.

Unfortunately, Kellogg's, the new owner of the RxBar, is going in the opposite direction with it. They are now using the *Rx* prefix as a foundation for a broader line of products, starting with, RX A.M. breakfast oats.[3]

But, hey marketers! Just because you can, should you?

ANCHORING FOR MORE

Let's go to another industry where I have spent a lot of time working, the credit cards. The best customers are those who borrow a lot at the relatively high interest rates that banks charge (and there are good reasons for that, by the way). They are wonderful because they depend on having access to credit to maintain their lifestyle and use the card for large purchases that they could not make otherwise. This could be anything from an unexpected medical expense to a dream cruise to the Bahamas with the family.

If you carry a balance with a credit card, you know that you have to make a minimum payment every month on the loan. This is the company's way of testing that you are good for the money and won't run away. You can always pay more than the required minimum, but not less without incurring a penalty. So here's a question for you.

If you are that consumer with a loan balance, how much should you pay? The minimum required payment or something more? Turns out that most (over half) balance-carrying customers pay something slightly more than the minimum regularly.

Now you are thinking, "Well, that's not surprising, people should pay what they can afford to pay back, right up to their payment capacity. If they can pay more, they should. Why pay more interest than you have to?"

When I was working with some of the largest credit card issuers in Latin America, here's what we discovered: people were using the suggested minimum payment as an anchor. In focus group discussions, they told us that if they paid something a little more than the minimum required payment, they felt like they were being fiscally more responsible.

Here's the rub. If you increased the minimum required payment, people would pay a little bit more than the new threshold. If you decreased the minimum payment, they would pay a little bit more than that reduced payment, or overall a little less. In other words, people were not paying according to their payment capacity but according to the suggested minimum. That is the good old *anchoring bias* at play for you. It is not just a curiosity; changing the minimum payment anchor can make hundreds of millions of dollars of difference to your profitability if you are a large credit card company.

Unfortunately, over time, many credit card companies lowered their required minimum payment, entrapping consumers in high-rate debt for a lifetime. This meant that if your credit card tagged the minimum payment at 2 percent of the owed balance, and the interest rate was 18 percent per year or 1.5 percent per month, you would repay roughly 0.5 percent of the principal per month. Seventy-five percent of your payment every month would be interest and you would repay your debt in 20 years or so. Since most people keep buying more things over time, in practice, they never repay their debt.

In the United States, where credit card debt now stands at nearly $1 trillion, the government decided that enough was enough. It passed the Credit Card Accountability Responsibility and Disclosure (CARD) Act in 2009, intervening with its own anchoring tactic. It required card issuers to specify on each monthly statement how much the consumer had to pay if they wanted to settle their full balance in three years and also how long it would take them to zero it out if they paid only the minimum. These new anchors led consumers to repay their debts slightly faster, but not that much more so.[4] Not all anchors work equally well.

If you are the marketer at the credit card company, what would you do? You could take the stand that no one is forcing anyone to take debt on their credit card or to make only the minimum required payment. You may also worry that you are taking advantage of a known human frailty. As a society, is it a good thing that millions of consumers are burdened with debt for life? Did it have to take an act of government to do anything at all?

Just because you can, should you?

MORE THAN PUTTING
TWO AND TWO TOGETHER

For my final case study on moral dilemmas for cognitive marketers, let's consider the psychological phenomenon called the *illusion* of causality.[5] The brain likes to connect the dots even when it should not. People tend to believe there is a causal connection between two events that are in reality unrelated.

Let me give you two random words—"boss" and "grand piano." What do you think of them? In numerous workshops around the world, when I do this same exercise, half my audience believes that I am going to say my boss is oversized like a grand piano, and the other half, that I'm plotting to drop one on her. To be clear, nothing can be farther from the truth: I am the managing director of my firm and I have no boss. I just picked those two words randomly, just as I explained.

This predisposition for causality makes consumers make all kinds of conclusions from conveniently provided end posts. And that gives marketers all kinds of ideas. It is kind of like the power of suggestion but without the actual suggestion and with only the hints.

Let me go back to our work on PediaSure. In that case, we were simply building on the moms' own beliefs around nutrition and its effects on their kids. They already believed that their children did not eat well. They were convinced that if their kids did not eat well, they would suffer from ungodly mental and physical dislocations in later life. We simply had to acknowledge these two goal posts and position PediaSure as the solution.

Now, there is in fact no evidence that suggests it would be better for kids to eat the same foods that adults do nor that if they don't, they will suffer any adverse health effects. Kids may very well eat the way they do because that is how nature wants them to. We simply don't know. We do see anecdotally that even kids who don't gobble up daily buckets of arugula turn out just fine.

But for the moms in Jakarta, the concerns around their children not eating the way they wanted them to were profound and made them feel awful. For us as marketers, it was easier to go with the flow, acknowledge their fears, and position PediaSure as an answer. It made for happier moms and kids and fewer mealtime battles.

Even so, our client, Abbott, was conscientious about not making an over-the-top claim and had invested in clinical studies to factually back up their core claim of balanced and complete nutrition. In contrast, many of their competitors in the Asian markets were unrestrained and promised unproven benefits like increased intelligence in the child using the illusion of causality.

In the pharmaceutical industry, drugs are serious business. Any claim you make must be supported by facts. Marketing by the illusion of causality gets the FDA's goat. Drug commercials commonly feature patients taking a medication and then dancing around like fireflies in the summer heat. After all, where is the proof that those specific activities will be possible from that particular drug for every patient, asks a testy FDA? Thus pharma companies have to qualify their claims and say that "individual results vary" or that only a certain percent of the patients on the drug achieve those results.

Warning letters from the FDA to drug manufacturers fly fast and furious after every perceived infraction and are dutifully recorded on a public website and make for some excellent in-between-flights reading,[6] if you are that kind of a guy (which I am). If you are so inclined, you can exploit the illusion of causality to make people draw conclusions about your products without saying the words.

But just because you can, should you?

THE DARK SIDE OF COGNITIVE BRANDING

There is a dark side to cognitive branding. We know that our brain processes information subconsciously or with low vigilance 95 percent[7] of the time. It takes mental shortcuts and is susceptible to making some choices that are not the most beneficial for us. That is just how the brain works and there is no getting around it. Armed with the new knowledge of the mechanics of the brain, marketers may be tempted to devise strategies that benefit their brands at the expense of the consumers. But just because they can, should they?

This is becoming a major issue to grapple with in the digital age that we live in, where brand stimulus can be delivered at lightning speed to millions of consumers. A 2019 study[8] by researchers at the University of Chicago found substantial use of "dark patterns" by a number of online retail brands. Dark patterns are "user interface design choices that benefit an online service by coercing, steering, or deceiving users into making unintended and potentially harmful decisions."

DARK PATTERNS AND THE TRUMP 2020 CAMPAIGN

When consumers are messaged by a brand they trust, they tend to do what it says without a lot of vigilance. That is our System 1 at work. Unscrupulous marketers use this fact to exploit their customers. Toward the tail end of the 2020 US presidential election, Donald Trump's campaign, which was running on fumes financially, adopted dark patterns as a mantra for their fundraising efforts.

It was business as usual for the campaign to create a virtual minefield of psychological traps on its online site to make donors unwittingly give a lot more than they planned to. For example, after you had committed to making a donation of say $100, the page would present a box that said in bold black letters "We need to know we haven't lost you to the Radical Left. If you UNCHECK this box, we will have to tell Trump you're a DEFECTOR and sided with the Dems. CHECK this box and we can win the House and get Trump to run in 2024." Yes, really! The box was prechecked with a tick mark and was then followed in nonbold, smaller type letters saying "Make this a monthly recurring donation." In other instances, the same small-type message made the donations weekly!

Confirmshaming is a dark pattern technique for guilting the user into opting into something they didn't intend to. The option to decline is worded in such a way as to shame the user into compliance. In this case you would be a defector lost to the radical left if you so much as dared to uncheck the box.

RoachMotel is a technique whereby it is easy for you to get into a situation but getting out is problematic. If you did get signed up for weekly recurring donations to the campaign, cancelling them would be an entire production.

Misdirection is when the site design purposefully focuses your attention on one thing to distract your attention from another. Here again, the first part of the message, which contains many of the things a Trump supporter might agree with, was prominent and the part about a monthly commitment was much less so and likely to be missed as routine fine print.

I didn't cherry-pick the preceding example. A *New York Times* investigation showed that the Trump campaign used dark patterns systematically and consistently to target their loyalists.[9] When Harry Brignull, a user experience designer, published his original list of dark patterns,[10] it was meant as a guide for marketers of what not to do. Who knew that the Trump campaign would make it their bible for exactly what to do? To be sure, Democrats too used some dark pattern techniques in their fundraising (which they absolutely shouldn't have), but nowhere near as much as the Trump campaign, which mastered it into a fine art.

For brand marketer, minding your manners is critically important. Acts like the preceding have real consequences in people's lives. The same story by the *New York Times* also highlighted the case of one Trump donor, a cancer patient, who gave a generous $500 to the campaign from his monthly income of $1,000, only to find that $3,000 had been withdrawn from his account over the next 30 days, leading his bank to bounce his scheduled utility and rent payments.

Marketers, no matter their political leanings, would do well to remember that their actions have real consequences on real people's lives. With knowledge comes responsibility.

The researchers revealed that 11 percent of the roughly 11,000 retail sites analyzed used such tactics. Remarkably, there is a whole industry of third-party suppliers that sell dark pattern engines for rapid deployment by any retail website. The researchers cataloged 15 different types of dark patterns, some of which use psychological approaches, such as artificial scarcity (loss aversion bias), suspect peer reviews (in-group bias), and confirmshaming. The latter refers to the practice of using negative language to describe actions that the consumer would take to reject a brand, for example, "No thanks, I don't want to take advantage of this incredible offer."

Online companies are investing heavily in the use of psychology in their branding and marketing. In 2015, Jeff Bezos, Amazon's CEO, set off alarm bells when he announced to shareholders that his company used 70 million psychological nudges per week through the company's Selling Coach program.

One concern is that in the gig economy, marketers have asymmetrically more information than their customers.[11] By choosing what they disclose, marketers can powerfully influence consumer behavior.

For example, when a website tells you that six people just bought the brand you are looking at, they know but fail to disclose that another 120 took a pass. Uber has come under scrutiny for using its information base to nudge drivers to work longer, which in turn keeps more drivers on the road and the price per ride low.[12] Instagram, WhatsApp, Twitter, and virtually all other social networks are under scrutiny for hooking consumers to their devices by offering the brain small emotional rewards in the form of pings, alerts, and notifications that can be addictive (hit the same neural reward centers that drugs of abuse do).[13]

These concerns are not new to marketers. By definition, any brand stimulus is going to subconsciously influence consumers, from the music you play in your store to the shape of your packaging. The harder question is, where do you draw the line?

THREE TESTS FOR
ETHICAL COGNITIVE BRANDING

Rather than be told by the government how to behave, marketers should regulate their own behavior themselves. To help determine where to draw the line on what's ethical, in my company, Cerenti, we developed three imperatives for testing whether the brand strategies we were proposing were ethical:

1. **Canonical Imperative.** Do to others as you would they do to you. Ask the question: If someone did this to me, would I be fine with it?

2. **Categorical (Kantian) Imperative.**[14] Do to others only that, which if done by everyone else too, would be good for society. Ask the question: If everybody started doing what I am doing, would that be a good thing?

    This particular rule is necessary because some people may have a low bar for themselves and others, and dubious behaviors would pass the first test above. For example, in a number of developing countries, some people are not only fine taking bribes but also giving them. In other words, bribing clears the canonical imperative in their case. However, the categorical imperative asks, what if everybody started accepting bribes to get things done? Would that be a good thing for society?

3. **Sunshine Imperative.** Do only that, which if made public, can be easy to defend and explain. Ask the question: If this story broke on page one of the *New York Times*, am I going to look like scum?

RxBar fails in the canonical imperative. Would you like it if brands that you buy were subtly embedding cues that make you believe they offer benefits that they actually don't? That they were recommended by doctors when they weren't?

Credit card companies that offer high interest rates and disproportionately low minimum payments that entrap people in debt failed all three tests. That is why they have earned a bad rap, become the punching bag for aspiring politicians, and been told by the government how to behave.

What about PediaSure implying that children will grow up healthy, physically and mentally, with its balanced and complete nutrition? I feel it clears all three tests fine. It meets the canonical imperative. Remember I told you Walt, the marketing director, used to give PediaSure to all his kids and drink it himself regularly. No problem with the Categorical Imperative as well. If all kids started doing what Walt's kids were doing, no harm done. There is certainly plenty of evidence to show that the vitamins and minerals that PediaSure offers are beneficial for the human body. Abbott also had done clinical studies that established that PediaSure was balanced and complete nutrition as defined by acceptable medical standards. One can reasonably expect those nutrients to contribute to the well-being of the kids. It also meets the test of the Sunshine Imperative, in that if it were published that there is no evidence that healthier eating makes for healthier adult lives, people would understand that those are the normal uncertainties of life.

KEY TAKEAWAYS

In some ways, this is the most important chapter in the book. Power with restraint is the best kind of strength of all. Cognitive brands work the way our brain works and for the good of our consumers. Stephen Genco puts it well when he says: "Covert persuasion is unethical if it disrupts, disregards, or attempts to displace a consumer's existing goals with new goals that benefit the seller but do so by damaging the health, wealth, or happiness of the buyer."[15]

I provide the three tests any branding program must pass for it to be an ethical cognitive brand:

- Canonical: Would you want somebody to do this to you?

- Categorical: Would it still be a good idea if everybody did this?

- Sunshine: Would you run for cover if everyone saw what you're doing?

In the next and final chapter, we close by taking a look at what lies in the future of cognitive branding.

CHAPTER 14

WHERE DO WE GO FROM HERE?

B rain sciences are advancing at a near breakneck pace. In the future, brand marketers will know more and be able to do more. Yet life will be harder, not easier. Some of that will be because we, brand marketers, will need to work hard to stay abreast of the scientific advances.

But the hardest part of the change will be the necessity of evolving ourselves and our own minds. Let's take a look at what's coming down the road and at what we have to rewire inside our own heads.

READ MY MIND

What if you could get a computer printout of exactly what the customer is thinking? Wouldn't that make life a lot easier? And that's the reason for the current fascination that many marketers have with the new wave of neuromarketing research.

For a long time, market research specialists have known that customers do not always say what they do, and in some cases, may not be aware of what they might do, when presented certain brand choices. This makes it hard to figure out through instruments like customer surveys and focus groups sessions—the workhorses of market research—which brands consumers will actually buy. So, it is tempting to ask if there is a way to stick a probe through customers' ears and get a true reading of their thoughts and intent, maybe even the subconscious ones that they are not aware of. For marketers, that would be really nice and convenient.

With advances in brain science, there are many different tools for peering into the brain. You can strap consumers to electronic devices, expose them to a brand stimulus, and see what lights up. While these techniques are still not completely developed, there is enough underway that it is worthwhile for marketers to start dabbling in such research and get their feet wet.

One of the more accessible and promising tools to use these days are eye scanners. They can be either mounted at the bottom of a computer screen or in the form of nonintrusive eyeglasses like wearable devices. These are available, along with appropriate software, at a relatively low cost. The devices track eye movement and pupil dilation.

If a research subject is watching a brand advertisement on a computer monitor, the marketer can tell what part of the screen the person looked at, how long it took them to get to the desired areas of the picture, what sequence of eye movements got them there, and the level of reaction. As we noted before, humans use relatively few visual cues to create an image and thus knowing precisely what parts in an advertisement or web page matter can be valuable information.

New Balance, the athletic shoe manufacturer, fine-tuned its television campaign by using eye trackers. They compared two campaigns, one based around the idea of the consumer feeling fiercely independent in their New Balance footwear and another around a community theme of "your friends and family rooting for you to do well." New Balance found that viewers engaged more intensely with the latter. Marianne McLaughlin, Global Consumer Insights leader at New Balance, said:

This allowed the company to efficiently zero in on the right campaign. Initially it was a learning curve—but the consistent delivery of highly impactful results (from eye trackers) built a level of trust, to the extent that today we require neuro evaluation of marketing, content, and programming. With a turnaround time of five to eight days, neuroscience compares favorably to more traditional approaches to creative testing. In the world of global fast fashion, we need to respond quickly. It's an absolute necessity.

That sums it up pretty well. You get the idea.

Besides eye tracking, a number of other tools are available to market researchers. Eye-tracking tools may be used in combination with software for facial expression analyses that can help you infer the type of emotional response and its valence (positive or negative).

Law enforcement agencies have long used lie-detectors that measure skin conductance (rate at which you sweat) to predict whether a suspect is telling the truth or not. That's galvanic skin response (GSR) measurement and may be used to sense subconscious arousal to a brand stimulus.

Electroencephalography (EEG) measures the brain's electrical activity and can help determine brain engagement, motivation, frustration, and cognitive workload. Academic researchers and those with a few million dollars to spare can buy a functional magnetic resonance imaging (fMRI) unit to directly peer into the brain's activity. fMRIs use changes in blood flow to detect areas of the brain that are in use and display them on computer screens in colorful three-dimensional plots.

Despite these technological advances, we are far from reading anybody's mind. And don't hold your breath, because we are not about to get there anytime soon. Even with the most advanced brain scanners, we can see that there is something going on in the brain, but interpreting what exactly it means is a whole different matter.

You may see that a subject is having an emotional reaction to your ad, but you can't tell what the emotion is or even if it is positive or negative. Research shows that the brain does not have hundreds of distinct neural areas dedicated to interpreting the multitude of emotions we feel. Instead, there may be just one core effect[1] that we feel, which is interpreted by the brain in a thousand different ways based on context.

In a sense, your brain is like your cell phone screen. Tapping any part of it activates the same electronic sensor (or core effect) that sits underneath the display, but what the action means depends on what particular application was running at the time. Context can make the same effect, namely a particular area of the brain lighting up, mean a million different things. You could try to uncover that meaning by combining the information from multiple devices, but is it any better than just doing a focus group?

In certain limited scenarios, researchers have had phenomenal success with neuromarketing-based methods. Researchers at Emory were able to predict a song's future popularity more accurately by observing fMRI signals within subject brains than by simply asking them how much they liked the music.[2] Similarly, a team led by Dr. Moran Cerf at Northwestern was able to predict the future success of movies with 20 percent greater accuracy than traditional methods by using EEG readings of audience members.[3]

So there's something there. If you have the budget, it is worthwhile for you to figure out which areas of your marketing research can benefit from neuromarketing. But don't ditch your conventional research anytime soon.

A summary of the most commonly used tools in neuromarketing is provided in the following table (see Table 14.1).

So what are marketers to do until such time as we can read people's minds with a handheld scope? My view is that good qualitative research is the key to uncovering insights that result in great brands. The supercomputer nesting inside our own skulls is not perfect but pretty darn good when suitably trained in the craft.

Those deep in the art of marketing sciences will immediately point out that methods like focus group discussions are overused and flawed. True, but so are all other methods, including particularly those based on neuromarketing. The real trick is to not rely too much on any one method, but to use many different ones.

When you are trying to understand the mind of a consumer, it is akin to understanding personal relationships. To decide how great a work col-

Table 14.1. Neuromarketing Techniques

	BRAIN SCAN		BODY SCAN		
	METABOLIC CHANGES	ELECTRICAL CHANGES	PHYSICAL CHANGES		Eye tracking
	fMRI (functional magnetic resonance imaging)	EEG (electro-encephalogram)	Biometrics	Facial coding	
Commonly Used Tool	(functional magnetic resonance imaging)	(electro-encephalogram)			
What it tracks	Which parts of a person's brain are active and how active they are	How stimulated is the brain	How normal is a person's sweating, breathing, and heart rate	How a person's facial muscles are reacting and changing	What a person is looking towards and whether the pupils are dilated
What it does in response to a brand stimulus	Maps oxygen and blood flow in regions of the brain known to be associated with specific functions or emotions	Detects electrical activity (usually ERPs)† caused by neurons firing in the brain at different frequencies and intensity	Uses a galvanometer and electrocardiogram (ECG) to measure changes in skin moisture (skin conductance) and heart activity	Uses cameras and software to detect and classify voluntary and involuntary movements of facial muscles into distinct expressions	Uses cameras and software to map pupil movement, angle, and dilation
What it could tell us about people	• How stimulated is the brain • What senses are being activated (sensory perception) • What is getting coded into memory and can be recalled • What emotions (including trust, craving, preference, loyalty) a person is feeling	• How attentive, engaged or excited is a person • How quickly a person recognizes or recalls a stimulus • Whether the person is reacting positively or negatively (valence)	• How stimulated is the person • What is the level of emotional engagement	• What are the conscious and subconscious emotional responses • Measures core emotions: anger, dislike, envy, fear, sadness, surprise, smile	• What in a visual draws focus, attention, excitement, or confusion • What parts of an image people scan for or focus on—and how quickly

(continued on next page)

Table 14.1. Neuromarketing Techniques (*continued*)

Common brand research applications	• Testing emotional and sensory response to new products or campaigns • Rebranding • Predicting choices • Identifying needs	• Testing video advertisements—including identifying key moments • Testing taglines and copy • Testing in-store experiences and website usability	• Testing video advertisements or trailers • Measuring emotional reactions in real-world environments	• Testing subconscious spontaneous emotional reactions to campaigns	• Improving web design • Testing store/shelf layout and customer experience • Testing package design • Establishing hierarchy of perception (what is noticed first/last)
What are the advantages	• Gold standard for predicting future decision-making and measuring specific emotions	• More portable and less expensive than fMRI • Extreme time-sensitivity allows researchers to pinpoint exact stimuli that cause reactions • Can measure rapidly changing reactions • Less intrusive	• Good portability and ability to detect a range of emotions • Non-intrusive	• Relatively ease in measuring spontaneous and unconscious reactions • Non-invasive • Less expensive • Easy to use	• Easy portability allows for in-field testing • Non-intrusive • Less expensive • Easy to use
What are the limitations	• Very expensive; limited to small sample sizes • Requires subject to lie still inside a lab machine, for a long time • Tested tasks can have limited complexity • ess time-sensitive than EEG	• Low spatial resolutions means it cannot measure precise emotions, only valence • May be overly sensitive to irrelevant stimuli	• Cannot tell the valence of emotion (excitement and stress look similar) • Physiologic responses lag several seconds behind brain activity making time-determinations impossible	• Some subjectivity in coding emotions, especially with a large range of facial structures	• Software and equipment can be expensive • Reliant on participant's eye-conditions • Considered to be less reliable; requires a large sample • Often used in combination with EEG

* Bercea, Monica Diana. "Anatomy of Methodologies for Measuring Consumer Behavior in Neuromarketing Research." (2012).
† ERP stands for event-related potential which is a specific neuron or neuron group firing as a result of a perceived stimulus.

league is, you may look at how good they are as an individual contributor when they have to produce a work product without help; as a team member when they have to deliver a result for which they must depend on others; and as a person who you might be stuck with at an airport for several hours and just have a chilled beer with.

Likewise, to get real insights into consumers, instead of just one method, use a mix of them, including in-depth individual interviews (IDIs), focus group discussions (FGDs), metaphor elicitation techniques (involves implicit association tests [IAT] like interpretive storytelling and image association), and in-home observational research.[4]

MAKING SENSE

While the senses are the gateway to our minds, there are more portals into it than you think, and in the future, we may discover more. As a marketer, you want to keep an eye on that too.

Senses have been regarded by philosophers as irreducible sensations. That means you cannot explain a sense to anyone who does not know it already. If one of your five senses has not worked from the time you were born, it is impossible for anyone to explain that sensation to you in a way that you could understand the experience of that sense.

We have more than five senses, maybe twice that or more.[5] For instance, there are senses in our body to track its balance and velocity. If you have ever walked headfirst into a solid wall while checking your Instagram feed from @lizzywithaquill and felt the world spin dizzyingly around, you have experienced what these senses do.

For companies whose brand experiences involve putting you in motion, these hidden senses are important to know and manage. Airlines have to design a flight takeoff and landing experience that does not cause nausea and for that reason don't have aircrafts take off faster and at sharper angles even though mechanically they could. Disney parks, on the other hand, may *want* you to feel that pit in your stomach on its *Star Wars* Rise of the Resistance ride when the ship jumps into hyperspace.

In the future, scientists may invent devices that generate entirely new human senses. For example, we may wear devices that allow us to sense electric fields in the way sharks do or the earth's magnetic field like bats do. Those would be the technological breakthroughs of a lifetime and would create a whole new dimension of brand experiences.

Already, gaming companies are playing with virtual reality (VR) systems that enhance our perceptions of reality. In the future, augmented senses will be as common as the Apple Watches and require marketers to rethink their brand experiences more expansively.

FIRE YOURSELF!

The hardest challenge for marketers lies not in tracking the technological advances but in evolving their own mindsets. Cognitive branding is like a new religion. You need to activate your System 2 processes to truly get it, but that is the mental process that is lazy and takes a lot of effort to use.

When I teach cognitive branding in workshops with companies, I see that people try to reduce it down to something that they know already. After all, if it is like something you already know, then there is no need to spend any time and effort on learning it. "Isn't this just like the functional and emotional branding?" they ask. Or "This is the same left-brain-right-brain research we have been doing, right?" chime in others. Nothing is farther from the truth (see the box Cognitive Branding Knowledge Essentials), but that is their System 1 trying to associate the new knowledge of cognitive branding to something familiar and old. It is a natural reaction, but also a reliable formula for not learning.

COGNITIVE BRANDING KNOWLEDGE ESSENTIALS

You may know cognitive branding already if:

- You are conversant with the following five fields of study and research:

    - Evaluative conditioning and priming (chapter on brand vibes)
    - System 1 process of the brain (chapter on instinctive brand sense)
    - System 2 process of the brain and behavior therapy principles (chapter on deliberative brand sense)
    - Self-determination theory (chapter on brand resolve)
    - Experiencing and remembering self-concepts (chapter on tales from the trenches)

- You have used the knowledge from these fields to design and execute your brands.

- You have both failed and succeeded on those efforts.

Cognitive branding is the forte of marketers who want to think about and constantly question what they see in customers and markets. Several of my clients have established incredibly detailed processes for launching innovative products. Every step in the process gets its own box with a carefully assigned step number (think something like "3.6.2") and customer research is churned out mechanically. Unfortunately, the better the process, the worse the outcome.

Process maps feel comfortable in corporate environments because they fit well with project management Gantt charts. They create an illusion of progress. Brand strategies arising from these are often unremarkable, falling deep into the sea of sameness. Cognitive branding does not fit neatly into the current boxes. Accepting that can be difficult but can help create spectacular brands that customers love.

Ravi Dhar, a behavioral sciences professor at the Yale School of Management who has done a lot of work on the psychology of consumer decision making, notes that change is hard because it creates uncertainty.[6] One of Dhar's executive program trainees, an insights executive from a bank, said, "What I learned after three days (in a class about behavioral sciences) is that I should fire myself, and we should do things totally differently." So true! For those with that kind of self-awareness, the rewards from cognitive branding are extraordinary.

The brand marketers of the future need to dive a lot deeper into the fields of psychology, behavioral science, and human emotion science. These areas are experiencing explosive growth, and marketers need to not only stay on top of the new research but also figure out how to apply it to their brands. They have to think more and strive to connect the dots better between science and consumer psychology. Marketing leaders will in most cases not be able to do it on their own without bringing specialists, schooled in behavioral sciences, into their departments and creating the experimental environment that the field needs to work in to be effective.

With many of our clients, we are setting up Cognitive Science Application Labs (CSALs) within their marketing departments. The CSALs are responsible for adapting principles from academic research to the business, testing them in field and monitoring their performance. The field of behavioral sciences is experimental and experiential in nature. Perfection follows from the rapid testing and refinement of new ideas. It takes creativity, new mindsets, and the acceptance of a bias for change.

In the coming years, we will continue to learn more and more about ourselves and how our brain works. What we know already today is game changing. No matter how that plays out, the future of cognitive branding will remain *Right Between Our Ears.*

ACKNOWLEDGMENTS

n my life, I have been fortunate to have had many teachers. Not just the ones in dusty classrooms, from St. Xavier's in Jaipur to Yale University in New Haven, but everywhere around me, from my brilliant peers at Cerenti and discerning clients around the world to my always-curious friends and family. I have soaked in what I learned from them like a wet rag under a gushing stream. In this book, I squeeze that rag and let the water drizzle out, if only to make room for more.

I would especially like to thank some of the early soldiers who slogged through the first draft of the manuscript, which at the time was more of a brain dump than a real book. Bill Dempsey—when he was not in a meeting with the four boards he is on, or biking the 50 miles that he regularly does in the Florida sun—was reading my notes and sending detailed emails with useful feedback. Alok Sharma, who himself is an in-demand, innovative analytic marketer, helped take the manuscript to a whole new level.

Sam Hill, one of the best writers I know, has given measured counsel throughout my journey as a fledgling writer, from the time we both worked at Booz Allen, to now, when he would have no reason to bother. Sam made sure I didn't embarrass myself then with my prose, or now.

Dane Tyson, who worked as a partner at Cerenti, warned me that his advice on the book would dwell solely on the negatives. That preamble was followed dutifully by a tightly wound, 3,000-word, single-spaced essay, with three levels of bulleted points delivering on the said premise—and thankfully so. Steve Genco, who is probably the most serious thinker about the implications of brain sciences for marketing, was generous with his time and provided several thoughtful suggestions on improving the core cognitive branding principles. His own book, *Intuitive Marketing*, is the most rigorous tome on cognitive marketing that readers wishing for deeper technical details on the underlying research would want to reach for.

Those brave souls were not the only ones to endure readings of the early manuscript. Jay Prenta, Shyam Khemani, Atul Mathur, Nikhil Pandit, Allan Weiss, Sharat Mathur, and Sharad Bhargava were among the many accomplished marketers who weighed in. In writing this book, I discovered that the publishing industry lives on a planet of its own, with its own unique laws of physics and mostly gravity. Anna Biehn, Michele Wucker, Philip Revzinn, and Hank Gilman offered valuable lessons on how to navigate the terrain.

Most of the ideas in the book came from my consulting practice. At Cerenti, we have had a rock-solid culture of holding ourselves accountable for ferreting out the truths in branding through unflinching and at times raucous debate. It eats up a lot of time, but often results in very cool insights for helping our clients build epic brands. So I thank the many colleagues who worked with me on our many branding engagements, including Sudeep Haldar, Aryaman Sudhama (spent a whole summer on research for the book), Danlei Yan, Rachel Lee, Kathryn Mertes-Egland, Dane Tyson, Lynn Whitman, Mark Grossman, Jim Evans, Dipanjan Chatterjee, Cesare Espinosa (deputized from Mastercard), Erik Leipman (on loan from Pinnacle Biologics), Rima Nair, Puja Lakhanpal, Constantin Loghinov, Silvana Hernandez, Jonathan SooHoo, Mike Connors, and Terioska Gamez. It was work for sure, but always amazingly fun.

Our best clients at Cerenti were exacting and pushed us to dig deep into the recesses of marketing to unearth the best answers for them. After all, it was their money and brands at risk. I want to particularly thank Matt Fisher, Willy Pardinas, Keli Walbert, Guillermo Herrera, Gustavo Abelenda, Ian Jarrett, Tim Walbert, Mark Silverman, Lutz Schlitz, Todd Smith, Brent Paul, Jorge Alfaro, Jaime Parades (always first to test cool new ideas), Kezia Zito, Erik Von Borcke, Greg Tatsukawa, John Lane,

Andy Leong, Vikram Karnani, Vivek Mohan, Susan Hazelwood, Paul Catenero, Ulises Vergara, John Kody, Aaron Lillybridge, Rafael Arana, Ignacio Lara, Prashant Shah, Alain Delongchamp, Jill Rahman, Joep Wijman, and Peter Kaemmerer.

I would also like to thank my agent, Esmond Harmsworth of Aevitas Creative, who, without a doubt, is among the best in the business and who I was truly lucky to find. Esmond is strategic and methodical, and you could easily imagine why I, as a consultant, would love that. More so, he knows exactly what he is doing even when you don't and gets the job done just when you think it is not going to be.

Donya Dickerson, the associate publisher at McGraw Hill, is a sheer delight to work with. The funny thing is that Donya describes my book way better than I do, and every time she does this, I notice something new about it. Now, isn't that wild? Last, but not least, I want to thank Kevin Commins, development editor, and Patricia Wallenburg for making what may well have been painful edit cycles, a piece of cake.

I also give a shout-out here to my good friend Hitendra Wadhwa, who teaches an inspirational course on inner personal leadership at Columbia University in New York. Two summers ago, he invited me to sit in on some of his classes and ruminate on what, at this stage of my life, my own purpose might be. That clarity followed from the team of super-bright students I was paired with, who asked of me, "Why haven't you written a book?" I didn't know why they asked such a peculiar question or have a great answer for them then. But now, here it is. Thank you, guys! You know who you are. Another friend, Anurag Sharma (Leo), author of the *Book of Value* and a popular professor of strategy at the University of Massachusetts, Amherst, gave valuable tips on how to get started on a book in the first place.

My family encouraged me throughout this project in innumerable ways. Actually, I'd like to say they were active collaborators at times and forced sounding boards at others (think mealtime entrapment). My two sons, who are normally a step ahead of me in all matters related to the emerging arts and sciences, and routinely skeptical of my theses, were a recurrent test bed for my ideas. Ishaan was among the few to suggest that methods developed in the practice of cognitive behavior therapy may be

a source of inspiration for choice paradigms. Ashwin was helpful in iden-
tifying tech brands for my case studies. My wife, Sujata, who has a natural
instinct for spotting great brands and buying them with class and flourish, helped research case studies on South Asian brands, which in my
opinion, play a starring role in some chapters of this book—as does she
in my life.

My parents taught me more things than I will ever remember and I
can imagine this book couldn't have come together without them. They
never asked for anything in return and would surely be embarrassed if I
did try to thank them. But I do hope they will derive the same pleasure
from this as they did from all other milestones in my life, and even when
now one of them is no more.

Just as I acknowledge many of my teachers in the preceding, the
two things I can be certain of is that I have neither named them all nor
thanked them enough. I hope they will rest content in the knowledge that
this book and what I have become would not have been possible without them.

NOTES

Chapter 1

1. https://youtu.be/q0hyYWKXF0Q, Tones and I, *Dance Monkey* (official video), You Tube.
2. David Court and Sandeep Dayal, "Beyond Behavioral Bounds," *Marketing Management*, September–October 2002, p. 28.
3. *Directory of Academic Experts in Behavioral Science, Ideas* 42, 2015, https://cpl.hks .harvard.edu/files/cpl/files/for_website_directory_of_academic_experts.pdf?m =1437146451.
4. June Gruber, *Human Emotion*, http://www.gruberpeplab.com/teaching/psych 131_summer2013/.
5. "Fact Sheet: BRAIN Initiative," The White House, Office of the Press Secretary, April 2, 2013, https://obamawhitehouse.archives.gov/the-press-office/2013/ 04/02/fact-sheet-brain-initiative.
6. R. H. Thaler and C. R. Sunstein, *Nudge: Improving Decisions About Health, Wealth, and Happiness*, New York: Penguin Books, 2009, p. 91.
7. A. Tom Horvath, Kaushik Misra, Amy K. Epner, and Galen Morgan Cooper, "Drug Seeking and Cravings: Addictions' Effect on the Brain's Reward System," Centersite.net, https://www.centersite.net/poc/view_doc.php?type= doc&id=48375&cn=1408.

Chapter 2

1. Enbrel TV commercial, "My Mom's Pain," iSpot.tv, https://www.ispot.tv/ad/ w1X2/enbrel-my-moms-pain.
2. Elizabeth A. Kensinger, "Remembering the Details: Effects of Emotion," *Emotion Review: Journal of the International Society for Research on Emotion*, vol. 1, issue 2, 2009, pp. 99–113, https://doi.org/10.1177/1754073908100432.
3. Ellie Parker and Adrian Furnham, "Does Sex Sell? The Effect of Sexual Program Content on the Recall of Sexual and Non-Sexual Advertisements," *Applied Cognitive Psychology*, vol. 21, issue 9, December 2007, pp. 1217–1228, https://doi .org/10.1002/acp.1325.
4. The Think, Feel, Act model is also a variation of the classic AIDA (attention, interest, desire, and action) model, which was invented as a sales, not marketing, tool.
5. George Lakoff and Mark Johnson, *Philosophy in the Flesh*, New York: Basic Books, 1999, p. 13, ". . . rule of thumb among cognitive scientists: unconscious thought is 95 percent of all thought," https://www.cse.iitk.ac.in/users/amit/books/lakoff -1999-philosophy-in-flesh.html.

6. Gerald Zaltman, *How Customers Think: Essential Insights into the Mind of the Market*, Harvard Business School Publishing, 2003, https://hbswk.hbs.edu/item/the-subconscious-mind-of-the-consumer-and-how-to-reach-it.

7. R. B. Zajonc, "Feeling and Thinking: Closing the Debate over the Independence of Affect," 2000, in J. P. Forgas (ed.), *Studies in Emotion and Social Interaction, Second Series*, Cambridge University Press, "Feeling and Thinking: The Role of Affect in Social Cognition," pp. 31–58.

8. Antoine Bechara, Antonio R. Damasio, "The Somatic Marker Hypothesis: A Neural Theory of Economic Decision," *Games and Economic Behavior*, 2005, vol. 52, issue 2, pp. 336–372, https://doi.org/10.1016/j.geb.2004.06.010, https://www.sciencedirect.com/science/article/pii/S0899825604001034.

9. George Lakoff and Mark Johnson, *Philosophy in the Flesh*, p. 20.

10. The dual processing theory of thought predates Kahneman's description of it; however, he deserves credit for making it come to life more memorably than had been done by those before him.

11. James N. Druckman, "Evaluating Framing Effects," *Journal of Economic Psychology*, 2001, vol. 22, pp. 91–101.

12. Heidi Mitchell, "Can a Person Learn While Sleeping?" *Wall Street Journal*, March 16, 2019, https://www.wsj.com/articles/can-a-person-learn-while-sleeping-11552744800; Wilhelm, I. Diekelmann and J. S. Born, "Sleep in Children Improves Memory Performance on Declarative But Not Procedural Tasks," *Learning & Memory*, April 25, 2008, Cold Spring Harbor Laboratory, vol. 15, issue 5, pp. 373–377, doi:10.1101/lm.803708.

13. For a good and accessible discussion on how we learn through processes of "incubation" and "percolation," see the book *How We Learn: The Surprising Truth About When, Where, and Why It Happens* by Benedict Carey, Random House, 2014.

Chapter 3

1. Lama Chahine and Ghassan Kanazi, "Phantom Limb Syndrome: A Review," *M. E. J. Anesth*, vol. 19, issue 2, pp. 345–55, 2007, https://pdfs.semanticscholar.org/0f8d/2b80b5c20ed0e21076de4b5ac48327ca05d2.pdf.

2. "Collections and Research Made by the Michigan Pioneer and Historical Society," *Historical Collections*, vol. 28, Annual Meeting 1898, 1900, p. 436.

3. Robynne Boyd, "Do People Only Use 10 Percent of Their Brains?" *Scientific American*, February 7, 2008, https://www.scientificamerican.com/article/do-people-only-use-10-percent-of-their-brains.

4. Jared A. Nielsen, Brandon A. Zielinski, Michael A. Ferguson, Janet E. Lainhart, and Jeffrey S. Anderson, "An Evaluation of the Left-Brain vs. Right-Brain Hypothesis with Resting State Functional Connectivity Magnetic Resonance Imaging," August 14, 2013, https://journals.plos.org/plosone/article?id=10.1371/journal.pone.0071275, https://doi.org/10.1371/journal.pone.0071275.

5. K. Roy, A. Jaiswal, and P. Panda, "Towards Spike-Based Machine Intelligence with Neuromorphic Computing," *Nature*, vol. 575, pp. 607–617, 2019, https://www.nature.com/articles/s41586-019-1677-2.

6. "Human Brain for Kids: Graphic on Functions of the Different Parts of the Brain," https://k8schoollessons.com/wp-content/uploads/2018/08/functions-of-brain.jpg.

7. Mercey Livingston, "Boost Happy Hormones Like Serotonin and Dopamine: Here's What You Can Do," November 18, 2020, *CNET*, https://www.cnet .com/news/boost-happy-hormones-like-serotonin-and-dopamine-heres -what-you-can-do/.
8. Educalingo, https://educalingo.com/en/dic-en/conation.
9. Kolby Wisdom™, http://www.kolbe.com/why-kolbe/kolbe-wisdom/.
10. Stephen J. Genco, *Intuitive Marketing*, Intuitive Consumer Insights LLC, 2019, p. 357.

Chapter 4

1. Kevin L. Rand and Stephen S. Ilardi, "Toward a Consilient Science of Psychology," *Journal of Clinical Psychology*, vol. 61, issue 1, 2005, pp. 7–20, doi: 10.1002/jclp.20088.
2. Nick McCullum, "Case Study: How 3G Capital Squeezed More Out of Heinz," *Sure Dividend*, September 4, 2017, https://www.suredividend.com/3g-capital -heinz.
3. David Hume, *A Treatise of Human Nature*, Book 2, Part 3, Section 2, New York: Oxford University Press, 2007.
4. Allan Chenworth, "Peering into the Brain with Chemical Biosensors," *Science & Technology Review*, Lawrence Livermore National Laboratory, October-November 2016, https://str.llnl.gov/content/pages/november-2016/pdf/11.16.3.pdf.
5. "Viser," https://en.wiktionary.org/wiki/viser#French.

Chapter 5

1. W. Hofmann, J. De Houwer, M. Perugini, F. Baeyens, and G. Crombez, "Evaluative Conditioning in Humans: A Meta-Analyzis," *Psychological Bulletin*, vol. 136, issue 3, 2010, pp. 390–421.
2. More precisely, in psychology, priming is a specific and different phenomenon whereby one stimulus is thought to subconsciously influence another that follows. This means that when certain thoughts are seeded in your mind, other related ones will be activated with greater ease in a process that psychologists refer to as "spreading activation." See also, Daniel Reisberg, *Cognition: Exploring the Science of the Mind* (2007), pp. 255, 517.
3. Dior J'Adore Absolu TV commercial, "The New Absolu: The Film," featuring Charlize Theron, song by Kanye West, 2018, https://www.ispot.tv/ad/davv/dior -jadore-absolu-the-new-absolu-the-film-featuring-charlize-theron-song-by -kanye-west.
4. https://www.afterellen.com/general-news/564111-when-subaru-came-out-the -birth-of-the-lezbaru.
5. https://www.benjerry.com/whats-new/2018/10/pecan-resistance-action.
6. "WEBFILM - Our blades are f***ing great," YouTube, https://www.youtube.com/watch?v=0YwMwTZw12k.
7. For a fabulous in-depth case study on the Dollar Shave Club, read the book *Billion Dollar Brand Club* by Lawrence Ingrassia, pp. 1–22.
8. K. M. Sheldon and A. J. Elliot (1999), "Goal Striving, Need Satisfaction, and Longitudinal Well-Being: The Self-Concordance Model," *Journal of Personality and Social Psychology*, 76(3), 482–497, https://doi.org/10.1037/0022

-3514.76.3.482. The self-concordance of goals (i.e., their consistency with the person's developing interests and *core values*) plays a dual role in the model. First, those pursuing self-concordant goals put more sustained effort into achieving those goals and thus are more likely to attain them. Second, those who attain self-concordant goals reap greater well-being benefits from their attainment.

9. David Marchese, "Ben & Jerry's Radical Ice Cream Dreams," *New York Times*, July 27, 2020, https://www.nytimes.com/interactive/2020/07/27/magazine/ben-jerry -interview.html.

10. Christopher Marquis, "Why Ben & Jerry's Won't Stay Silent on White Supremacy—or Other Social Justice Issues," *Forbes*, June 9, 2020, https://www .forbes.com/sites/christophermarquis/2020/06/09/why-ben--jerrys-wont-stay -silent-on-white-supremacy-or-other-social-justice-issues/?sh=665ebf936f07.

11. Jelani Cobb, "Behind Nike's Decision to Stand by Colin Kaepernick," *New Yorker*, September 4, 2018, https://www.newyorker.com/news/daily-comment/behind -nikes-decision-to-stand-by-colin-kaepernick.

12. Soo Youn, "Nike Sales Booming After Colin Kaepernick Ad, Invalidating Critics," ABC News, December 21, 2018, https://abcnews.go.com/Business/nike-sales -booming-kaepernick-ad-invalidating-critics/story?id=59957137.

13. Burwell v. Hobby Lobby Stores, Inc., Wikipedia, https://en.wikipedia.org/wiki/ Burwell_v._Hobby_Lobby_Stores,_Inc.

14. Mary Hanbury, "The Rise and Fall of Victoria's Secret, America's Biggest Lingerie Retailer," *Business Insider*, February 20, 2020, https://www.businessinsider.com/ victorias-secret-rise-and-fall-history-2019-5.

Chapter 6

1. Sadahiko Nakajima, Mariko Yamamoto, and Natsumi Yoshimoto, "Dogs Look Like Their Owners: Replications with Racially Homogenous Owner Portraits," *Anthrozoos*, vol. 22, issue 2, June 2009, https://go.gale.com/ps/anonymous?id=G ALE%7CA207324088&sid.

2. T. L. Chartrand and J. A. Bargh, "The Chameleon Effect: The Perception–Behavior Link and Social Interaction," *Journal of Personality and Social Psychology*, 76(6), 1999, pp. 893–910, https://psycnet.apa.org/doiLanding?doi= 10.1037%2F0022-3514.76.6.893.

3. Eric Jaffe, "Mirror Neurons: How We Reflect on Behavior," Association for Psychological Science, May 1, 2007, https://www.psychologicalscience.org/ observer/mirror-neurons-how-we-reflect-on-behavior.

4. George Lakoff and Mark Johnson, *Philosophy in the Flesh*, New York: Basic Books, 1999, p. 20, ". . . rule of thumb among cognitive scientists: unconscious thought is 95 percent of all thought," https://www.cse.iitk.ac.in/users/amit/books/lakoff -1999-philosophy-in-flesh.html.

5. Interestingly, one possible short cut to opening your mind and rewiring your System 1 circuits is through the use of psychedelic drugs. Recent research suggests that psychedelics, like MDMA, LSD, and psilocybin (magic mushrooms), may alter the biochemical bonds in the brain's neural network. Research from Johns Hopkins University showed that adult mice that had stopped learning certain new social skills by a certain age could be rewired with MDMA to learn those skills, just like younger mice. Now, because System 1 is capable of borrowing its knowledge from the System 2 of others, you might be tempted to try psychedelic drugs. After all, if researchers at Hopkins, with their prodigious System 2 brains,

think there is something to it, does not your System 1 tell you this is a possibility? Before you proceed, you may want to remember that the subjects in this research were dispensable, "we'll make more" rodents. On a more serious note, research with psychedelics is expanding with human subjects and is showing promise in a number of common mental diseases.

6. Tim Henderson, "Too Many Pedestrians Injured by Looking at Their Phones," Governing.com, December 11, 2014, https://www.governing.com/topics/transportation-infrastructure/too-many-pedestrians-injured-by-looking-at-their-phones.html.

7. S. J. Maglio and T. Reich, "Choice Protection for Feeling-Focused Decisions," *Journal of Experimental Psychology*, January 16, 2020, https://www.researchgate.net/publication/338635749_Choice_protection_for_feeling-focused_decisions.

8. Kahneman. *Thinking Fast and Slow*, Chapter 5, "Cognitive Ease."

9. Tatiana Homonoff, PhD (NYU Robert F. Wagner School of Public Service), Lee-Sien Kao (ideas42), Doug Palmer (ideas42), and Christina Seybolt (University of Chicago Energy & Environment Lab), "Skipping the Bag, Assessing the Impact of Chicago's Tax on Disposable Bags," September 2018, https://www.ideas42.org/wp-content/uploads/2018/09/Bag_Tax_Paper_final.pdf. In their study, they say that while "82% of customers used disposable bags prior to the tax, this fraction declined to 40% after the tax was implemented. In contrast to the overwhelming impact of the tax, a five-cent bonus for reusable bag use had almost no impact on disposable bag use, evidence consistent with a model of loss aversion."

10. Andrew K. Przybylski, Kou Murayama, Cody R. DeHaan, and Valerie Gladwell, "Motivational, Emotional, and Behavioral Correlates of Fear of Missing Out," *Computers in Human Behavior*, vol. 29, issue 4, pp. 1841–1848, doi:10.1016/j.chb.2013.02.014.

11. "Announcing the Fyre Festiva," YouTube, January 12, 2017, https://youtu.be/mz5kY3RsmKo.

12. Sandeep Dayal, Helene Landesberg, and Michael Zeisser, "How to Build Trust Online," *McKinsey Quarterly*, 2003.

13. Michael I. Norton, Daniel Mochon, and Dan Ariely, "The IKEA Effect: When Labor Leads to Love," *Journal of Consumer Psychology*, vol. 22, issue 3, July 2012, https://dash.harvard.edu/bitstream/handle/1/12136084/norton%20mochon%20ariely%20third%20round%5b1%5d.pdf?sequence=3&isAllowed=y.

14. Tang TV advertisement in Pakistan, YouTube, 2018, https://youtu.be/yfpEQn9XNDM.

15. Lizzie Widdicombe, "How Everlane Hacked Your Wardrobe," *New Yorker*, September 25, 2017, https://www.newyorker.com/culture/on-and-off-the-avenue/how-everlane-hacked-your-wardrobe.

16. Laura Stevens, "On Amazon, Fake Products Plague Smaller Brands," *Wall Street Journal*, July 19, 2018, https://www.wsj.com/articles/on-amazon-fake-products-plague-smaller-brands-1532001601.

17. Sascha Topolinski and Fritz Strack, "Scanning the 'Fringe' of Consciousness: What Is Felt and What Is Not Felt in Intuitions About Semantic Coherence," Department of Psychology II, Social Psychology, University of Wuerzburg, Germany, *Consciousness and Cognition*, 18(3), September 2009, pp. 608–618, https://doi.org/10.1016/j.concog.2008.06.002.

18. Guinness TV commercial, "Wheelchair Basketball," iSpot.tv, https://www.ispot.tv/ad/7bSd/guinness-wheelchair-basketball.

19. Guinness reveals "Made of More" advertising campaign created by AMV BBDO, TheDrum.com, October 1, 2012, https://www.thedrum.com/news/2012/10/01/guinness-reveals-made-more-advertising-campaign-created-amv-bbdo.
20. Stephen J. Genco, *Intuitive Marketing*, Chapter 7, pp. 115–130.
21. As a side note, I would add that rheumatologists have had the last laugh over their peers. When Remicade, a cutting-edge biologic drug, was launched, it was a "buy-and-bill" medication, meaning that the physician would buy the drug and earn a markup on it each time it was used. Also, the drug was one of the most expensive ($20,000 to $30,000 per year) at the time and infused in the physician's office only, which meant there was a ton of money to be made. Rheumatology was overnight transformed from being one of the lowest compensated medical professions to one of the highest—certainly leaving primary care physicians in the dust.
22. "Who Sharpened Occam's Razor?" IrishPhilosophy.com, http://www.irishphilosophy.com/2014/05/27/who-sharpened-occams-razor/.
23. Aristotle, Book 1, Part 25, "Analytica Posteriora," in Richard McKeon (ed.), *The Basic Works of Aristotle*, Modern Library Classics, 2001.
24. George Lakoff and Mark Johnson, *Philosophy in the Flesh*, p. 20.
25. Robert Cialdini, *Influence: The Psychology of Persuasion*, New York: Harper Business, 2006.
26. Celebrex TV commercial, "Body in Motion," iSpot.tv, https://www.ispot.tv/ad/7V7z/celebrex-body-in-motion.

Chapter 7

1. Benjamin Koellmann, "Smart Cookie," *Business Today*, March 31, 2013, https://www.businesstoday.in/magazine/lbs-case-study/how-kraft-foods-won-over-customers-in-china-and-india/story/193162.html.
2. S. G. Hofmann, A. Asnaani, I. J. Vonk, A. T. Sawyer, and A. Fang, 2012. "The Efficacy of Cognitive Behavioral Therapy: A Review of Meta-analyzes," *Cognitive Therapy and Research*, vol. 36, issue 5, pp. 427–440, https://doi.org/10.1007/s10608-012-9476-1. In a number of clinical trials, cognitive behavior therapy (CBT) has been shown to be superior to medicines like SSRIs in the case of a number of common psychological disorders, https://www.ncbi.nlm.nih.gov/pmc/articles/PMC3584580/table/T1/?report=objectonly.
3. David D. Burns, *Feeling Good: The New Mood Therapy*, New York: Harper, 1999.
4. Evan Mayo-Wilson, Sofia Dias, Ifigeneia Mavranezouli, Kayleigh Kew, David M. Clark, A. E. Ades, and Stephen Pilling, "Psychological and Pharmacological Interventions for Social Anxiety Disorder in Adults: A Systematic Review and Network Meta-analyzis," *Lancet Psychiatry*, 2014, vol. 1, pp. 368–76, September 26, 2014, https://www.thelancet.com/journals/lanpsy/article/PIIS2215-0366(14)70329-3/fulltext.
5. "Follow the Frog," YouTube, https://www.youtube.com/watch?v=3iIkOi3srLo.
6. Opdivo TV commercial, iSpot.tv, "A Chance to Live Longer," https://www.ispot.tv/ad/wIsF/opdivo-a-chance-to-live-longer.
7. In fact, the cost of the treatment can exceed $250,000 as many patients require a combination of expensive drugs. Deena Beasley, "The Cost of Cancer: New Drugs Show Success at a Steep Price," Reuters, April 3, 2017, https://www.reuters.com/article/us-usa-healthcare-cancer-costs/the-cost-of-cancer-new-drugs-show-success-at-a-steep-price-idUSKBN1750FU.

8. K. Witte and M. Allen, "A Meta-Analyzis of Fear Appeals: Implications for Effective Public Health Programs," *Health Education and Behavior*, vol. 27, issue 5, pp. 591–615, 2000. G. Hastings, M. Stead, and J. Webb, "Fear Appeals in Social Marketing: Strategic and Ethical Reasons for Concern," *Psychology and Marketing*, vol. 21, issue 11, pp. 961–986, 2004.

9. "CDC: Tips from Former Smokers—Terrie's Tip Ad," YouTube, March 15, 2012, https://www.youtube.com/watch?v=5zWB4dLYChM. Terrie unfortunately died in 2013. The CDC released the following statement "The Centers for Disease Control and Prevention (CDC) mourns the passing of Terrie Hall, one of the people featured in CDC's Tips from Former Smokers® (Tips®) national tobacco education campaign. Terrie, 53, died Monday, September 16, 2013, from the cancer she fought so bravely during the final 13 years of her life. 'The passing of this public health hero is a loss for us all, and a reminder to heed her warning about the dangers of smoking,' said Tim McAfee, MD, MPH, director, Office on Smoking and Health," https://www.cdc.gov/tobacco/campaign/tips/stories/anti-smoking -champion-terrie-hall-dies.html#:~:text=The%20Centers%20for%20Disease%20 Control%20and%20Prevention%20(CDC),during%20the%20final%2013%20 years%20of%20her%20life.

10. "The Facts About Scare Tactics," Regional Center for Health Communities, Metrowest, Education Development Center, http://masstapp.edc.org/sites/ masstapp.edc.org/files/Talking%20points%20about%20scare%20tactics_0.pdf.

11. Enbrel TV commercial, "My Mom's Pain," iSpot.tv, https://www.ispot.tv/ad/ w1X2/enbrel-my-moms-pain.

12. Xarelto TV commercial, "Not Today," iSpot.tv, https://www.ispot.tv/ad/Z5DV/ xarelto-not-today.

13. https://en.wikipedia.org/wiki/Dumb Ways_to_Die.

14. "Dumb Ways to Die," November 15, 2012, YouTube, https://www.youtube.com/ watch?v=IJNR2EpS0jw.

15. Daisy Dumas, "Being Dumb Is Almost Cool with Surprise Advertising Hit," *The Sydney Morning Herald*, November 19, 2012, https://www.smh.com.au/ technology/being-dumb-is-almost-cool-with-surprise-advertising-hit-20121118 -29k6z.html.

16. "The Warby Parker Marketing Strategy Decoded," *TapJoy*, September 19, 2019, https://www.tapjoy.com/resources/warby-parker-marketing-strategy/.

17. Danny Parisi, "They Have One Goal, Take Over the World," *Glossy*, May 16, 2019, https://www.glossy.co/fashion/they-have-one-goal-take-over-the-world-how -independent-eyewear-brands-compete-with-the-behemoth-of-essilorluxottica.

18. Carey K. Morewedge and Colleen E. Giblin, 2015, "Explanations of the Endowment Effect: An Integrative Review," *Trends in Cognitive Sciences*, vol. 19, issue 6, pp. 339–348, doi:10.1016/j.tics.2015.04.004. PMID 25939336, http:// careymorewedge.com/papers/EndowmentReview.pdf.

19. https://www.ispot.tv/ad/7Jim/prudential-the-prudential-magnets-experiment.

20. Stephen Pulvirent, "The Untold Story of Watchmaking's Most Iconic Advertising Campaign: The 'Generations' Campaign of Patek Philippe," *Hodinkee*, December 27, 2016, https://www.hodinkee.com/articles/untold-story-patek-philippe -generations-advertising-campaign.

21. Slavoj Žižek, *Less Than Nothing: Hegel and the Shadow of Dialectical Materialism* London: Verso, 2012.

22. Edward Jay Epstein, "Have You Ever Tried to Sell a Diamond?" *The Atlantic*, February 1982, https://www.theatlantic.com/magazine/archive/1982/02/have -you-ever-tried-to-sell-a-diamond/304575/.
23. Actually, wurtzite boron nitride and lonsdaleite are harder and rarer in nature. Lonsdaleite is sometimes formed when graphite meteorites slam into Earth, while wurtzite boron nitride is created under extremely high temperatures and pressures in volcanic eruptions. Jessica Griggs, "Diamond No Longer Nature's Hardest Material," *New Scientist*, February 16, 2009, https://www.newscientist.com/ article/dn16610-diamond-no-longer-natures-hardest-material/#ixzz68b0Laio9.

Chapter 8

1. Steve Genco provides a great overview of such research in his book *Intuitive Marketing* in Chapter 11, "Consumer Goal in Action," pp. 197–223. As I mentioned in an earlier chapter, he elegantly simplifies the problem of inaction by suggesting two *universal* motivations that drive behavior. The first is a desire to be happier and better off tomorrow than today. And the second is a need to feel good about ourselves and others.
2. M. Milyavskaya and K. M. Werner, "Goal Pursuit: Current State of Affairs and Directions for Future Research," *Canadian Psychology/Psychologie Canadienne*, vol. 59, issue 2, 2018, pp. 163–175, https://doi.org/10.1037/cap0000147.
3. B. S. Wiese, "Successful Pursuit of Personal Goals and Subjective Well-Being," in B. R. Little, K. Salmela-Aro, and S. D. Phillips (eds.), *Personal Project Pursuit: Goals, Action, and Human Flourishing*, Lawrence Erlbaum Associates Publishers, 2007, pp. 301–328, https://psycnet.apa.org/record/2006-11798-011.
4. Juliano Laran, Chris Janiszewski, and Anthony Salerno, "Exploring the Differences Between Conscious and Unconscious Goal Pursuit," *Journal of Marketing Research*, June 1, 2016, https://doi.org/10.1509/jmr.13.0263.
5. K. C. Berridge and M. L. Kringelbach, "Pleasure Systems in the Brain," *Neuron*, vol. 86, issue 3, 2015, pp. 646–664, doi:10.1016/j. neuron, 2015.02.018, https:// www.ncbi.nlm.nih.gov/pmc/articles/PMC4425246/.
6. Clark Buckner, "4 Chemicals That Activate Happiness, and How to Gamify Them," *Technology Advice*, October 30, 2017, https://technologyadvice.com/ blog/information-technology/activate-chemicals-gamify-happiness-nicole-laz-zaro/. Dopamine is involved more with anticipation and striving than the actual "happiness" feeling. Oxytocin makes us feel empathy with and closeness to others. Serotonin puts us in a good mood. Endorphins mask pain or discomfort and help with the fight-or-flight response. The exact role of each chemical is under debate and study. The general idea that specific neurochemicals contribute to a sensation of happiness is well established.
7. UPMC, "Neurosurgery and Brain Health, How Brain Chemicals Influence Mood and Health," September 4, 2016, https://share.upmc.com/2016/09/about-brain -chemicals/.
8. This is real enough that people whose reward systems are compromised can suffer from serious disorders like anhedonia (lack of pleasure) or dysphoria (negative affect or emotions).
9. Gregory P. Strauss, et al., "Anticipatory vs. Consummatory Pleasure: What Is the Nature of Hedonic Deficits in Schizophrenia?," *Psychiatry Research*, vol. 187, issue 12), 2011, pp. 36–41, doi:10.1016/j.psychres.2011.01.012, https://www.science direct.com/science/article/abs/pii/S0165178111000461?via%3Dihub.

10. Richard M. Ryan, and Edward L. Deci, "Self-Determination Theory and the Facilitation of Intrinsic Motivation, Social Development, and Well-Being," *American Psychologist*, vol. 55, issue 1, January 2000, pp. 68–78, doi: 10.1037110003-066X.55.1.68, https://selfdeterminationtheory.org/SDT/documents/2000_RyanDeci_SDT.pdf.

11. R. M. Ryan and E. L. Deci, *Self-Determination Theory: Basic Psychological Needs in Motivation, Development, and Wellness*, New York: Guilford Publishing, 2017.

12. Japan Dentures Recycling Association, https://disposalknowhow.com/dentures/.

13. Steve Genco captures these concepts simply but in much greater detail in his book *Intuitive Marketing*, pp. 208–210.

14. National Car Rental TV Commercial, "Control Enthusiast" Feat, Patrick Warburton, Ad ID: 1161927, ispot.tv. https://www.ispot.tv/ad/7EJ5/national-car-rental-control-enthusiast-feat-patrick-warburton.

15. Tanya Gazdik, "National Car Rental Extends 'Go Like A Pro,'" *MediaPost*, September 12, 2016, https://www.mediapost.com/publications/article/284369/national-car-rental-extends-go-like-a-pro.html.

16. Mastercard Baseball Commercial, YouTube, https://youtu.be/71KAO_bmc2o.

17. Mastercard, "McCann-Erickson and a Campaign That Never Got Old? Priceless." https://www.aaaa.org/timeline-event/mastercard-mccann-erickson-campaign-never-got-old-priceless/.

18. Ancient Indian philosophers were so unhinged by the idea that material pleasures (derived from *prakriti* or creation) could never deliver eternal happiness that they posited that real happiness could only be achieved by relieving the mind of all desires. Patañjali, in the *Yoga Sutra*, regards the mind as an unwelcome appendage to the soul (*purusha*). By stilling the mind (ceasing thought, cognition, ideas, and images—or together, the *vrittis*) through meditation, one can liberate the soul to return to the eternal reality (*Brahma*). This, by the way, was a huge leap of faith by Hindu philosophers, who chose not to dwell on the possibility that vacuuming the mind of all might lead merely to an empty mind rather than any broader reconciliation with the universal soul (*moksha*). If everyone did this, we would not need brands, as no one would be wanting or buying anything. Luckily, even most Indians treat these ideas as only a compartmentalized thought experiment, and most yoga enthusiasts worldwide are not clued into its actual purpose and treat yoga (a dumbed-down adaptation of Lord Shiva's dance, *tandav nritya*) as a stretching exercise. For a good discussion on the Hindu philosophy of Yoga, read *The Yoga Sutra of Patañjali*, by Edwin F. Bryant.

19. Esteban Ortiz-Ospina and Max Roser, "Happiness and Life Satisfaction," 2017, *Our World in Data*, https://ourworldindata.org/happiness-and-life-satisfaction. It is noted that an average happiness score of 7 is likely to be seen in more developed countries like the United States. In countries like Burkina Faso, where there is political turmoil and basic needs of the population are not met, the score is lower around 4.5. They also note the Easterlin paradox, named after Richard Easterlin. At the heart of the paradox was the fact that richer countries tend to have higher self-reported happiness, yet in some countries for which repeated surveys were available over the course of the 1970s, happiness was not increasing with rising national incomes.

20. Paul Bloom, "The Good Life: Happiness, Open Yale Courses," https://youtube/7dep9KPWp3g?t=1200. Paul Bloom of Yale, who has a phenomenal lecture on this topic, does point out that there are exceptions to the rule of regression to the

mean for happiness. For example, he informs us, breast enhancement and reduction surgeries do make women sustainably happier.

Chapter 9

1. George Lakoff and Mark Johnson, *Philosophy in the Flesh*, New York: Basic Books, 1999, p. 20, ". . . rule of thumb among cognitive scientists: unconscious thought is 95 percent of all thought," https://www.cse.iitk.ac.in/users/amit/books/lakoff -1999-philosophy-in-flesh.html.

Chapter 10

1. "A Brand New World," *Economist*, January 25, 2020, https://www.economist.com/ business/2020/01/23/it-has-never-been-easier-to-launch-a-new-brand.
2. Zelle is a way to easily send small sums of money to anyone with a bank account from a mobile phone. See zellepay.com.
3. Allison Gauss, "6 Socially Responsible Companies to Applaud," Classy, https:// www.classy.org/blog/6-socially-responsible-companies-applaud/.
4. https://www.pfizer.co.uk/tackling-rise-antimicrobial-resistance, Pfizer UK.
5. Tom Huddleston Jr., "How Allbirds Went from Silicon Valley Fashion Staple to a $1.4 Billion Sneaker Start-Up," CNBC, December 18, 2018, https://www.cnbc .com/2018/12/14/allbirds-went-from-silicon-valley-staple-to-billion-sneaker -startup.html.

Chapter 11

1. "Hallucinations: Symptoms & Signs," MedicineNet, https://www.medicinenet .com/hallucinations/symptoms.htm.
2. https://youtu.be/tV2RLLtOgL4?t=312.
3. Kahneman, Diener, Schwartz, "Objective Happiness," Kahneman, *Well-Being: Foundations of Hedonic Psychology*, Russell Sage Foundation, 1999.
4. This connecting of the dots is sometimes referred to as a Bayesian inference model of the brain.
5. Elaine Cassel, "Behavioral Science Research Leads to Department of Justice Guidelines for Eyewitness Evidence," *Virginia Lawyer*, February 2000, https:// www.vsb.org/docs/valawyermagazine/feb00cassel.pdf.
6. Daniel Kahneman, "Evaluation by Moments: Past and Future," in D. Kahneman and A. Tversky (Eds.), *Choices, Values and Frames*, New York: Cambridge University Press and the Russell Sage Foundation, 2000, pp. 693–708.
7. Evan Weingarten, Gal Zauberman, Kristin Diehl, "Duration Sensitivity of Key Moments," *Cognition*, vol. 214, 2021, https://doi.org/10.1016/j.cognition .2021.104750. (https://www.sciencedirect.com/science/article/pii/S00100277 21001694). My take: The practical question at hand is whether faster response times translate into superior experiences for the customer. Earlier work by Fredrickson and Kahneman suggested that what defines our memory of an experience is it peak and end (think of it as the climax and the end). This is called the Peak-End Rule. This led to the theory of "Duration Neglect." That says that the duration of an experience does not matter, only its peak and end. Translate that as customer response time is not important, only the quality of the experience is—and that latter is defined by the climax and how the experi-

ence ended. This latest research by Zauberman and others confirms the Peak-End Rule, but says that duration indirectly affects the experience. This is because in a negative customer experience, if the response time is longer, the worst parts of the experience (negative peak and end) appear worse than they actually are to the customer.

8. Steve Gillman, "The Science of Tipping: 16 Proven Ways to Increase Your Tip Income," The PennyHoarder, March 26, 2015, https://www.thepennyhoarder.com/make-money/side-gigs/how-to-get-more-tips/.

9. Jill Rosen, "Element of Surprise Helps Babies Learn Best," *Johns Hopkins Magazine*, https://hub.jhu.edu/2015/04/02/surprise-babies-learning/.

10. https://www.preventivmeasures.com/.

11. https://www.youtube.com/watch?v=gP92j-uEnps.

12. Tanya Lewis, "Pi, Anyone? The Secret to Memorizing Tens of Thousands of Digits," *LiveScience*, March 13, 2015, https://www.livescience.com/50134-pi-day-memory-experts.html.

13. Guinness World Records, https://www.guinnessworldrecords.com/world-records/most-pi-places-memorised?fb_comment_id=752963494793308_901656546590668.

14. Tank Garage Winery, https://www.tankgaragewinery.com/product/2016-Lords-of-the-Boulevard-Red-Wine-Napa-Valley?.

15. "Reunion," Google Search, YouTube, https://www.youtube.com/watch?v=gHGDN9-oFJE.

16. Norbert Schwarz, Herbert Bless, Herbert Strack, Gisela Klumpp, Helga Rittenauer-Schatka, and Annette Simons, "Ease of Retrieval as Information: Another Look at the Availability Heuristic," *Journal of Personality and Social Psychology*, vol. 61, issue 2, 1991, pp. 195–202, doi:10.1037/0022-3514.61.2.195, https://psycnet.apa.org/doiLanding?doi=10.1037%2F0022-3514.61.2.195.

17. Christopher Chabris and Daniel Simons, *The Invisible Gorilla: How Our Intuitions Deceive Us*, June 7, 2011.

18. https://www.bing.com/videos/search?q=the+invisible+gorilla&view=detail&mid=76C696714DFD83C1468A76C696714DFD83C1468A&FORM=VIRE.

19. Old Spice, The Man Your Man Could Smell Like, YouTube, https://www.youtube.com/watch?v=owGykVbfgUE.

20. https://www.inc.com/articles/201108/5-marketing-lessons-from-old-spice.html.

21. https://www.change.org/p/fairfield-pool-278-meadow-street-fairfield-ct-demand-removal-of-sexist-billboard.

22. L. Geraci, M. A. McDaniel, T. M. Miller, et al, "The Bizarreness Effect: Evidence for the Critical Influence of Retrieval Processes," *Journal of Applied Research in Memory and Cognition* 41, 2013, 1228–1237, doi:10.3758/s13421-013-0335-4, https://www.ncbi.nlm.nih.gov/pubmed/23737359.

Chapter 12

1. Robin Givhan, "Seriously, Prada, What Were You Thinking? Why the Fashion Industry Keeps Bumbling into Racist Imagery," *Washington Post*, December 16, 2018, https://www.washingtonpost.com/arts-entertainment/2018/12/15/seriously-prada-what-were-you-thinking-why-fashion-industry-keeps-bumbling-into-racist-imagery/.

2. Clarinda Rodrigues, "Multisensory Brand Communications: Capturing the Hearts and Minds of Consumers," Chapter 6 in *Brand Touchpoints* (Marketing

and Operations Management Research), Aparna Sundar (Editor), Nova Science Pub Inc. (July 6, 2018); https://novapublishers.com/shop/brand-touchpoints/.

3. "Scent Marketing in Flagship Store Burberry Regent Street," https://www.zaluti .com/blog/scent-marketing-in-flagship-store-burberry-regent-street.

4. "Inside the Retail Strategy of Burberry," *Insider Trends*, January 16, 2018, https:// www.insider-trends.com/inside-retail-strategy-burberry/#ixzz6NT422F3i.

5. Sara Baskentli and Maureen Morrin, "Understanding the Role of Crossmodal Processes in Branding," Chapter 9 in *Brand Touchpoints* (Marketing and Operations Management Research), Aparna Sundar (Editor), Nova Science Pub Inc (July 6, 2018); https://novapublishers.com/shop/brand-touchpoints/. The authors show that stimulus to one sense can influence perception of another sense. For example, round shapes versus angular (visual stimulus) are associated with the perception of sweeter taste. Round shaped candy will taste sweeter than star shaped candy with edges. Yellow colored colas will taste more citrusy than chocolate-colored ones. This may happen due to past associations, impact of linguistic metaphors or neural structures of the brain.

6. G. White, S. Fishbein, and J. Rutsein, "Passionate Love and the Misattribution of Arousal," *Journal of Personality and Social Psychology*, vol. 41, 1981, pp. 56–62, doi:10.1037/0022-3514.41.1.56, https://psycnet.apa.org/record/1982-05734-001.

7. https://www.ispot.tv/ad/wBUg/prudential-the-prudential-walkways-experiment#.

8. April H. Crusco and Christopher G. Wetzel, "The Midas Touch: The Effects of Interpersonal Touch on Restaurant Tipping," December 1, 1984, https://doi.org/ 10.1177/0146167284104003.

9. Whitepaper: Mega Tips—Scientifically Tested Techniques to Increase Your Tips, Dr. Michael Lynn, Associate Professor, School of Hotel Administration, Cornell University, 2004. http://doclibrary.com/MSC99/DOC/megatips0529.pdf.

10. "Experts in Emotion 6.3—Matthew Hertenstein on Touch," YouTube, May 20, 2013, Experts in Emotion Series; Director: June Gruber, Yale University, https:// youtu.be/uRW_UA7Yx04.

11. "I'd Like to Buy the World a Coke," The Coca Cola Company, https://www.coca -colacompany.com/news/id-like-to-buy-the-world-a-coke.

12. Ricki Green, "Coca-Cola Connects Indians and Pakistanis Together Through a Live Communications Portal Via Leo Burnett Chicago and Leo Burnett Sydney," Campaign Brief, May 20, 2013, https://campaignbrief.com/coke-connects-indians -and-paki/.

13. Coca-Cola Small World Machines—Bringing India & Pakistan Together, May 19, 2013, https://www.youtube.com/watch?v=ts_4vOUDImE&feature=youtube.

14. Lawrence Williams and Joshua Ackerman, "Please Touch the Merchandise," *Harvard Business Review*, December 15, 2011, https://hbr.org/2011/12/please -touch-the-merchandise.

15. Sonic Magic, "The Wonder and Science of Sound," May 24, 2019, CBC-TV. https://www.cbc.ca/natureofthings/m_features/the-psychology-of-sound.

16. K. M. Knoferle, E. R. Spangenberg, A. Herrmann, et al, "It Is All in the Mix: The Interactive Effect of Music Tempo and Mode on In-Store Sales," *Marketing Letters*, vol. 23(1), 2012, pp. 325–337, https://doi.org/10.1007/s11002-011-9156-z.

17. Joel Beckerman, *The Sonic Boom: How Sound Transforms the Way We Think, Feel, and Buy*, Mariner Books, October 21, 2014, p. 53, https://www.amazon.com/Sonic -Boom-Sound-Transforms-Think, ebook/dp/B00K9W842A.

18. *The Fajita Effect, How the Sound of a Sizzle Made the World Crave Chili's*, Houghton Mifflin Harcourt, *Medium*, October 21, 2014, https://medium.com/galleys/the-fajita-effect-504838a5f2f0.
19. C. Gomez-Diaz and R. Benton, "The Joy of Sex Pheromones," *EMBO Reports*, vol. 14, issue 10, 2013, pp. 874–883, doi:10.1038/embor.2013.140, https://www.ncbi.nlm.nih.gov/pmc/articles/PMC3807217/.
20. Alison Motluk, "The Rules of Attraction, Tinkering with Pheromones Turns Fruit Flies into Indiscriminate Lovers," *University of Toronto Magazine*, November 18, 2009, https://magazine.utoronto.ca/research-ideas/science/the-rules-of-attraction-fruit-fly-phermones-joel-levine/
21. "From Signature Fragrances to Curated Background Music," *Equal Strategy*, https://www.equalstrategy.com/portfolio/media-scent-marketing-music-styling/.
22. "Sales of the Leading Liquid Laundry Detergent Brands of the United States in 2018," Statista, https://www.statista.com/statistics/188716/top-liquid-laundry-detergent-brands-in-the-united-states.
23. A. V. Jaeggi and C. P. Van Schaik, "The Evolution of Food Sharing in Primates," *Behavioral Ecology and Sociobiology*, vol. 65, 2011, p. 2125, https://doi.org/10.1007/s00265-011-1221-3.
24. Comité Champagne, "Champagne Only Comes from Champagne, France," https://www.champagne.fr/en/tasting-and-appreciation/champagne-tasting-experience/language-of-the-senses.
25. Julie Beck, "Our Moods, Our Foods: The Messy Relationship Between How We Feel and What We Eat," *The Atlantic*, March 6, 2014, https://www.theatlantic.com/health/archive/2014/03/our-moods-our-foods/284238/.
26. Martin Lindstrom, *Brand Sense: Sensory Secrets Behind the Stuff We Buy*, New York: Free Press, 2005.

Chapter 13

1. Alejandro Cremades, "How This Entrepreneur Turned A $10,000 Startup Investment into a $600 Million Acquisition," *Forbes*, March 26, 2019, https://www.forbes.com/sites/alejandrocremades/2019/03/26/how-this-entrepreneur-turned-a-10000-startup-investment-into-a-600-million-acquisition.
2. https://www.merriam-webster.com/dictionary/Rx.
3. Cathy Siegner, "RXBAR's Prescription for the Future: New Name, New Products, Changes in Leadership," FoodDive, March 7, 2019, https://www.fooddive.com/news/rxbars-prescription-for-the-future-new-name-new-products-changes-in-lea.
4. Jialan Wang and Benjamin J. Keys, "Perverse Nudges: Minimum Payments and Debt Paydown in Consumer Credit Cards," *Penn Wharton Public Policy Initiative*, Book 25, 2014, http://repository.upenn.edu/pennwhartonppi/25.
5. H. Matute, F. Blanco, I. Yarritu, M. Díaz-Lago, M. A. Vadillo, and I. Barberia, "Illusions of Causality: How They Bias Our Everyday Thinking and How They Could Be Reduced," *Front Psychology*, vol. 6, 2015, p. 888, doi:10.3389/fpsyg.2015.00888.
6. https://www.fda.gov/drugs/warning-letters-and-notice-violation-letters-pharmaceutical-companies/warning-letters-2019.
7. George Lakoff and Mark Johnson, *Philosophy in the Flesh*, New York: Basic Books, 1999, p. 20, ". . . rule of thumb among cognitive scientists: unconscious thought

is 95 percent of all thought," https://www.cse.iitk.ac.in/users/amit/books/lakoff
-1999-philosophy-in-flesh.html.

8. Arunesh Mathur, Gunes Acar, Michael J. Friedman, et. al, "Dark Patterns at Scale:
Findings from a Crawl of 11K Shopping Websites," *Proceedings of the ACM on
Human Computer Interaction*, vol. 3, CSCW, Article 81, November 2019, https://
arxiv.org/pdf/1907.07032.pdf.

9. Shane Goldmacher, "How Trump Steered Supporters into Unwitting Donations,"
April 3, 2021, https://www.nytimes.com/2021/04/03/us/politics/trump
-donations.html.

10. https://www.darkpatterns.org/types-of-dark-pattern.

11. Alex Rosenblat and Luke Stark, "Algorithmic Labor and Information
Asymmetries: A Case Study of Uber's Drivers," *International Journal of
Communication*, July 30, 2016, https://papers.ssrn.com/sol3/papers.cfm?abstract
_id=2686227.

12. Noam Scheiber, "How Uber Uses Psychological Tricks to Push Its Drivers'
Buttons," April 2, 2017, https://www.nytimes.com/interactive/2017/04/02/
technology/uber-drivers-psychological-tricks.html.

13. D. M. Kuss and M. D. Griffiths, "Social Networking Sites and Addiction: Ten
Lessons Learned," *International Journal of Enviromental Research and Public Health*
vol. 14, 2017, p. 311, https://www.mdpi.com/1660-4601/14/3/311.

14. This comes from the great German philosopher, Immanuel Kant, from his 1785
work *Groundwork of the Metaphysics of Morals* and states, "Act only according to
that maxim whereby you can, at the same time, will that it should become a universal law."

15. Stephen J. Genco, *Intuitive Marketing*, Intuitive Consumer Insights LLC, 2019,
p. 350.

Chapter 14

1. L. F. Barrett, "Solving the Emotion Paradox: Categorization and the Experience
of Emotion," *Personality and Social Psychology Review*, vol. 10, issue 1, 2006, pp.
20–46, doi:10.1207/s15327957pspr1001_2. PMID 16430327.

2. Gregory S. Berns and Sara E. Moore, "A Neural Predictor of Cultural Popularity,"
Journal of Consumer Psychology, June 8, 2011, https://doi.org/10.1016/j.jcps.2011
.05.001.

3. Kayla Stoner, "Brain Waves Predict Success of Advertisements—Neuroscience
Technique Measures How Well Films Will Do at Box Office," *Northwestern Now*,
March 16, 2017.

4. Robin Higie Coulter and Gerald Zaltman, "Using the Zaltman Metaphor
Elicitation Technique to Understand Brand Images," *NA—Advances in Consumer
Research*, vol. 21, eds. Chris T. Allen and Deborah Roedder John, Provo, Utah,
Association for Consumer Research, 1994, pp. 501–507, https://www.acrwebsite
.org/volumes/7644.

5. Philip Perry, "Think You Have Only 5 Senses? You've Actually Got About 14 to
20," *Big Think*, May 2, 2018, https://bigthink.com/philip-perry/think-you-have
-only-5-senses-its-actually-a-lot-more-than-that.

6. Hal Conick, "Read This Story to Learn How Behavioral Economics Can Improve
Marketing," American Marketing Association, January 12, 2018, https://www
.ama.org/marketing-news/read-this-story-to-learn-how-behavioral-economics
-can-improve-marketing/.

INDEX

ABOUT THE AUTHOR

Sandeep Dayal is the managing director for the marketing powerhouse Cerenti Marketing Group, which has been rated by *Forbes* as one of America's Top Management Consulting Firms for the prior six years in a row. Previously, he has worked for McKinsey and Booz, two of the world's top strategy consulting firms. In his 25-years-plus consulting career, he has had a unique vantage point from which to work with and shape some of the world's most amazing brands—with nearly 100 engagements spanning 30-plus companies.

Dayal is a marketing visionary, and many of his articles, including those on building trust online, creating digital brands, and deciphering the consumers' behavioral bounds, have proven to be remarkably prescient in predicting major marketing shifts. It is from this work deep in the trenches, alongside some of the world's top marketing executives, that he has developed a practical and game-changing framework for building what he has christened as cognitive brands.

Dayal holds a Master's in Public and Private Management degree from the Yale School of Management.

He can be reached at www.sandeepdayal.com.